Holland America Cruises
ms Prinsendam

1980
Orient/Alaska Trans-Pacific Cruises

Singapore, Philippines, Hong Kong, Japan, Alaska.
Special port of call, Shanghai (People's Republic of China).
Optional tour to Peking.

29 days Singapore to Vancouver, April 28
27 days Vancouver to Singapore, September 30
Fly free between the U.S. West Coast and Singapore.

BURNING
COLD

THE CRUISE SHIP
PRINSENDAM
and the
GREATEST SEA RESCUE
OF ALL TIME

H. PAUL JEFFERS

ZENITH PRESS

For the men and women of the U.S. Coast Guard
and all who fought to save the passengers, officers, and crew
of the *Prinsendam* and in memory of Mary Lou Shanley.

This edition published by Zenith Press, an imprint of MBI Publishing Company,
Galtier Plaza, Suite 200, 380 Jackson Street, St. Paul, MN, 55101-3885 USA.

© H. Paul Jeffers, 2006

MBI Publishing Company Books are also available at discounts for in bulk
quantities for industrial or sale-promotional use. For details write to Special
Sales Manager at MBI Publishing Company, Galtier Plaza, Suite 200,
380 Jackson Street, St. Paul, MN, 55101-3885 USA

Cover by Rochelle Brancato
Layout by Tom Heffron

Cover photo © Shutterstock

On the title page: The cover of the brochure for the 1980 Trans-Pacific cruises.
Author collection

ISBN: 0-7603-2079-9
ISBN-13: 978-0-7603-2079-2

Printed in the United States

CONTENTS

"It is really a question of whether
the Good Lord will give us enough time."

–Admiral Richard Schoel
U.S. Coast Guard Co-ordination Center,
Juneau, Alaska, October 4, 1980

Looking for the Prinsendam

The press wire service bulletin on the morning of October 4, 1980, was brief. The U.S. Coast Guard reported that a fire was sweeping through the Holland America Line cruise ship *Prinsendam* in the Gulf of Alaska, forcing more than three hundred passengers and two hundred crew to abandon the ship 175 miles south of Valdez.

As assignment editor and producer at all-news radio station WCBS in New York, I made the *Prinsendam* the top item during three days of follow-up reports. The story was so dramatic in all its aspects that it overshadowed the presidential election campaigns of Jimmy Carter and Republican challenger Ronald Reagan. Accounts took precedence over the continuing national embarrassment over Americans being held hostage in Iran for more than a year, a war between Iran and Iraq, New York City's dire financial straits and skyrocketing crime rate, the American League playoff series between the Yankees and the Kansas City Royals, the announcement that movie star Steve McQueen had a rare form of lung cancer, and a heavyweight title fight between Muhammad Ali and Larry Holmes. The race to save the *Prinsendam* combined superb technology, daring, bravery, ingenuity, and undaunted spirit. As developing news was banged out by the wire services, we learned of efforts to pluck mostly elderly passengers from lifeboats one at a time to helicopters, an oil supertanker, and a Coast Guard cutter in tempestuous seas and shuttle them to Valdez and Sitka while the *Prinsendam* continued to blaze.

Accounts from dazed passengers to a swarm of reporters and TV camera crews provided details of what happened during those bitterly cold hours on the stormy, deep, and dangerous waters. It was compelling stuff. But newsworthiness is as fleeting as time. Three days after the first bulletin, the saga of the *Prinsendam* was no longer at the top of newscasts. Within a week, it was history. News and the world moved on, leaving the full story of the *Prinsendam* unrecorded for a quarter of a century. Yet it's as gripping a drama as Walter Lord's epic *A Night to Remember* about the *Titanic*, with all the tension of *The Terrible Hours* and *The Perfect Storm*. The story of the *Prinsendam* stands not only as a saga of people struggling against the odds to survive on the sea in the dead of night, but also as a riveting record of how the United States Coast Guard rallied to confront the greatest challenge in its history.

Long forgotten by most people, except those who had been involved in the race to save lives in the Gulf of Alaska, the *Prinsendam* suddenly surfaced in my consciousness after two decades. Having had some success writing books in a thirty-three-year career in broadcast news, I had decided to see if I could make a living solely as an author. Always looking for the next book project, I was kicking around ideas with my literary agent, Jake Elwell, in early 2003. He asked, "Did you ever hear of the *Prinsendam*?"

Distant snippets of memory stirred. "It caught fire and sank off the coast of Alaska," I said, "about twenty years ago."

"It was in 1980. My grandparents were on it with hundreds of senior citizens. He was the publisher of the newspaper in Worcester, Massachusetts. The day after they were rescued by the

Coast Guard, she was interviewed on the *Today Show*. I have the tape and an article he wrote. How about doing a book on the race to save the *Prinsendam?*" Jake asked.

Dubious about being able to find anyone to interview from a ship fire twenty-three years ago–people who were old back then and had probably long since died–I bravely told Jake that I would look into what might be available on the subject. There wasn't much. In an Internet search, I found references to some magazine articles from the early 1980s. The index of the *New York Times* listed a few news accounts and a promising sidebar about a New York couple who had been aboard. An e-mail inquiry to Coast Guard historian Scott T. Price in Washington, D.C., elicited a pledge of help, but with a disheartening response that there was little in Coast Guard headquarters files, and whatever might be in the national archives was most likely on the West Coast. Confident that newspapers in Alaska would have given the story a lot of coverage, I envisioned having to travel thousands of miles for a book that might never happen, at a cost that might not be feasible in terms of the advance payment from a publisher, *if* Jake found one interested in considering the proposal, *should* I succeed in digging up enough information to write one.

While I was busy with other projects, I didn't abandon the *Prinsendam*. I continued my search for sources, primarily on the Internet, using every key word I could think of, from "Prinsendam" and the names of Coast Guard ships that I knew had been involved to U.S. and Canadian air force units that had participated. These efforts produced a little more information, but not nearly enough to write a book.

In the hope that a Web site for former Coast Guardsmen might be productive, I posted a notice of my interest in finding anyone who had served on the command ship *Boutwell* or the two cutters that took part in the rescue. Continuing my Internet search for any new sources, I discovered in early 2004 the Web site of the Burlingame Historical Society in California. It cited a talk that had been given the previous autumn by *Prinsendam* passenger Jeannie Gilmore.

Contacting the historical society, I asked to be put in touch with her. The response provided not only her phone number, but the amazing revelation that she possessed a treasure trove of newspaper clippings, magazine articles, photographs, and other material, *and* that two friends, Fiona and Stephen Hamilton, had created a DVD containing forty-five minutes of newscasts recorded during the rescue by Jeannie's sister, Mary Lou Shanley of San Jose, California, from the television networks and local stations. In our initial phone conversation Jeannie said that she was "thrilled that someone is finally going to write this." As people faced with the possibility of being in a book inevitably do, she asked, "Who's going to play me in the movie?" I said, "Why, Julia Roberts, of course." Jeannie liked that idea.

During a week-long visit in July 2004, I interviewed Jeannie and her daughter Carole, and they gave me all of the material they had accumulated. Jeannie was approaching her eightieth birthday, but she was as vibrant as she had been in 1980. She provided names of others who had been on the cruise or had taken previous *Prinsendam* excursions. Travel writer Morgan Lawrence gave me insights into the ship's earliest years of service. Colin Flynn of Redwood City, California, provided information on his parents, Jim and Kitty, who were on the ill-fated cruise.

Shortly after returning to New York, I got an email from a *Boutwell* crew member, David Hughes. His unexpected reply to my posting in May 2004 on the former Coast Guardsmen Web site resulted in my obtaining his memories and photographs he had snapped, and the name of another retired *Boutwell* crewman, Thomas Ice. Still on active duty, Chris Macneith led me to one of the first women graduates of the Coast Guard Academy, *Boutwell* engine-room officer Monyee Kazek. Accounts of actions by the *Boutwell*'s rescue teams were provided by former–Boatswain Mate Peter Marcucci and Master Chief Petty Officer Kenneth Bradbury. Chief Gun Fire Controller Robert Gershel shared his extensive files. Invaluable insights into air-sea rescue and other aspects of the operation came from the supertanker *Williamsburgh*'s First Assistant Radio Officer David J. Ring Jr.

Suddenly, writing a book that at first blush had seemed impossible had become a reality. As I discovered rich details and more names of passengers on the ill-fated *Prinsendam*, my file expanded from a few shreds of information to a formidable stack, along with an ample archive of photographs and interviews with passengers by newspaper and TV reporters at the time. The official report of the investigation by Dutch authorities contained a minute-by-minute account from the discovery of the fire and efforts to quell it to the decision to abandon ship and rescue efforts. Included were data on the *Prinsendam*'s construction and history since its launching in 1973, along with information on her officers and crew. My file had also expanded with articles by passengers and information on the ships and aircraft that took part in the largest and most complex air-sea rescue ever attempted.

Undertaking a neglected story of heroism and the implacable human spirit dealing with trouble at sea stirred my lifelong fascination with the romance of ocean travel, the seemingly inborn magnetism of the oceans running throughout the story of mankind, and the writer's timeless lure of the sea. Believing that if I took a ship voyage I ought to be going somewhere for a purpose, I had never been interested in booking a cruise with the only goal of hedonism. I had twice crossed the Atlantic from Southampton, England, to New York on *Queen Elizabeth 2*. The journeys were in the late summer and autumn. On each I found myself on stormy waters and temporarily seasick, but quite delighted to be bounced around by gale-force winds and waves high and rough. Daring them as I stood on deck feeling the lash of driving rain and slashing ocean, I knew that I was among thousands of passengers and crew, but I felt like the ancient mariner of Samuel Taylor Coleridge's epic poem: "Alone, all, all alone; Alone on a wide, wide sea." And I remembered a line from Walt Whitman: "Joyous too we launch out on trackless seas, fearless for unknown shores." He was speaking of the soul, but it didn't matter. When you're on a ship, even if it's an ocean liner, you feel as if you are at heart a sailor. Felix Riesenberg, in *Vignettes of the Sea*, wrote that the ocean has always been a seducer. It was "a careless lying fellow, not feminine, as many writers imagine, but strongly masculine in its allurement." All ships were females that the manly sea "caresses and chastises as the case may be." So in this book, the *Prinsendam*, Coast Guard cutters, and other ships are referred to in the female gender.

The tradition of assigning female gender pronouns to ships had been an issue between me and the copy editor of my book *Colonel Roosevelt*. It dealt with Theodore Roosevelt and the Spanish-American War. Infected with a fever of political correctness, the copy editor had changed all my "she" references to every ship of the American and Spanish fleets to "it." After I fired off a broadside of objections to this outrageous attempt to scuttle centuries of naval and merchant-marine practice to the editor who had signed the book, the copy editor was torpedoed. All the ships in what Roosevelt's friend John Hay, U.S. ambassador to England in 1898, called "a splendid little war" remained feminine. I have often wondered how Herman Melville would have reacted if the mid-1990s political correctness had somehow taken hold in the nineteenth century and he'd gotten back the manuscript of *Moby Dick* with every "she" stricken for "it." And the same for every author of tales about the seas, ships, and sailors who scanned the broad horizon for whales and let out the exultant cry, "Thar she blows."

Like those salty yarns, this book is in the great tradition of seagoing stories since time immemorial in which venturers from land confronted not only an emergency on a ship and the power of an indifferent and ageless ocean, but came to grips with our tenuous mortality.

CHAPTER 1

Once in a Lifetime

*T**he Prinsendam*

Small. Snug. Welcoming. Personal. Intimate. It didn't offer the daunting majesty of the *QE2* crisscrossing the Atlantic or the crowded behemoths that plied the turquoise Caribbean. It was the kind of cruise ship where you might get to know almost all your traveling companions. But the destinations were the most alluring attractions. In the words of the old popular song, "far away places I've been longing to see" once were only names on maps in geography class or fleeting images in the short subjects at the movies on Saturday nights called travelogues that always seemed to end with the narrator saying, "And so we bid farewell to . . ." There was a hint, if not a promise, of thrilling adventures awaiting everyone who ventured afar. A mystery, perhaps, in which you might run into a real-life Charlie Chan. Or romance! A man might meet someone like Deborah Kerr in *An Affair to Remember* and a woman might find a dashing, handsome Paul Henreid and fall instantly in love like Bette Davis abandoning her old-maid inhibitions on a ship in *Now, Voyager* as she found herself enchanted while Henreid's character lit two cigarettes at once, one for her, one for him.

Luggage-laden passengers who boarded the *Prinsendam* with memories of the ships in movies brought not only images of romance and adventure but a hilarious sequence in *A Night at the Opera*, with the Marx Brothers and others jammed into a tiny stateroom and tumbling out of it when the door was opened. No one who had seen *A Night to Remember* or had read the Walter Lord book went to sea without thinking about the *Titanic*. And there was TV's *The Love Boat*.

If amour were not to be found on the *Prinsendam*, there would certainly be wonderful food from dawn to the witching hour. "Have a full breakfast or lunch at pool side or step inside our air-conditioned Lido Restaurant–dressed for the sun," said the brochure. "Enjoy a variety of sizzling breakfast favorites, and cold and hot luncheon specialties. Or eat in the more formal dining room. If you wish, have a continental breakfast in your stateroom." For dinner every night, "chefs outdo themselves creating delicious specialties. From hors d'oeuvres to soups, fish, roasts, poultry and salads to extravagant desserts, followed by a presentation of cheeses and fresh fruits. Later, your sea-sharpened appetite will lead you to the tempting array of delicacies at the Midnight Buffet."

Dancing after dinner. Deck promenades. Enlightening talks by experts on this and that in the auditorium. All this was promised right there in the Holland America Line's lively brochure. "If you've already seen the Western half of the world, let us take you on a once-in-a-lifetime journey to the other half–the world bordered by the Pacific." A lavish color-illustrated twenty-page "Orient-Alaska Trans-Pacific Cruises" brochure for 1980 advertised a voyage to Alaska, Japan, Hong Kong, and the Philippines, with an optional port call in the People's Republic of China and a voyage to exotic Indonesia. "No matter how many cruising adventures you've thrilled to in the past," it pledged, "this is the one you're likely to remember the longest."

The newest member of Holland America's five-ship fleet, the *Prinsendam* offered 201 air-conditioned, tastefully furnished staterooms and luxurious amenities within an atmosphere of high adventure and excitement. Six decks—Sun, Bridge, Promenade, Main, and A and B—were "devoted to the luxurious vacation life you expect, with an ambiance of intimacy and charm." Days at sea would "rival the pleasures of the most expensive resorts." Bask in the sun. Swim. Enjoy deck sports. Play chess. Go to the movies. See sports events and documentaries in color on videocassettes presented on a wide screen. If you enjoyed bridge, "an extensive program is conducted by a 'Travel-With-Goren'" expert who offered lectures, party bridge, and duplicate tournaments sanctioned by the American Contract Bridge League.

You could "develop a new craft or artistic pursuit—or work at a familiar one." Choose from a variety of other events, "all carefully planned by your Cruise Director to fill your days." For a "nightlife filled with variety," you could dance to the ship's orchestra, join newfound friends for a drink in the inviting Prinsen Club, take pensive walks on deck, "gazing out at the shimmer of starlight on the sea." When time came to sleep, you'd "feel luxuriously at home in a tastefully appointed stateroom." Outside AA double rooms called cabins deluxe on the Sun and Bridge decks and the double BB, CC, DD, and EE rooms to single rooms (FF, GG, HH, and JJ) on Main, A, and B decks provided private bathrooms with either a tub or shower, toilet, two channels of music, telephone, individually controlled air conditioning, and wall-to-wall plush carpeting. You were invited to fall asleep in the anticipation of tomorrow, knowing that you and the ship were in the care of Dutch officers, "famous for seafaring throughout the centuries," and your "friendly Indonesian crew."

At midship were two elevators and a grand stairway. On the Promenade Deck was the swimming pool, overlooked by the Lido Terrace. Those who preferred libations indoors could go to the main lounge or get a forward view from the Prinsen Club bar, with dance floor, adjacent to the duty-free shopping center.

Vivacious and gregarious, fifty-five-year-old elementary school teacher and education adviser Jeannie Gilmore had set her heart on exploring the shops and stores in every port of call on the *Prinsendam*'s itinerary. She had no qualms about taking a couple of weeks away from her husband Bill and their home in Burlingame, California, to spend freely for touristy souvenirs in Ketchikan, Alaska, clothing in Hong Kong, wood carvings and embroidery in Manila, antique stone temple dogs in Shanghai, perhaps a kimono in the Ginza district of Tokyo, and jewelry in Singapore before fulfilling a dream of sipping a Singapore Sling at the bar of the famous Raffles Hotel. The idea of taking the twenty-seven-day cruise had been her mother's. At age seventy-seven, Neva Hall was an enthusiastic traveler for whom neither years nor frailty would ever be impediments.

As publisher of the Worcester, Massachusetts, *Telegram-Gazette*, Richard Steele was an influential figure in the state's third-largest city. A Republican who was also a friendly foe of the Kennedys, he was an experienced journalist with an interest in getting a look inside Communist China, if only briefly and as a tourist. Resembling and admiring of Jackie Kennedy, Louise Steele had prepared for formal-dress dinners by packing heirloom jewelry and evening gowns. She felt as excited as the first time she sailed off as a young woman to take in the splendors of Europe. Her sights were now set on shopping in Tokyo and meeting their daughter Barbara and her husband in Singapore. Daughters

Virginia and Nancy had been invited but had not wanted to be away from their own families for such a long time.

For Irving and Isabella Brex of Seattle, Washington, the cruise was a once-in-a-lifetime event, and likely their only opportunity to explore the Orient. They were elderly and Irving had diabetes. His condition required Isabella, a retired nurse, to administer insulin injections. Although their friend Paul P. Noyes of Burlingame, California, was eighty-six years old and had only recently suffered a head injury in a fall, he was a lively fellow and had been a boon companion on other trips. Booked into a Double-A outside cabin deluxe on the Sun Deck were former New Jersey state senator Fairleigh Dickinson (chairman of the New Jersey university bearing his name and a former Coast Guardsman) and his wife, Betty. Also quartered on the Sun Deck were Max and Edith Kleeman. On B Deck in an F inside single was teenager Mike Nelson, whose parents were in a double on the Main Deck. In an outside single room on A Deck, Barbara A. Meade was an ocean cruise first-timer. She was determined to pay close attention to instructors during a fire drill on the Promenade Deck as they demonstrated the proper way to wear the life vests that were stowed in every cabin. She had packed for the trip according to the advice in the travel brochure; "just in case" the weather was warmer than expected, a bathing suit would be a good thing to bring along.

Sailing for reasons as varied as the places they were leaving behind were Earl Andrews of Redding, California, a World War II veteran; Jack Barclay from Calgary, Alberta, an official of a Canadian oil firm; Leo Brackman, a Los Angeles sculptor; and John Courtney and Edwin Ziegfeld, retired college art professors. Mrs. Ann Corey of Silver Spring, Maryland, was with her seventy-five-year-old mother, Mrs. Stanley Foster, of Sun City, Arizona. Attorney John W. Gyorokos of Huntington Beach, California, was with his wife, Ginny, daughter Sandra, age nineteen, and eighteen-year-old son Gene. Sixty-year-old Betty Milborn, from Tucson, Arizona, was looking after her aunt, Betty Clapp, who was planning to celebrate her seventy-ninth birthday on October 21 in Peking, China.

Frazier Reed of San Jose, California, had recently retired from the insurance business. Joan Thatcher was a Berkeley, California, minister. Elizabeth "Betsy" Price of Palo Alto had taken trips on other cruise ships. Herman and Sally Solomon were residents of the Woodland Hills section of Los Angeles. They owned a sporting-goods store. Also in the retail merchandise business, Edward Brennan was president of Sears, Roebuck and Company. A 1955 graduate of Marquette University, he'd begun his business career selling men's furnishings at a Sears store in Madison, Wisconsin. Brennan held various positions in buying, marketing, and store management and had recently been elected company president.

With free return airfare, the rates according to accommodations per person were:

Outside double-room cabins deluxe AA, Sun and Bridge decks: $5,075

Outside double room BB, Main Deck: $4,625

Outside double room CC and DD, Main and A and B decks: $4,345 to $4,140

Inside double room FF, Main and A and B decks: $3,625

Outside single cabins deluxe A, Sun and Bridge decks: $8,375

Outside single room B, Main Deck: $7,630

Outside single room C, Main and A and B decks: $6,520

Outside single room D, A and B decks: $5,795

Outside single room E, A and B decks: $5,435

Inside single room F, Main and A and B decks $5,075

Addition of a thirteen-day Indonesian cruise ranged from $8,030 to $7,645.

These prices were assuaged, perhaps, by a Holland America policy that no tipping was expected. Dispensing with gratuities in 1970, the company adopted the tradition of European hotels of adding a service percentage to the accommodation charge. While the company boasted that the policy had been successful, ocean-travel historian John Maxtone-Graham observed in a chronicle of the era of the great steamships, *The Only Way to Cross*, published in the year the *Prinsendam* was launched (1973), that the Dutch stewards "refuse tips not only in public but in private as well, when there is no superior about to remind them." The brochure for the 1980 Orient/Alaska Trans-Pacific Cruises advised passengers, "Because you pay nothing extra for food aboard ship, your room, entertainment on board and all that great service, you'll find taking a cruise can cost less than many other kinds of vacations." It was also the policy to operate with a "no cash" system on board. The means of exchange was vouchers (except in the gift shop and shore excursions office), with the amounts charged to the passenger's account at the end of the voyage. Credit cards and personal checks were not accepted for payment of shipboard accounts. The official currency was the U.S. dollar. Other money was exchangeable at the prevailing rate.

All passengers were required to possess a valid passport, proof of smallpox vaccination and inoculation against cholera, with a typhoid shot recommended. Should anyone get seasick or otherwise take ill, an infirmary was staffed by a physician and registered nurse, with a "nominal fee" for the doctor. Other amenities were a "modern, fully air-conditioned beauty parlor," fully equipped laundry, pressing and dry-cleaning service, ship-to-shore telephone, and a limited number of safe-deposit boxes for money, jewelry, and other valuables. The gift shop accepted American Express, Visa, and Mastercard.

For anyone who didn't bring a camera, the ship's photographer took pictures of most events. Terry Allen had snapped photos of thousands of Holland America Trans-Pacific tourists on the twice-yearly outings on the *Prinsendam* since it began service in April 1973. Registered in the Netherlands Antilles, the *Prinsendam* made its shakedown cruise to Bali. On board to look after and assist members of the press and travel writers on another voyage in 1979, travel writer and publicity adviser Morgan Lawrence had no difficulty promoting features of a ship whose enticements were self-evident: A large silver bowl of caviar at the entrance to the dining salon. Comfortable cabins and rooms. Lavish décor in the public spaces, and handsome appointments everywhere. Efficient officers, courteous and helpful young crew members, and an eager-to-please staff arranged onboard activities and assisted in planning port-of-call adventures ashore. Allen knew the motorship stem to stern, from the Sun Deck to the engine room and from each of its six decks to the wheelhouse.

The commander on this journey, Captain Cornelius Wabeke, was marking his thirtieth year as a Holland America master. His chief officer was also a Holland America veteran, H. E. Valk. Second officers were Matthew Oosterwijk and P. W. Schol. Third and fourth officers were Paul Welling and S. L. Douwes. Chief engineer Albertus Boot supervised Second Engineer Officer John Repko, Third Engineer Officer Jacob van Hardeveld and Assistant

Engineer Officer Robert Kalf. Other officers were First Electrician G. J. ten Voorde, and Chief Radio Officer J. J. A. van der Zee. Hotel manager D. Zeller had a staff of stewards and hostesses to attend to the passengers' needs and caprices, along with tour director Gene Reid and Reid's wife, Diane, who was in charge of arranging shore excursions.

Entertainers hired for the cruise included pianist Richard Yanni. Jack Malon, a magician from New York, traveled with his wife, Beatrice. They and Las Vegas comedian Roger Ray would entertain the passengers with a troupe of young singers that presented evenings of Broadway show tunes, accompanied by the ship's small orchestra. Offstage, twenty-three-year-old Peter Kapetan planned to prepare for visiting Japan by reading the novel *Shogun*. On the entertainer roster as a lecturer, John Graham had left a career in the foreign service, trying to help resolve contentions in the third world, hopefully to the benefit of the United States. He had spent a year dealing with an arms embargo against South Africa. After a failed try at establishing a consulting business and in need of an income, he listened to a friend's suggestion that easy money could be made giving lectures on cruise ships. As promised, Graham recalled, "the pay was great." He also got to bring along his thirteen-year-old daughter, Malory. Free to speak on any subject he chose, Graham noted that many if not the majority of passengers were senior citizens. Part of his job was "waltzing widows with blue hair around the dance floor."

Observing the passengers boarding the *Prinsendam*, Richard Steele hoped that those who were his age or older shared his feeling of anticipating what people of a certain generation in the history of the United States used to call a "swell" time. Back when ship comings and goings that newspapers in harbor cities listed as "arrivals and departures" were as routine as the weather forecasts and yesterday's sports results, those were the days when steamships were seen off by crowds amid a blizzard of streamers and confetti and bon voyage parties in staterooms called to an abrupt halt by the shouted warning, "All ashore who's going ashore!"

A *Prinsendam* passenger wishing to throw such a party had been notified by the Holland America company, "We're all in favor of this old sea tradition, and we'll be glad to help with yours." Arrangements for liquor and soft drinks could be made by using a special preference form that came with the ticket and asked what a passenger wished for the party, as well as the number of trays of sandwiches.

The only apprehension that Steele felt as he watched his fellow passengers and admired the ship was a wire report he'd read on a teletype in his newspaper's editorial room of a typhoon called Thelma moving north in the Pacific toward Alaska.

CHAPTER 2

"I Hope it Doesn't Sink!"

The *Prinsendam* was tiny compared to the immense ocean liners of the time. In the age of speed, people in a great hurry to come and go quickly embraced the intercontinental airplane that shrank both time and distance. In interest of the march of progress and modern efficiency the jet had diminished the pleasure of going somewhere. The same fate had befallen long-distance trains. The romantic Richard Steele missed the old ways of travel. He had always agreed with the poet Edna St. Vincent Millay. In 1921 she wrote that "there isn't a train I wouldn't take, no matter where it's going." Or a steamship.

Though not a poet, one of Steele's favorite authors, Ian Fleming, creator of master spy James Bond, knew about the lure of trains. While Agent 007 waited in the railroad terminal in Venice, Italy, for the arrival of another mysterious beauty to flee with her aboard the Orient Express, he pondered the majesty of the long-chassied German locomotive under the arc-lights. He thought it panted quietly with the labored breath of a dragon dying of asthma. Wisps of steam rose from the couplings between royal-blue carriages. Another mystery writer, perhaps Eric Ambler, saw an earlier Orient Express as a proud dowager lifting the hem of her skirts to dance her way across Europe. Great American trains such as the Broadway Limited, the twentieth century pulling into Grand Central Terminal with some movie star aboard, and the California-bound Santa Fe Chief were also gone, or sad shadows of what they were. The same happened to ocean liners, leaving only the *QE2* and gigantic cruise ships heading out to tropical islands within easy reach of the United States, but without genuine destinations or meaningful purpose.

Or maybe, Steele thought, he was just getting old.

If so, he was still the romantic of his youth. That part of him beheld the *Prinsendam* and saw "a bejeweled beauty." Sparkling lights hung from her masts and superstructure. They shone from portholes. She was bathed in floodlit brilliance. Instead of standing on a dock waiting to go on board, he ought to be in Massachusetts, seeing that his newspaper was properly informing its readers about the race for president and all the other events called "news" on the last night of September. But Louise wanted to see Japan, and there was no denying her dreams, now or ever.

She had enjoyed planning this trip, making the arrangements, buying the right wardrobe, sorting through her heirloom jewelry for the exact bauble for this dress or that one, and making sure that Steele's tuxedo was pressed and his patent leather shoes were presentable.

Looking at the festive throng on the dock, Steele played the old newsman's game of sizing up people and conjecturing as to the journalist's five W's. Who were they, where did they come from, when had they decided to go, what did they plan to do in faraway places, and why?

Most seemed to be his age, and many very much older.

Given the steep cost of sailing on the *Prinsendam*, they certainly must have reached a point in their lives where they were more than able to afford it.

For some it was a last chance for an adventure, like aging ex-president Theodore Roosevelt setting off to explore a Brazilian jungle river because, as he'd explained, it was his "last chance to be a boy again."

Perhaps this trip was one that *Prinsendam* passengers had been putting off for years, and possibly all their lives.

Henry Heinichen, a retired army colonel, and his wife, Leila, had sailed on the *Prinsendam* several times. For Muriel Marvinney and her friend Agnes Lilard of Short Hills, New Jersey, it was the first time. Widows, they had sought each other's company. Golfers, they belonged to the Canoe Brook Country Club in Summit, New Jersey. Looking up from a teed-up ball one day, Agnes exclaimed, "Muriel, how would you like to take a cruise to the Orient?"

"You're kidding," Muriel replied.

"No, I'm not. I saw an ad in the paper about a month-long cruise to Red China, Japan, and Singapore. A few other places, too."

Muriel thought a moment and said, "Sounds good to me."

Of the on-the-spot decision Muriel recalled, "Our families are wonderful. We're both fortunate that our children and grandchildren live nearby and visit us. But, loving as our children are, and with all the dear friends both Ag and I have, there is a kind of invisible barrier for us as widows. You're always the fifth wheel at social gatherings. It's not deliberate, mind you. As Agnes says, 'After all, the world goes two by two.' Despite that, the two of us kept busy and interested and involved, and our lives were full. When we broached the idea of our taking 'a slow boat to China,' our children were all for it. The more I thought about it, the more exciting the idea seemed. All summer we pored over brochures like a couple of kids."

After a round of bon voyage parties, they flew from Newark to Vancouver. Muriel found the ship "wasn't as large as I had thought it would be," but she was impressed that it had "one of those impressive Dutch names."

From its beginning, Holland America Line had named its ships after the cities, towns, and villages of the Netherlands or Dutch colonies, among them *Schiedam, Zaandam, Volendam, Ryndam,* and *Rotterdam.* The *Prinsendam* had the name of an island at the south end of Sunda Strait off the southwest tip of Java, Indonesia. The suffix "dam" designates a passenger ship. Original funnel colors were black and yellow with green-white-green bands of equal width. The company's flag bore equal horizontal stripes of green, white, and green. The *Prinsendam* had an orange smoke funnel and a logo of parallel blue-and-white stripes. The mast was topped with a radar antenna. A pair of motor launches and lifeboats hung from davits. The hull was red below the waterline and deep blue above it, with the name "Prinsendam" in white. She looked pretty, exquisitely graceful, and enticing.

Although travel writer Carolyn Stuff was not with the passengers on September 30, 1980, she had learned about the *Prinsendam* the year before. She had discovered, as the Steeles, Jeannie Gilmore, and all the passengers would soon learn, that on a small ship "you acquire a warm proprietary feeling such as you have for your home." Having experienced the ship on a cruise of the Indonesian archipelago in the winter of 1979, Stuff had been attracted by "the music" in the names of ports: Singapore, Penang in Malaysia, Belawan, Sumatra, Java, Bali, and Jakarta. It was a music of "a specific Pacific kind, a melody that we too seldom hear," and for which the *Prinsendam* was built, to "thread through narrow waters to ports where few liners can find a harbor." Created primarily to ply Pacific waters, the *Prinsendam* made Alaska runs to reposition it for the Asiatic island cruises.

"It seemed to me at once spacious and cozy," Stuff recalled, "but certainly not small." Unlike smaller ships she had known, she could entirely circle the Promenade Deck, with five laps equaling a mile of walking or jogging.

Opportunities for vigorous exercise were not the appeal of a *Prinsendam* cruise for John Courtney, age sixty-nine, and his companion, Edwin Ziegfeld, three years older. Both were retired from administrative positions in college art departments. Courtney had been department chairman at Jersey City State College in New Jersey. Ziegfeld was on the faculty of Columbia University's Teachers College. Courtney had sold his house in Redding, Connecticut, and Ziegfeld a home in New York's Greenwich Village to settle in a commodious apartment in Mount San Antonio Gardens in Claremont, California. Their plans for a seven-week holiday in the Orient included the Indonesian sojourn. Ziegfeld bought an expensive Retina 3 camera and a telescopic lens. A mostly new wardrobe had been selected for cold and hot climates. Each had brought $2,000 in American Express traveler's checks. To save adding a thousand dollars for a high deck to the $6,000 they'd paid for tickets, they were booked into an outside room on the lowest (B). It had rooms 401 to 468 and crew quarters. The A Deck had staterooms numbered 301 to 376 and the hospital. The Main had 202 to 244, the main foyer and the formal dining room, with a shaft running from the engine room through above decks to the funnel. Promenade Deck, with no cabins or rooms, consisted of an aft sun deck and outdoor swimming pool overlooked by the Lido Restaurant, a large lounge midship, the forward shopping center on the port side and the cinema on starboard. Facing the prow behind the gift shop was the Prinsen Club with a bar and circular dance floor. The Bridge Deck had a sports area aft, rooms 151 to 172, the wireless room, offices, and the wheelhouse. The top Sun Deck had rooms 101 to 116 and sports areas.

Passengers boarded through the main foyer and were greeted with the efficiency and courtesies Holland America required of its employees and officers in crisp white uniforms. They provided directions to decks and rooms, assisted with luggage anyone wished to have in-cabin, and gave assurances that any to be stored in the hold would be carefully and safely handled. Deck plans that helped passengers move around the ship and locate amenities had been placed in each room. Also awaiting each passenger in the rooms was a table designation for dinners. If none had been requested at the time the cruise was booked, the assignment was made by the maître d'hôtel. However a table at dinner was chosen, it would be for the entire cruise. Seating for breakfasts and lunches was random.

The hustle and bustle of finding rooms reminded Steele of checking into vacation hotels with Louise and as a journalist and later as a newspaper executive arriving alone at professional and political conventions. The *Prinsendam*'s corridors were narrower, but not as tight as the passageways of sleeping cars on long-distance trains. Rooms were masterpieces of maximized use of limited space. Rectangular outside cabins deluxe had two single beds against walls at right angles with a table and lamp separating them, a desk and chair, and a bathroom with tub and a small closet. Outside double rooms and inside singles were similar in layout, but narrower and with a shower. Inside doubles were square and had a smaller desk. The décor in all was hotel-room modern. Windows were portholes. They could not be opened and were revealed or hidden with ceiling to floor sliding drapes.

At the Vancouver hotel where the Steeles had stayed the previous night, Louise had sent her young grandson, Jake Elwell, a postcard with a picture of the *Prinsendam*. She wrote a little joke: "I hope it doesn't sink!"

As eight p.m. neared, the Steeles in cabin 342 on A Deck and the passengers from cabins deluxe of the Sun Deck to doubles and singles on the lowest deck (B) abandoned "settling in," as cruise veteran Elizabeth Price called it, and made their way outside again by elevator or stairs to the Promenade, Bridge, and Sun decks for the excitement of departure. Looking at the Vancouver skyline on a clear and cool Tuesday evening, then gazing down at a small crowd waving them bon voyage on the pier, Jeannie Gilmore put an arm around her mother, thought of her husband, Bill, and their daughters, Carole and Chrissy, and felt a tug of homesickness.

Before going out on deck, Isabella Brex made sure that Irving had taken his insulin shot and that he'd put on a sweater. Bud Damarell and William Powell were anticipating finding the bar and toasting their first night at sea with bracing drinks. Earl Andrews couldn't help thinking back to being jammed between other GIs on a troop ship sailing off to win World War II. John Courtney and Edwin Ziegfeld beamed with the realization of their dream of a Pacific odyssey. Joan Thatcher thought of her congregation in Berkeley and said a silent prayer. From stem to stern, hundreds of people who had responded to the lure of an ocean-crossing, either because of superb advertising by Holland America Line or simply a desire to get away from the world and their routine lives for a while, felt and thought the same. They were thrilled, excited by the fact of sailing away with strangers, anticipating making friends that might remain so after the trip, missing those they were temporarily leaving behind, trying to imagine the wonders that lay ahead, and hoping they would experience all the things the travel brochure had promised.

Captain Cornelius Wabeke had the responsibility to take his ship to sea and gave the order to do so to the officers around him and those in the engine room whose charge it was to supervise the crew and engineering staff. Chefs, cooks, and waiters were preparing to serve the first meal to more than three hundred hungry passengers. The three bar staffs stood prepared to mix and pour. The stewards and porters were on hand wherever they might be needed to assist the lost or the confused and busy securing baggage. Chief housekeeper H. van Duren was confident that the *Prinsendam* was shipshape. Hotel manager D. Zeller, first and second maître d'hôtel W. de Vis and J. W. Dansberg agreed. Both the gift shop and the duty-free stores were fully stocked. The front office was open with ample safe-deposit boxes for anyone who desired one. In the radio room, First Radio Officer J. J. A. van der Zee was on station to send and receive messages, with second radio officer J. A. van der Werf on call, should he be needed. They were keeping up to date on the location and direction of Typhoon Thelma.

Born in the mid-Pacific on September 27 between 140 and 150 degrees east, Thelma had been officially designated "Typhoon 198017," meaning she was the seventeenth of the season. Her maximum winds were clocked at fifty-five knots. Movement north and east would bring Thelma close to Alaska as the *Prinsendam* sailed from Vancouver, assuring that for part of the cruise the ship would encounter rough sea conditions. The ship had been equipped with state-of-the-art stabilizers, but Dr. Y. Menger would undoubtedly find himself treating more than the customary number of cases of *mal de mer* when the *Prinsendam* left the shelter of Alaska's Inland Passage and entered the high ocean waters.

In addition to the international Morse code for signaling SOS in the event of a crisis, many ships plying the world's oceans in 1980 were equipped with a new alert system known as AMVER. Originally called Atlantic merchant vessel emergency reporting and renamed as the automated mutual-assistance vessel rescue, it retained its acronym. The "automated" in the name referred to its use of computers that had been nonexistent when the AMVER system began operating globally in 1958. The new technology produced an electronic surface picture (SURPIC) of an area of the ocean and indicated locations of AMVER-participating ships within it. During the 1960s and 1970s, the system had been a vital element in the Mercury, Gemini, Apollo, and Skylab space programs. By 1980, AMVER-equipped ships around the globe and the control center processed two thousand reports a day. In its most spectacular success, the life of a Scottish seaman aboard the motor vessel *Tyne Bridge* was saved when a SURPIC sweep located a passenger ship with a doctor on board. Based at the Department of Transportation Systems Center, Washington, D.C., AMVER employed a Control Data Corporation mainframe computer.

In an office adjacent to the radio room as the *Prinsendam* eased away from the pier, the ship's purser, A. J. M. Boxebeld, and hotel manager Zeller checked the passenger manifest and counted

320. Officers, crew, and other Holland America personnel aboard totaled 204. In the first-night-aboard tradition of passenger ships, guests were not expected to dress up for their first meal. As they entered the dining room, they were greeted by Captain Wabeke, the hotel manager, and officers, with the ship's photographer snapping them with the captain.

At each of the place settings the large menu for the welcome dinner had a floral picture (iris) on the cover. The bill of fare was on facing pages in English on the left and Dutch on the right. The choices lived up to the brochure's promise that the chefs would "outdo themselves" creating delicious specialties. After a choice of juices (tomato, grapefruit, clam, and apple), the menu listed:

Hors d'Oeuvres
Pâté of Strasburg goose liver
Smoked salmon, sturgeon, and river eel with capers
Fresh melon scoops in cup, port wine
Assorted Baltic and Dutch relishes

Soups
Consommé Asparagus, Alba-Velouté Trafalgar
Apple-Vichyssoise Glacée

Fish
Poached Tranche of Turbot, melted butter
Farinaceous Ravioli al Sugo di Carne

Entrée
The Planked Steak (Prime Sirloin Steak as you like it and done to your taste)

Special du Chef: Braised Leg of Lamb, Provençale (Tomato sauce with onions, garlic, peppers, olives. Anchovies)

Poultry
Brandied duckling, spiced dressing
Royal Ann Cherry Compote

Vegetables
Cauliflower Mornay, glazed carrots, stuffed tomato
Buttered pilaw rice

Potatoes
Fines herbes, rissoles, nuggets
Baked Idaho potato with sour cream and scallions

Salads and dressings
Crisp lettuce, mixed greens, and grand bean salad
French, Russian and Blue Cheese dressing
Low calorie: Salad Neptune (Artichoke bottom with lobster, celery, hard boiled egg and pimento on a bed of crisp lettuce, mayonnaise or Thousand Island dressing)

Cheeses
International cheese from the tray
Dutch rusks, crackers, pumpernickel, crisp bread

Sherbet
Sherbet "Morning Star" (Watermelon)

Desserts
Coupe "St. Jacques"
Carmelita Cake, Stefaner Rollade
Bavarois Diplomate, Friandises
Butter-pecan, vanilla, and peach ice cream

Fruit
Selection of fresh fruit
Figs and dates, Steminger in syrup, mixed nuts

Beverages
Coffee, tea, chocolate, milk.

(Wine, champagne, beer, and liqueurs were available on request for an additional charge that would appear on the passenger's shipboard account at the end of the trip.)

Jeannie Gilmore had chosen the first dinner sitting because she thought a later serving would be too late and waiting might tire her mother. Also at table nine for four were Mrs. Ann Corey and her mother, Mrs. Stanley Foster, an early dinner being indicated by Ann for the same reason. John Gyorokos and wife Ginny and their teenage children shared a table for six with Mr. and Mrs. Solomon. By chance or design, all the places were soon filled and the feasting began. Among those in the second seating, Elizabeth Price and her traveling companion, Lynn Detroit, on their fourth cruise together, dined with Australians. Len Bennett was from Perth and May Caodel from Adelaide. Both named places to see on the Indonesian option that they had found especially interesting during vacation sojourns from their homeland.

Preferring to enjoy cocktails before dinner, Richard and Louise Steele had indicated a later seating. Either by happenstance or by whim, the maître d' had gone over the roster of those who had not specified a table preference and matched Polish-sounding names, Marjorie and Richard Cezikowipz of San Bruno, California, were at a table with Elizabeth Czetwrtynski and her husband of Tryon, North Carolina. Two and a half years after a stroke, Marjorie had almost recovered totally but still had leg weakness and relied on a wheelchair. While they dined, brief life stories were swapped, their families and careers discussed, and hopes for smooth sailing expressed, along with why they were on the cruise, what they looked forward to doing and seeing, comparing accommodations, and agreeing that the *Prinsendam* was a truly beautiful little cruise ship.

By the time dinner service was completed, she was well underway. The sky was partly cloudy, the night air comfortable, and the ocean placid. Most passengers went off to bed. Some strolled the Promenade Deck. A few occupied chairs on the Lido Terrace facing the stern and gazed at the white trail cut into the dark water by the ship's wake, growing wider and less defined the farther the ship moved. No one decided to take a dip in the swimming pool. At the opposite end of the Promenade Deck the Prinsen Club was experiencing a very lively trade in nightcaps and the selling of Cuban cigars, barred to connoisseurs in the United States since President John Kennedy slapped on a trade embargo to signify America's displeasure with communism that had been imposed by dictator Fidel Castro just ninety miles from Miami. Enjoying the knowledge of partaking Cohibas that would be illicit at home, retired Colonel Henry Heinichen and World War II vet Earl Andrews coddled snifters of brandy and bantered yarns about their active-duty days. The cigars led to how it was too bad that the 1961 Bay of Pigs invasion had failed and that Castro had his Red neck saved in the Cuban Missile Crisis of 1962 by Kennedy and Soviet boss Nikita Khrushchev. Staring at the real prospect of thermonuclear war, they'd hastily cut a deal to save face, national pride, and several thousand years of civilization.

Had Richard Steele been part of the conversation between the retired soldiers, he could have given them the journalism side of the crisis and how ABC's Washington correspondent John Scali had been a secret communication channel for both sides in clandestine meetings that were real-life cloak-and-dagger stuff with none of the flash of the James Bond books and films. If the barstool talk dwelled on Kennedy, he had plenty of tales to tell about him and the rest of the clan that had become the most famous names in Massachusetts since Sam, John, and John Quincy Adams and found "the Kennedys" twentieth-century American royalty. Steele also could have related the shock, sadness, and anger he'd felt when United Press International flashed the news that shots had been fired at Kennedy's motorcade in Dallas on November 22, 1963, followed by another flash that the president was dead. If any in the Prinsen Club were interested, he had yarns about the scramble to cover the assassination and its aftermath because for the Worcester *Telegram-Gazette* it was also a local story. But were he to launch into such stories, Louise was likely to switch the subject to Kennedy's glamorous and fashionable wife, Jackie.

Like Jeannie Gilmore after she was certain that her mother was comfortably in her bed, rather than settle themselves in the bar, Richard and Louise walked around the Promenade Deck with him puffing the day's last cigar. They found little about the *Prinsendam* to match the TV series *The Love Boat*. Captain Wabeke was nothing like the fictional ship's master, Captain Merrill Stubing, played by Gavin MacLeod. Nor was the compact *Prinsendam* like the show's expansive *Pacific Princess,* except that the luxury cruise ships' destinations were exotic places. There was certainly a difference in their passengers' ages. If those aboard the *Prinsendam* as she headed in the night for Ketchikan were cast in a weekly television show, Richard thought, the name of the cruise ship would probably be *The Old Codger Boat.* But youth was the currency of the TV generation, and the effect of *The Love Boat* was that people believed cruise ships were settings for falling in or out of love and that the captain, officers, hostesses, bartenders, and the crew were there solely to guide passengers' lives, not run a ship.

As Richard and Louise strolled the Promenade Deck with little resemblance to actors in a television show, he counted six lifeboats and two motor launches. Life preservers were hung on railings at convenient spots, but they struck him as more decorative than reliably useful in an emergency. The most essential safety device was a life jacket provided for each individual, with their use to be demonstrated by the crew at the outset of a voyage. Because an exhibition of life-vest use had not taken place, he supposed it would occur tomorrow, along with a practice by the crew in lowering the lifeboats. The vast majority of the mostly Indonesian crew, he thought, seemed quite young, but he reasoned that he'd reached an age when everyone in the crew was very youthful looking. He and Louise had arrived at that time in their long lives when a trip on a Love Boat meant a drink before dinner, satisfying food, a walk in the night sea air, and a good night's sleep.

With the lights out in their room, waiting for slumber to come, Richard listened to the distant hum of the engine deep below and felt the very subtle swaying of the ship.

CHAPTER 3

Shipshape

For Holland America Line, 1980 was its 107th year of carrying passengers on what the firm's centennial commemorative book had called "A Bridge to the Seven Seas." Founded in Rotterdam on April 18, 1873, as the result of the reorganization of the financially struggling Plat, Reuchin & Co., it was named Nederlandsch-Amerikaansche Stoomvaart Maatschappij (NASM). The primary purpose was providing transportation of goods and people to America. Because the company received no aid from the Dutch government and Holland had no naturally deep harbors, the dimensions of ships were restricted and growth of the company proved slow. The new entity's prize property, the *Rotterdam*, had made her maiden voyage from the Netherlands to New York in October 1872. Weekly sailings by it and additional ships to the United States alternated from the ports of Rotterdam and Amsterdam. Purchase of seven British steamers put the company in a stronger position to compete with larger lines, such as Red Star and Cunard, for the Atlantic route. In 1890 it was profitable enough to buy its Hoboken, New Jersey, dock.

Five years later, the *Rotterdam* sailed from Holland to Copenhagen, Denmark, and back on a short summer voyage that introduced the "cruise." On June 15, 1896, NASM changed its name to Holland Amerika Lijn. By the firm's twenty-fifth anniversary it was operating six ships and claimed to have carried ninety thousand cabin passengers and four hundred thousand in steerage from Europe to America. From the 1890s to the 1920s its ships conveyed more than ten percent of the New World's immigrants. By its centennial year (1973), the total exceeded eight hundred fifty thousand. On the second Holland America Line cruise (1910), the luxurious *Statendam* went from New York to the Mediterranean and the Holy Land. During World War I, the line lost six ships and twelve employees in submarine attacks. While the *Statendam* was in Belfast, Ireland, for safekeeping, the British took it over and converted it to a troop ship and named her *Justicia*. Back in full service following the war, the line built four combined passenger and cargo ships and expanded its cruise service to include the Caribbean and an around-the-world voyage (1926) that offered a "floating university." At the start of World War II the line had twenty-five ships. When Germany occupied the Netherlands, a Dutch government in exile was established on its liner *Westerland*, berthed at Falmouth, England. Other ships of its fleet were used as troop transports and sailed half a million miles, carrying four hundred thousand men.

During the 1950s and 1960s, Holland America's advertising slogan was, "It's good to be on a well-run ship." In 1968 the company boasted that its flagship *Nieuw Amsterdam II*, the *Rotterdam V*, and *Statendam IV* were cruising nearly full time. That year *Rotterdam V* became the first passenger ship to employ a "hotel manager." Holland America was also the first line to adopt the "Lido" dining concept of casual attire and a wide variety of selections in the dining room. In 1969, as transoceanic travel by jet airliners was rapidly outmoding crossings by ship, the line began promoting "Holland American Cruises." It also began recruiting dining room staff in Indonesia, with a training program in Bandung that used actual Holland America Line place settings. The first graduates of the school began working on the *Ryndam* in 1970.

Abandoning transatlantic operations in 1971, Holland America redeployed the *Nieuw Amsterdam* to Port Everglade, Florida, for cruises of ten and eleven days. It also acquired one million shares of the Alaska tour company Westours at $1.25 a share, giving Holland America controlling interest. Registering its ships in Willemstad, Curaçao, Netherlands Antilles, it also introduced midnight blue to the hulls of its passenger ships. On its one-hundredth anniversary, the fleet consisted of four cruise vessels, four cargo transports, and three cargo-container ships.

To mark its centennial in 1973 the company commissioned *A Bridge to the Seven Seas,* a large, lavishly illustrated book by two authors with the same name, Dick Schaap. The one in Amsterdam wrote it in Dutch. The Dick Schaap in New York was the famous sports writer/columnist and best-selling author of *Instant Replay.* He translated the book into English. Because the *Prinsendam* hadn't been completed as they wrote, it was depicted in a photograph of a model, looking rakish against an almost cloudless sky.

"Cruising," they wrote, "is not the boring life of the elite rich, as it once was painted. Rather, it is the place for the sea-minded. It is the place for people who see mystery in the ocean, mystery in its strength and restlessness. And cruising is the place for those who truly care to see how others live." To travel, to explore the world, and the thrill, the two Schaaps continued, "is so much greater by ship. Sailing on the running tide, with the sound of water and the sight of water. Then returning home to tell about double vacations; the one of incomparable atmosphere on a large and social floating ship hotel; the one of interesting adventures away from the ship." In 1973, Holland America was looking forward to the launching of its first purpose-built cruise liner. An 8,566-ton, 452-foot passenger motor vessel, the *Prinsendam* was to have a twin sister ship, scheduled for service in 1974. These additions to the fleet, said Holland America, were designed to "open up new and exciting fly/cruise possibilities" by offering alternating identical fourteen-day cruises from Singapore to the Indonesian islands. But an opportunity to acquire a pair of liners from the Moore-McCormack line scuttled the order for a second ship that had been placed in December of 1970 with the Dutch ship-building firm, N. V. Scheepswerft en Machinefabriek "De Merwde" v/h Van Vliet & Co. Work began on building "Hull No. 606" with the laying of the keel in October 1971 and a goal of completing the $27 million ship and delivering her in the spring of 1973. Seven months after the keel-laying, the hull was launched (July 7, 1972) and sent to Wilton-Fijenoord shipyard in Schiedam, Netherlands, to be outfitted.

Construction of a passenger ship required adherence to safety specifications and rules of international agreements that established standards for placement and structures of watertight doors to separate sections of ships carrying more than thirty-six passengers. In preparatory talks about the building of the *Prinsendam* between the owners, Holland Amerika Lijn, and the Netherlands government's shipping inspection department, the company said that it wished the *Prinsendam* to comply with all standards of watertight compartmentalization, engine design, fuel-supply system, and engine-room firefighting systems, as well as those affecting the bilge pumping system.

The machines that powered the *Prinsendam* were four eight-cylinder, 4,000 horsepower engines, numbered one, two, three, and four, placed from port to starboard. Those to port could be coupled to drive the port propeller shaft and the starboard pair the starboard propeller shaft. The screws were variable pitch, with an alternator forward of each inner engine shaft. These supplied all electrical power when the ship was underway. The auxiliary engine room's two alternators supplied power when not underway. The main and auxiliary engine rooms were separated by a watertight bulkhead with a watertight door. Another watertight bulkhead was set forward of the auxiliary engine room.

Plans for the main engines' fuel-supply system called for them to run on heavy oil as well as diesel oil. The heavy oil was primarily for starting the engines and maneuvering. It was pumped to a settling tank (number nineteen) on the starboard side by an automatic pump. Another tank on the port side contained clean oil for emergencies. A heavy fuel oil separator drew fuel from tank nineteen starboard and pumped clean oil to the heavy-oil service tank and was always kept full. Overflow went back to tank nineteen starboard through an overflow glass. Clean oil in the service tank (number twenty) was drawn out by low-pressure fuel-booster pumps. Various auxiliary equipment included a quick-closing valve on the service tank, booster pumps (one running and one on standby), two fuel heaters (operating and standby), a viscosity meter, and a pressure valve.

The eight-cylinder engines were connected to fuel lines by rubber tubes that were to be replaced every two years because they were continuously subjected to short pressure impulses and more vibration in eight-cylinder engines than six- and nine-cylinder engines. These stresses could result in leaks. Another vulnerability was a hollow-bolt connection on the high-pressure pump. The bolt could be damaged if it were tightened too much, causing a crack in the small fuel supply and return holes under the bolt head.

Firefighting equipment consisted of pumps in the main engine room, auxiliary engine room, and stabilizer room. These were electrically powered, centrifugal, self-priming pumps. A bilge/fire pump was also installed. Pressure lines were connected with water mains on A Deck. Fires in the engine room were extinguished with water, foam, six portable extinguishers in the main engine room, four in the auxiliary engine room, and one each in the stabilizer room and a connecting tunnel. A system of pumping carbon dioxide that could feed the fire-quenching gas to both engine rooms simultaneously was controlled from the Bridge Deck. Fire detectors were situated in the engine room and connected to alarms in the control room. Seven fire dampers could be operated from the Bridge Deck, on the port side, the Sun Deck, and the lounge on the Promenade Deck. Fire hydrants fitted with hoses and nozzles were positioned throughout the ship, along with portable extinguishers. Fire stations were on B Deck aft of the engine room, the Main Deck, and on the Promenade Deck next to the movie theater. The stations were equipped with two to four heat-resisting suits, flashlights, fifty kilograms of dry extinguishing powder, gas masks, and breathing apparatus.

These systems and the design and construction of the *Prinsendam* complied with Method III of specifications contained in the agreement of the International Congress of Safety of Life at Sea (SOLAS). While it dictated a sophisticated automated fire-detection system and use of fire-retardant surfaces in all passageways and cabin bulkheads, Method III did not require installation of a shipwide sprinkler system. The *Prinsendam* also met all standards of the U.S. Coast Guard and would pass a routine inspection a few months before the September 30, 1980 sailing. Ten watertight bulkheads with twenty-five watertight doors divided the ship into eleven sections. Three life boats were on the starboard side of the Bridge Deck; number one was a motor launch that could hold forty-three people. The lifeboats had a capacity of ninety-nine each. Between them were six inflatable life rafts that could hold twenty-five each. The port side had six rafts and three boats designated two (motor launch), four, and six. Each motorized boat was equipped with a radio transmitter. When the cruise ship was at anchor in port, rather than at dockside, the motorboats could ferry passengers ashore.

Holland America planned to take delivery of the *Prinsendam* in late April 1973 and send her on an inaugural cruise to Singapore on June 1. But the schedule went awry on April 24 when a fire started in a refuse bin in the barroom. The blaze quickly spread to the electrical wiring. Out of control for an hour and a half, the fire spread smoke and soot throughout the ship, ruining the interior. A survey of the damage found a need to not only clean and repair the cabins and public areas, but to rewire the electrical system. Estimating this would take five months, Holland America canceled all Indonesian cruises and set November 30, 1973 as the date for the *Prinsendam*'s debut, sailing from Rotterdam. She was ready on November 12, leaving eighteen days to get her sea-ready. To the relief of the company, she departed on time, with brief stops at Southampton, England; Lisbon, Portugal; several African ports; and Jakarta, Indonesia, en route to a festive Singapore welcome on January 11, 1974. Three days later, she commenced her first cruise.

With a length of 427 feet and a width of 62 feet (139 by 19 meters), the *Prinsendam* had a passenger capacity of 452, but was limited by Holland America to a maximum of 375 for cruises. Her maximum cruising speed was nineteen knots. The sales brochure for 1974–1976 cruises advertised a ship that was "elegant, comfortable and designed for cruising to exotic and undiscovered places . . . a dashing vessel, with a delightful life-style all her own." Available were fourteen-day Indonesia Adventure Cruises from October 21, 1974 to April 21, 1975, and a second from November 10, 1975 through April 12, 1976. Seven-day Secret Ports cruises went from Singapore, and Mystery Island cruises left Jakarta every other Monday. An ambitious traveler with time to spare could choose a twenty-three-day inclusive tour from Amsterdam (reachable from New York on KLM Royal Dutch Airlines 747 jets) to Singapore and Bangkok, Thailand, or go from Los Angeles to Tokyo, Singapore, and the Indonesia islands.

Travel advisor and writer Morgan Lawrence gave the *Prinsendam*'s debut a glowing review. Other assessments by invited members of the press and the first paying passengers agreed. Some called her a mini-liner. Others saw a "luxury cruising yacht." A 1975, Holland America's "Mariner News" publicity brochure announced an expansion of the *Prinsendam*'s itinerary to Alaska, with cruises from May to November, starting in Vancouver and ending in Singapore.

The sales brochure for 1978–1979 exclaimed, "As you cruise between two continents on the ms *Prinsendam*, you'll enjoy some of the most magnificent accommodations afloat. We think you'll agree–a once-in-a-lifetime journey deserves a one-in-a-million ship."

The enticement had persuaded travel writer Carolyn Stuff to book an odyssey through the Indonesian archipelago. "I was fortunate in having friends aboard," she recalled, "so each evening we met for cocktails in the lounge, frequently after having gone our separate ways during the day." On succeeding nights, dinner menus featured cuisines–French, Swiss, Dutch, German, and, inevitably, Indonesian, Stuff wrote, "in overwhelming abundance from caviar to *mousse au chocolat*." And there were lunches, afternoon snacks, midnight buffets, and "early bird coffee and continental breakfast in the Lido Café or terrace beside the pool."

By all accounts, the *Prinsendam* was a honey of a ship.

CHAPTER 4

Drill

For a moment after Jeannie Gilmore awoke at first light on Wednesday, October 1, 1980, she didn't know where she was. She definitely wasn't in her bed in Burlingame, California. In that split second, she was aware of a slight swaying of the small, dim room and thought she felt the beginning of an earthquake. Realizing that she was on a ship took an instant and came with a smiling memory of last night's splendid dinner and the delightful walk around the Promenade Deck. A glance at the other bed assured her that her sleeping mother was fine. With a glimpse at a bedside wind-up travel clock with an alarm that she'd set for eight o'clock, she saw that it was just past seven. She decided to let her mother sleep until then, at least.

According to the itinerary, the *Prinsendam* would not reach its first stop, Ketchikan, until eight the next morning. Passengers could go ashore for an eight-hour period for a feel and taste of the town that called itself the salmon capital of the world. In the meantime, they would spend their first day at sea in a variety of activities available on Holland America's wonderful little cruise ship. Or just pass the time loafing or in a deck chair looking at the ocean. At some point, she supposed, the crew would show everyone what to do in case of an emergency, from putting on a life-preserver vest to knowing which of the lifeboats would be theirs. But *not* until after breakfast, please, Jeannie thought, intending to go back to sleep until the alarm clock went off.

Still not adjusted to the time difference between the East and West Coasts that air travelers called jet lag, Richard Steele had found himself wide awake at four in the morning, instead of his usual seven o'clock awakening in Worcester, Massachusetts. Were he at home, he would turn on a radio or the TV to get the news from the previous night. He had boarded the *Prinsendam* to get away from journalism, but that goal was easier to say than it was to realize. He wouldn't see a newspaper until the ship got to Ketchikan, assuming that the town had one, or that Wednesday eastern papers would be available, which he doubted. This possibility caused him to wonder if the radio operator in the *Prinsendam*'s wireless room followed the practice of counterparts on ocean liners of the past by posting a summary of the day's current events. Unable to go back to sleep, he rolled out of bed and went to a porthole to check the state of the weather. The sky was clear and the water looked calm. He dressed and donned a light windbreaker to go out to light up a cigar and go down to the Promenade Deck for a walk. Leaving the cabin, he encountered an impossibly boyish-looking crewman swabbing the deck.

Obviously startled to see a passenger awake and out hours before dawn, the youth smiled and made a slight bow. "Good morning, sir. Everything okay, sir?"

"Yes, thank you," Steele replied. "It's just the jet lag, you see."

"Breakfast," said the crewman, resuming his work, "is served starting at seven o'clock."

By then, Steele thought as he struck a match that the wind immediately extinguished, he might be hungry enough to eat.

Stepping into the passageway between the Lido and the lounge, he managed to light the cigar and saw through an open door that other equally youthful crewmen were readying the Lido for the first wave of breakfast-seeking passengers. Returning to the deck, he was passed by a man who looked seventy, at least. In a purple jogging outfit, he was running as if Satan himself were in hot pursuit of his immortal soul.

From Los Angeles, David Levin was seventy-seven and a believer in physical fitness and healthy eating. In his youth he'd been a surfer, long before wet suits were as common on the beaches of Southern California as the seals that their black suits resembled. Well before hordes of muscular young men carried boards as if they'd invented them and years prior to a quintet of kids called the Beach Boys hit the pop music charts with "Surfin' USA," Levin had been riding the waves. A jog, run, or walk around the Promenade Deck five times came to a mile.

As the sun rose above the Alaskan mountains, the *Prinsendam* awoke slowly. Early birds drifted to the Lido Club and main dining room, enticed by the aroma of coffee and the smell of bacon and pancakes. Sleepy eyes and smiles of recognition greeted people who had been strangers before last night's dinner. Thoughts turned to plans for the day. An activities sheet slipped under cabin doors during the night listed the choices—a morning lecture in the theater on the subject of what to expect in Ketchikan, craft lessons in the lounge, a magic show following dinner, a showing of the movie version of the musical *South Pacific*, gift shop hours, shuffleboard on the sports deck, skeet-shooting from the fantail, and instructions on the use of life vests with a lifeboat drill at eleven o'clock on the Bridge Deck. The sheet warned that the drill was *"Required of all Passengers."*

Having gone through such what-to-do-in-an-emergency demonstrations on ocean liners, Richard Steele assumed that some *Prinsendam* passengers wouldn't take the drill seriously. History recorded that few had bothered in 1979 on the Italian-registered *Angelina* that had a kitchen fire and sank. Fortunately there were no casualties because she was berthed in St. Thomas in the U.S. Virgin Islands and most of the passengers were ashore. This had not been the outcome when the Greek liner *Lakonia* burned off Madeira on a Christmas cruise in 1963 and 125 people died. Two years later, ninety perished in a fire on the Panamanian-registered *Yarmouth Castle*, bound from Miami to Nassau. A blaze that began in a storage room had engulfed lifeboats and radio equipment. Only the speedy response of rescue ships on July 25, 1956, prevented all but 50 of the 1,700 passengers on the *Andrea Doria* from being lost after she collided with the freighter *Stockholm* in thick fog off the coast of Nantucket.

Passengers on the *Prinsendam* were expected to bring their life jackets so they could be instructed on how to wear them. During the drill, lifeboat assignments would be given. Crewmen would demonstrate—and practice—lowering the boats. They were also to show how to operate the lifeboat's rowing mechanism. It consisted of four moveable overhead metal contraptions that looked like long chinning bars. Extending from one side of the boat to the other, they were a substitute for oars. Reaching up and pulling and pushing them activated a small propeller below the boat.

Part of the exercise that did not involve passengers was a test of the watertight doors, controlled from the bridge. Another boat drill by the crew would be conducted at Ketchikan. While the ship was moored with the port side against the dock, the starboard boats would be lowered to the water. Under command of the senior second engineer officer a small fire drill would be held by an engine-room fire team.

Steele found the lifeboat drill efficient and impressive. "Everyone inventoried, each assigned to specific boats, everyone in a life jacket," he noted. "The boats are not lowered all the way. Who cares? We'll never use them. The all-clear whistle blows. We scurry back to the Lido Deck to play and relax."

The signal for an emergency, noted Edwin Ziegfeld, would be ringing of a bell, one long and three short. During the drill, he snapped a few pictures with his new camera and got a funny shot of John Courtney in a life jacket. After they returned the jackets to their cabin, they made their way to the Lido for breakfast.

With the emergency drill completed, Captain Wabeke shifted his attention to the latest weather report from the wireless room, particularly to the location of Typhoon Thelma. From experience in dealing with typhoons on such a track he was confident that Thelma's only effect on his ship when she headed for open ocean after a stop at Ketchikan and a cruise of Glacier Bay would be rain, strong winds, and choppy water. Within the subpolar zone, warm air moving north from the mid-Pacific and cold air coming south from the Arctic clashed most strongly during the cold half of the year. As solar energy falling on the arctic regions diminished, the phenomenon known as the Aleutian Low strengthened in September, eventually producing storms to blanket the forty-ninth state with ever-deepening snow. This was why Holland America Line cruises in Alaskan waters commenced in April and ended in October. Should Thelma prove to be a dangerous storm, the *Prinsendam* would remain in the Inland Passage until the typhoon disintegrated. The weather advisory indicated that she was already losing her punch.

If not, passengers who did not have sea legs would be in for a few hours of rough going and the infirmary would experience a brisk business dispensing seasickness remedies. For now, however, it was smooth sailing, on course and on time for the passengers' rendezvous with their first chance to collect souvenirs in the quaint old fishing town of Ketchikan.

There wasn't much that the lecturer in the theater on the Promenade Deck could tell Jeannie Gilmore and her mother, Neva Hall, about the self-advertised salmon capital of the world. They'd been there. Fellow sojourners who hadn't and wanted a preview learned that Ketchikan dated back to 1883, when Portland, Oregon, businessmen hired Mike Martin to look into possibilities of building a cannery on Ketchikan Creek. By the early 1900s the population was eight hundred. Fishing, mining, and logging made it an important trading community. In 1980 the main industry was tourism. Of course, natives had been there long before. They'd called it "Hatch Kanna," meaning "spread wings of a thundering eagle." On the western coast of Revillagigedo Island, 679 miles north of Seattle and 235 miles south of Juneau, it had the benefit of a maritime climate of warm winters and cool summers. Average annual rainfall was 130 inches and the yearly snow amounted to thirty-two inches.

Among the audience at the lecture, Alex Composito of Seattle, Washington, had not in his wildest imagination ever contemplated either visiting Ketchikan or joining a cruise. When he traveled, it was by airplane and was related to his wholesale clothing import business. His venture on the *Prinsendam* was the result of two personal disruptions in his life. At the age of fifty-five, after twenty years of marriage, he found himself a divorced man. It was neither his fault nor his wife Ellen's. With their children grown up and gone, he and Ellen had just drifted apart. The other event leading to being on the ship was the death five months ago of his father, Tony, of a heart attack at the age of seventy-five. He'd died without taking Alex's mother, Theresa, age seventy-two, to Japan to see where he'd been stationed in the navy during the Korean War. With the *Prinsendam* cruise paid for, and feeling a need to get away and come to terms with the end of his marriage, and feeling that his mother also ought to get away for awhile, Alex suggested that he accompany her. They shared a cabin that Tony had selected on B Deck. What no one but Alex and Theresa knew was that she had brought an urn containing Tony's ashes and planned to scatter them at sea as the ship approached Yokohama. Had the former sailor lived a little longer to realize his nostalgic dream he probably would have noted that the *Prinsendam* was now gliding through slightly choppy water.

In the hospital in the bow of A Deck the effect of the increase in the sway and roll of the ship had presented Dr. Menger a few requests for seasickness treatment. Below in the engine room, Second Engineer Officer de Boer and greasers Zainai Abidin and Mohamad Ali sipped coffee during a break, their ears accustomed to the noise of four engines. At the bottom of the ship they felt none of the swaying and rolling that was noticeable to some passengers on the upper decks. Leaving the wheelhouse to Chief Officer H. E. Valk, the *Prinsendam*'s skipper, Captain Wabeke, was in his quarters also having a mug of coffee while studying the chart of Ketchikan's harbor and a report on weather conditions provided by the wireless room. Nothing he read relating to Thelma provided any reason for concern. The *Prinsendam* had experienced worse typhoons during the summertime Asian cruises. As to Ketchikan, he'd taken the ship into the port many times. He was satisfied with how the emergency drill had gone and looked forward to greeting each of his passengers at the evening's first dress-up dinner when women who chose to don evening dress would look lovely and the men who wore tuxedos handsome.

The bill of fare already being prepared by the chefs was their Epicurean Dinner. Its courses offered the Javanese Temptation of broiled fresh rock lobster tails, fried sirloin steak "Julius Caesar" topped with Strasburg goose liver pâté rolled in raw ham, Piccate di Vitello alla Lombarda (young veal morsels turned in light hazelnut butter), and Shaslik Tashkent, described on the menu as "dainty minions of tender lamb, submerged in aromatic spices and brandy to absorb its exquisite flavor," broiled on a skewer. For the weight-conscious there was the low-calorie Waistline Salad. As on ocean liners, time on cruise ships was measured in eating, from breakfast to lunch, light fare in the lounge in late afternoon, and dinner to midnight supper. All around the Promenade Deck between eating as the ship passed eastward of the Queen Charlotte Islands archipelago of more than 150 islands on route to the Nicholas Passage and the Tongass Narrows to Ketchikan, more than three hundred relaxed and well-fed passengers did whatever caught their interest. Many lounged on the Lido Deck. A few souls defied cool air temperatures by trying out the swimming pool. Above on the Bridge Deck sports area, John Courtney and Edwin Ziegfeld joined Ethel and Francis Burrowski of Miami, Florida, in a shuffleboard match as the Solomons watched. Betty Milborn and her aunt were inside browsing in the gift shop. Barbara Clark had decided to get her hair done in the beauty parlor. Dr. Stanford and Eleanor Farnsworth paused in a starboard-side stroll of the Promenade Deck to have a closer look at their assigned lifeboat and agreed that it seemed awfully small.

Settled in the lounge with her mother after breakfast, Jeannie Gilmore wondered how husband Bill and daughter Carole were getting along without her as she leafed through a booklet containing details of Indonesian shore excursions, including Bali, "island of enchantment, of tranquil beauty, island of temples and ceremonies." Ever-gregarious, her mother, Neva Hall, was making a new friend of fifty-nine-year-old Dorothy Harrington and swapping stories about Harrington's splendid hometown, San Francisco. A hostess, identified by a small nameplate as S. Stevens, drifted through the lounge asking couples, small groups, and individuals if they were satisfied with the service and their accommodations. Assured that they were, she moved on.

Light rain greeted the *Prinsendam* as she eased into Ketchikan's harbor early on Thursday morning, October 2, but the sky brightened to afford a day of sightseeing and shopping along the rustic boardwalk of Creek Street. Muriel Marvinney bought "an exquisite pair of tiny mukluks" (soft fur-lined Eskimo boots) for her baby grandson. Among Jeannie Gilmore's purchases made in Hill's Indian Crafts at Vancouver were a scenic print for twenty-five dollars and two small totem poles for twenty-eight dollars and fifty-three dollars. Whatever irresistible treasures and trinkets Ketchikan shops offered remained to be discovered. Determined to take presents home to her students, she bought several tiny totem poles and other native handicrafts. For herself she purchased a small painting of a mother and her children by a local artist because she was drawn to its life-affirming symbolism.

Jim and Kitty Flynn of Redwood City, California, mailed a postcard with a picture of the ship to their son Colin that said, "It's raining here. Got off the ship this morning & walked a few blocks. Ship small, but comfortable. Everyone very friendly. Had some rough seas last night, but didn't disturb us. Didn't like our 'table mates,' so we are changing to an early seating this evening. Danced till 12:30 last night to good little orchestra. Lots of white evening jackets at Captain's party. Love, The Sailors."

While the passengers were ashore in Ketchikan the lifeboat crews practiced lowering boats. When the *Prinsendam* was again underway in the late afternoon, the sun was peeking through breaks in the clouds. Entertainment after dinner featured Jack Malon's magic tricks, jokes by Roger Ray, and a young Greek musician, billed only by his first name. Yanni Chryssomalis was raised in Kalamata, Greece. A graduate of the University of Minnesota with a bachelor's degree in psychology, he'd been the keyboardist for Minneapolis-based rock band Chameleon and later became nationally known in the United States as Yanni through private-label albums of his own music sold directly through commercials on television.

For the most scenic portion of the Alaskan leg of the voyage during a leisurely cruise of Glacier Bay on Friday, October 3, a U.S. Park Service ranger delivered a lecture on the history of one of America's most spectacular national parks. The original inhabitants of Glacier Bay, Tlingit (pronounced klink-it) Indians lived in the region of what was now Glacier Bay National Park and Preserve until the end of the Little Ice Age. Advancing glaciers forced them to abandon their villages and move to Hoonah, across Icy Strait. In 1794, British exploration ship *Discovery* captained by George Vancouver anchored in Point Althorp as a survey crew under command of Lieutenant Joseph Whidbey maneuvered longboats through ice-choked waters of Icy Strait and created a survey chart that recorded an indentation in the shore topography that "terminated in solid compact mountains of ice."

The glacier that filled the bay was then in rapid retreat, producing a floating icepack and a projection into the strait that reached almost to Lemesurier Island. Historians noted that even as Glacier Bay lay encased in ice, natives carried on their activities in many locations along the nearby coast. In 1879, explorer and naturalist John Muir relied on Tlingit guides in a search for glaciers, adventure, and spiritual enrichment. The first of distinguished scientists/naturalists to visit the region, he made his last trip to Glacier Bay in 1899 with an expedition organized by American railroad tycoon Edward Harriman. The sojourn included scientists, artists, writers, and photographers in an exploration from Alaska's southeast boundary to the Seward Peninsula. It remained in Glacier Bay five days. Soon after the Harriman expedition left, an earthquake shook the glacier named for Muir and unleashed masses of floating ice that prevented later ships from closely approaching the glacier for a decade. Steamship companies removed Glacier Bay from their itineraries.

Scientific interest in Glacier Bay remained high in the years after Muir and Harriman. After numerous visits, William S. Cooper, a plant ecologist studying the return of plant life to the recently de-glaciated terrain, persuaded the Ecological Society of America to spearhead a campaign for its preservation. The effort resulted in President Calvin Coolidge signing in 1925 a proclamation creating Glacier Bay National Monument. When a military air base built during World War II was converted to civilian use, Park Service planners had envisioned a lodge and administration area at Sandy Cove, accessible only by boat, that could be linked to the new airport by a few miles of road. Despite appeals from local homesteaders and national conservation organizations, fourteen thousand acres of land, including the Gustavus airport, were removed from the monument in 1955. Post-war prosperity and interest in outdoor recreation led to the development of parklands for visitors. In 1956, National Park Service director Conrad Wirth announced Mission 66. A ten-year program of planning and development for national parks, it was intended to coincide with the fiftieth anniversary of the founding of the Service. Glacier Bay was part of Mission 66 with funding for construction of the lodge, a dock, administration building, employee housing, and other facilities at Bartlett Cove. In the Alaska National Interest Lands Conservation Act of 1980, the park was extended to the Alsek River and Dry Bay.

Because of these improvements, Glacier Bay returned to itineraries of cruise ships and afforded Holland America an opportunity to maximize the value of the *Prinsendam* through repositioning trans-Pacific cruises from Vancouver to Japan by way of Ketchikan. To enhance the passengers' experience of quiet contemplation of Glacier Bay's natural wonders the engines were stopped. Muriel Marvinney would recall, "We silently drifted close to the towering walls of ice. The sun intermittently peeking through gray banks of clouds glanced off the blue-streaked glaciers, so that they sparkled like sapphires." For Jeannie Gilmore the glaciers were "turquoise-blue." Glaciers were not snow white or silver, as one might expect, the park ranger explained, because they absorbed all hues of the light spectrum except blue.

When Captain Wabeke commanded that the ship's four engines be restored to life after hours of long silences that were broken only by the occasional click of camera shutters and lowered voices, as if the passengers feared uttering a loud remark or making a sudden noise would shatter the ice like a delicate piece of crystal, the ship moved across the bay as slowly and gracefully as a swan on a pond. She glided toward a narrows that would be *Prinsendam*'s passage to the open ocean and her awed passengers' last stretch of serene water.

Having coursed north and east from the mid-Pacific, the season's seventeenth typhoon had arrived in the Gulf of Alaska, bringing rain and strong winds that stirred large waves with frothy white caps and deep troughs. Clouds that had parted to allow countless photographs of sun glinting on the ice slabs of Glacier Bay gathered above rugged terrain bracketing the ship. The weather was recorded fair, with a moderate sea and a high south-southwest swell. The chief officer and senior second engineer did not stand watch on the bridge. Available for this purpose were two second and third officers.

As the *Prinsendam* headed for the Unimak Passage at four thirty p.m. on October 3 to start the ten-day voyage toward a place that Americans who experienced World War II, such as U.S. Army veteran Earl Andrews, remembered their Japanese enemies' propaganda hailing as "The Land of the Rising Sun," passengers began to realize that there could be more to cruising than the glories and the luxuries described in the travel brochures. Since leaving Vancouver it had been smooth sailing. The decks had been level, handrails in passageways mostly untouched, and the going steady. Now the footing was becoming a little less sure.

The ship pitched and rolled on the high swells. Her jaunty bow dipped. The stern rose. The *Prinsendam* suddenly seemed as light as a cork. For two nights and two days the cruise had been as tranquil and pleasant as promised. Now, being on the

Prinsendam began to take on the aspects of riding a roller coaster. Passengers who had praised themselves for not getting seasick and had silently mocked those who did suddenly felt a little queasiness in their stomachs. Entering the dining room for the first sitting, Jeannie Gilmore noticed quite a number of vacant chairs. The bouncy going didn't bother Muriel Marvinney. She would recall having "a lovely" dinner that night with her intrepid friend Agnes Lilard. They were joined for the meal by equally dauntless friends that they'd made at breakfast on the first day out. Grace and Paul Miller were "the kind of caring people who make you feel totally at ease."

In a cruise diary that Muriel had decided to keep, she had recorded, "The scenery, as our ship made its way up Alaska's coastal inland waterway that first day, was gorgeous. There were towering cliffs on either side of us, and when the channel would narrow down they'd loom over us." Glacier Bay was "untouched by man since creation's dawn" and made her feel insignificant in comparison. She wrote, "We felt God."

Groaning in his cabin on B Deck, Alex Composito was feeling like hell. He had thought that lying down would help. As the bed rocked, he quickly realized he was mistaken. Unfazed by the rough conditions, his mother made him feel as if he were a kid again, telling him to cut out the complaining and find the ship's doctor and get something to settle his stomach. Rousing at last, he searched the deck plan for the hospital and hoped he'd reach it without throwing up in a corridor on the way. He arrived at the hospital door and found a line of similarly green-looking and miserable sufferers. Among them was the musician Yanni, hoping but doubtful that he'd feel better and not have to cancel his evening performance.

To serve however many passengers appeared in the dining room the ship's kitchen staff and waiters who had experienced bouts of rougher weather than this went about their business as if the *Prinsendam* were tied up in port. Beyond the swinging doors astern of the two-hundred-seat dining room the kitchen was a world apart from the plush décor of the rest of the ship. Built for utility, its walls were gleaming steel. The metal flooring was ribbed to prevent slipping. Dinner plates and other chinaware were stacked in cage-like holders. Table tops, counter surfaces, and stoves had raised edges to keep items from sliding to the floor. Cooks were sure-footed as they moved from refrigerators stocked with tons of staples and delicacies to preparation areas and stoves. Waiters trained in the Indonesian school and honed by experience carried food-laden trays from the heat of the kitchen to the tables of the air-conditioned dining room with nimble dexterity.

Three decks down, the engine room officers and crew were oblivious to the weather. In charge were the junior second engineer officer and third engineer officers, P. Aarnoutse and J. J. C. van Hardeveld. Fourth engineer officers F. J. R. Fabriek and J. C. Dörr and assistant engineer officer R. Kalf divided engine room watches. Because of the timing of meals they were scheduled to be relieved at midnight.

To prepare for the sumptuous food that Holland America Line had promised cruisers, Jeannie Gilmore and her mother had spent months slimming their waistlines, followed by a shopping spree for new clothes in smaller sizes. Determined to look her best, Jeannie bought a red suit. Because she would be taking a month off from teaching children confined to homes or hospitals with illnesses, she hired substitutes. Standing in line to board the flight that took them to Vancouver with yellow Holland America tags on her luggage, she noticed a couple with bags bearing the same identification. Naturally friendly, she'd introduced herself to Jim and Kitty Flynn, then asked him what he did for a living.

He replied. "I usually don't tell my profession to people that I just met. When I do, they feel uncomfortable and nervous."

Jeannie replied, "Now I am *really* curious."

Flynn smiled. "I own a mortuary."

"That's wonderful," Jeannie said with a laugh. "If anything terrible happens, you'll know just what to do."

This black humor seemed not quite so amusing a short time later on the airplane to the port of Vancouver when the seat next to Jeannie was taken by a man to whom she posed the same question. He replied that he was a missionary en route to an overseas posting. Gazing intently at Jeannie, he asked, "Are you prepared to meet your maker?"

Thinking this was an odd thing to ask someone going on a trip, she vehemently replied, "No. I'm going on a cruise, I'm going to have a wonderful time, and I plan to come back alive. I'll meet my maker in due time, but not right now."

Like many of the passengers, Jeannie had taken the emergency drill lightly and went up to the Promenade Deck without taking her life jacket. Now, as the ship was tossed about on its way to open ocean, she was wearing her favorite pearl necklace as she and her mother sat at table-for-four number nine and quickly realized they would be dining alone. Feeling empathy for those who were seasick, she enjoyed dinner, admired a fancy chocolate sculptured dessert that looked too gorgeous to eat, and felt sorry for the chef who had labored all day to create it, only to find the dining room more than half empty.

Jeannie recalled, "By then the ship was really rocking. My mom did not look well and said she was going down to the room."

Feeling fine herself, Jeannie went to the main lounge, anticipating taking in the evening's entertainment. Putting on a show aboard a ship in stormy weather proved challenging. The star, Yanni, offered a couple of songs but announced he was too ill to go on. With some of the young Broadway show singers laid low by seasickness, the remaining performers managed to do a few numbers. Nor did the orchestra fare well. While Jeannie felt sorry for the musicians having to play in such conditions, she couldn't help being amused by the plight of the poor violinist as he gripped a pillar to keep from being pitched off the bandstand. Suddenly feeling a need to throw up, he bounded down and rushed to the exit.

With live entertainment scuttled, Jeannie decided to see the night's feature film in the cinema. A remake of the 1934 tear-jerker *Little Miss Marker* that starred Shirley Temple and Adolph Menjou, this version had an all-star cast, including Julie Andrews, Walter Matthau, Tony Curtis, Bob Newhart, and Brian Dennehy, portraying Depression-era gamblers created by Damon Runyon in a story about a little girl who was left by Matthau's character as an IOU for a debt. Like the dining room, the theater was almost empty. Among those spared from seasickness was Edwin Ziegfeld. Alerted with the rest of the passengers that the evening's dinner dessert was to be spectacular sculptures in chocolate, Ziegfeld had taken his camera. His traveling partner, John Courtney, had felt too poorly to leave their cabin. Giving in to Louise's desire to see the film, Richard Steele endured a movie that he believed should have been left un-remade. When Louise returned to their cabin a few minutes after midnight, he went down the grand staircase to the Promenade Deck with the intention of enjoying the day's last cigar in the lounge, rather than daring the boisterous weather by taking a stroll on a rain-slicked rocking deck.

A spacious room at midship between the forward movie theater-lecture hall, shopping area, and intimate Prinsen Club and the aft Lido Restaurant, the spacious lounge's character and décor resembled a lobby of an upscale European tourist hotel. The only difference was pictures on the walls, depicting colorful tropical scenes of the *Prinsendam*'s Pacific Ocean itineraries. Chairs and sofas that were filled during the day were abandoned. A tan padded cover draped a baby grand piano on a small bandstand. The only patrons of the nine-stool bar to port at the rear of the lounge were three middle-aged men who evidently believed that the best way to deal with a stormy sea was to fortify themselves with tightly held glasses of strong drink.

Feeling no desire for post-midnight male companionship, Steele settled in a plush chair next to small table with an ashtray to pack his pipe. Lighting it, he thought about the movie he'd just seen and imagined what the original author of the story, Damon Runyon, would make of a situation involving three men at a bar and one sitting by himself in the lounge of a ship on a storm-tossed Alaskan waterway. What might Runyon see in the three drinkers and the solitary watcher? Which would become the story's main character?

Amused by the question, he decided that because Runyon had been a newspaperman he would choose the aloof pipe-smoker and fashion him as a guy with a card in his wallet or pinned to his shirt or coat that bore the most magic word in the dictionary of occupations: PRESS. He would be a man that the card had admitted to corridors of power, the smoke-filled rooms of men who decided who should wield it, lavish festivities in ballrooms and banquet halls, tenements and back alleys where murders had been committed, and anywhere else in an exciting, usually perilous world. The bar setting was just right. Hard news and stiff drinks were companions.

Chasing news, Runyon's character would have had rum and Coca-Cola highballs and gin martinis in long-stemmed glasses he had been told were modeled on a woman's breast. He'd have savored Manhattans in Manhattan, Old Fashioneds at the bar in the Astor Hotel in Times Square in New York, creamy Brandy Alexanders in the Starlight Room of the Waldorf-Astoria, tequila across from the Alamo, ouzo in Athens, Bushmills Irish whiskey in Belfast, tangy Thai beer in Bangkok, Budweiser from cans in Saigon, champagne in an elegant Wagons-Lit bar car of the Orient Express as though he were Hercule Poirot solving the murder in the Calais coach or James Bond in *From Russia With Love*, and gin and tonic at Harry's Bar in Venice, pretending he was Hemingway and waiting to have a drink with Ingrid Bergman or Gary Cooper.

In carrying out jobs he'd have been handed by an assignment desk, he might find himself pushed around, insulted and frequently ignored, or glad-handed and slapped on the back. He'd be conned, cajoled, flattered, seducer or seduced, and occasionally scared. As to who would play him in the movie, who would be a better fictionalized Richard Steele than Walter Matthau?

With his fanciful rumination ended, Steele looked across the empty lounge to the bar and saw that the trio of drinkers was gone. For an instant he had an eerie feeling that somehow while he had been thinking about a movie involving the news business, everyone had abandoned the ship. Returning to his cabin, he found Louise asleep. As he started to undress, something somewhere in the buffeted ship creaked. With wind-whipped rain pelting the panes of the two portholes, he had to steady himself against a sudden roll to port.

On B Deck, John Gyorokos had shed his three-piece black velvet tuxedo and hung it in the closet. Elizabeth Price was settled snugly in bed to read the Glacier Bay literature that had been handed out by the park ranger. The reverend Joan Thatcher never went to sleep without opening her Bible to read the ninety-first Psalm and its ever-assuring second verse: "I will say of the Lord, He is my refuge and my fortress: my God; in Him will I trust." John Courtney and Edwin Ziegfeld scanned the next day's activity sheet. Because of the rough waters, Betty Milborn had eaten a light meal of consommé and salad. Her aunt had enjoyed both a full meal and telling those at their table of her plans for celebrating her seventy-ninth birthday in Peking, China.

On the desk as Jeannie Gilmore put on a short nightgown lay a stack of postcards, with stamps, to be mailed from Yokohama, to her husband Bill and daughter Carole in Burlingame, her second daughter Christine, students and other teachers, and numerous friends. Pointing to a string of pearls still around Jeannie's neck, Neva Hall gave Jeannie a stern motherly look and demanded, "Are you planning to sleep with them on?"

"Mom, if the ship goes down," Jeannie replied, jokingly, "they're going to the bottom of the ocean with me."

CHAPTER 5

XXX

A t 12:40 a.m., Saturday, October 4, 1980, third engineer Jacob Van Hardeveld and assistant engineer Robert Kalf had been on watch in the engine room for ten minutes. Change of officers at 2400 hours (midnight) was delayed a half hour because of schedule modifications that the unfavorable weather conditions had imposed throughout the ship. While the passengers could retreat to their beds or brace themselves with drinks at the lounge bar, officers and crew had to carry out not only their routine tasks, but secure and batten down anything in the floating hotel that might become a hazard. Anticipating rampant seasickness, stewards and porters had placed brown paper "barf" bags in every passageway and stairwell. Deck crews stowed or tied down chairs and tables. Some windows and portholes were covered with plywood. In sections of open decks, ropes to serve as handrails had to be strung. Covers of lifeboats were checked. Officers shifted from four six-hour watches to three of eight hours' duration. Anyone who was not on duty was placed on standby status.

Mohamad Ali had come on duty at 0010 hours and immediately began the routine tasks required at the start of the shift. In the sensible terminology of equipment maintenance jobs in motorship engine rooms his job title was "greaser." It was a good job that had taken him from his village in Indonesia to parts of the world that his parents could only try to imagine. He spoke passable English and had learned all the Dutch officers' commands that he needed to know to do his job, using a language that was a combination of his native tongue and a few nautical phrases in English. He'd quickly gotten used to being teased occasionally about having the same name as the famous American boxer, although the first name was spelled differently. The fighter and the greaser also contrasted in physique. The black champion boxer was taller, fuller, broader and powerfully muscular. The Ali of the *Prinsendam* had tan skin and the small, lithe body suited to squeezing into tight places.

When Third Engineer Van Hardeveld and Assistant Engineer Kalf came on watch, Ali was between engines two and three. Pausing a moment between tasks, he watched as Kalf changed a filter in the fuel supply line. At the start of a watch, checking the filter and changing it if needed were routine activities. What was not ordinary was a flash of blue flame near cylinder seven of main engine number two and an alarm signal. When Ali saw a squirt of oil in the direction of engine number three, he dashed up to the control room on B Deck and breathlessly exclaimed in his second language, "Sir, plenty oil main engine two."

Grabbing a dry-powder fire extinguisher, Ali rushed back to engine number two and found a fire.

Having heard the alarm signal, Assistant Engineer Officer Kalf had also looked toward the engine and seen oil spurting near fuel-pump cylinder number seven of main engine two. On the way to the auxiliary room, he passed Ali carrying the dry-powder extinguisher. Kalf switched on the starboard auxiliary alternator to prevent an interruption in electric power. In the control room, Van Hardeveld told him to shut down all ventilator fans in order to prevent the spread of thick black smoke throughout the engine room. Kalf realized that the task could not be carried out because the ventilator fans' control switch was at the opposite end of the smoky engine room.

At fifty minutes after midnight, Van Hardeveld left the control room. Entering the engine room, he saw smoke and flames near engine number two, somewhere between fuel cylinders four and eight. Hoping to stop what was obviously a leak in the high-pressure fuel-supply line, he ordered the number two engine shut down and number three thrown out of gear. This left engines number one and four to drive both propellers and maintain the ship's maneuvering ability and speed. But cutting off number two also shut down its alternator, shifting the full electrical load for the ship to number three. With the engine-room alarm ringing and smoke billowing, he stood on cylinder number two of engine number one and sprayed the fire with dry powder. It seemed to snuff it out.

Returning to the control room on B Deck to obtain breathing apparatus, Van Hardeveld found Chief Engineer Officer Albertus Boot, First Electrician G. J. ten Voorde and other officers. He explained the situation and returned to the engine room to look for the location of the fuel leak. Unable to find it and determine its extent, he saw Second Engineer Officer J. F. Repko and Ali using a fire hose to cool the exhaust gas duct. Their belief that the crisis was controlled was shattered a moment later with a burst of flames that made staying in the engine room untenable. Van Hardeveld directed Repko to close the quick-release fuel valves and fire dampers in the engine room, then stopped numbers one, three, and four himself and went to the Bridge Deck fast.

In the wheelhouse, Second Officer Matthew Oosterwijk had been determining the ship's position when he heard the fire alarm. A display panel showed it was in the engine room. This was confirmed immediately by Chief Engineer Boot by telephone from the control room. As Oosterwijk summoned Captain Wabeke to the wheelhouse, Boot requested that the engine room and all watertight doors be closed.

Meanwhile, Second Engineer Officer de Boer, Third Engineer Officer Aarnoutse, and Fourth Engineer Officer Dörr went forward on A Deck to the midship elevators to go down to B Deck and via an emergency exit to the stabilizer room. Finding the watertight door closed, they opened it manually. When they reached their destination, the auxiliary engine room was full of smoke. Dörr had breathing gear and entered to prepare the port auxiliary alternator for starting. Turning it on, he found that the revolutions of the starboard alternator decreased. Suspecting that the equipment was not receiving cooling water, he returned to the stabilizer room and explained the problem to De Boer. He told Dörr to open a connecting valve between the fire main and a line that provided sea water.

At the same time in the wheelhouse, discussion centered on pumping carbon dioxide gas into the now sealed engine room to extinguish the fire. Doing so would mean that the engine room could not be entered until all the CO_2 was pumped out, perhaps not for hours. The chief engineer reported that all engine-room personnel had gotten out and were accounted for and that relevant watertight doors and entrances to the engine and stabilizer rooms had been closed.

The captain gave the order to use carbon dioxide.

One of Holland America's most experienced captains, Wabeke had commanded all but one of the line's superb "dams," but he had never faced the duty that only a ship's master could perform. He told Second Radio Officer J. A. van der Werf to alert the U. S. Coast Guard station at Kodiak that the *Prinsendam* was in trouble by sending out the signal "XXX."

Transmitted at 1:08 a.m., the triple-X signal sought assistance without the urgency of the Morse code distress call that people the world over knew as SOS. The sending of dots and dashes to represent letters of the alphabet by wire was invented by Samuel F. B. Morse, a portrait painter, and introduced in 1844. It had been used in the first transatlantic radio transmission by Guillermo Marconi in 1901. The SOS alert had its most spectacular success in 1912 after the ocean liner *Titanic* struck an iceberg. Operating at 500 kilohertz (kHz), just below the lowest AM radio frequency, the Morse distress system had a range of approximately 1,200 nautical miles during the day and farther at night. Receiving stations heard *Prinsendam*'s XXX not only in Kodiak and other locations on the U.S. Pacific coast, including Seattle and San Francisco, but in New Zealand as well. With the advancement of communications technology and the use of stationary earth-orbiting satellites, the Morse system had become relegated to a back-up system on most modern oceangoing ships to communications by satellite, known as COMSAT. The *Prinsendam* was equipped with both, but as the engine-room fire spread to other areas of the ship, COMSAT would be rendered useless.

Citing the ship's radio call sign (PJTA), the message that went out said:

PASSENGER SHIP PRINSENDAM/PJTA POSITION 57-38 DEGREES NORTH AND 140-25 DEGREES WEST.

FIRE! FIRE IN THE ENGINE

ROOM FLOODING ENGINE ROOM WITH CARBON DIOXIDE.

CONDITIONS UNKNOWN. PASSENGERS 320. CREW 190.

Wabeke's next responsibility was to inform everyone on board of the emergency and not create panic. Through loudspeakers in all parts of the ship and passengers' rooms he said in a commanding but, he hoped, reassuring tone, "This is your captain speaking. We have a small fire in the engine room. It is under control, but for your own safety, please report to the Promenade Deck."

CHAPTER 6

A Hell of a Way to Meet People

Nearly a quarter of a century after Mohamad Ali saw a flash of blue and squirting oil in the engine room, Jeannie Gilmore compared the following moments to the dog in the Sherlock Holmes story that didn't bark in the nighttime. "When a ship's engines stop running," Jeannie said, "you notice it." Obviously, she thought at the time, the *Prinsendam* wasn't stopping to let someone off in the Gulf of Alaska.

"Something," she said to her mother, "is definitely amiss."

A moment later, the captain's voice gave the reason and directed passengers to go to the Promenade Deck. Flinging aside a blanket, Jeannie said, "Mom, put your coat on." Handing Neva Hall her purse with long straps, she said, "Hang this around your neck." Jeannie did the same, got into a coat and put on a furry white cap that, according to her husband Bill, looked as if a rabbit had decided to take a nap on her head.

Leaving the cabin, they found the passageway full of black smoke. Holding hands, they felt their way to a stairway that was less smoky and went from the Main Deck to the place on the Promenade Deck that had been designated as their gathering point during the emergency drill. As they came outside, several crewmen carrying long-handled axes dashed in front of them. The small crowd watched them with expressions that seemed bemused, rather than anxious.

Someone uttered a racist joke. "Now I know what they mean," he said with a laugh, "when they talk about watching a Chinese fire drill."

The prevailing mood, Jeannie noted, seemed almost festive. More and more people came on deck, adding to the party-like mood. "I must say," exclaimed an elderly man in pajamas and with a drink in hand, "this is a hell of a way to meet people."

When the alarm sounded, Muriel Marvinney's head had just hit the pillow, she would relate later. Bolting up in bed, she thought her alarm clock had gone berserk. Realizing that the clanging was in the corridor, she and Agnes Lilard got up and went to the door. Muriel's hand shook as she opened it. In the confined space, the air reverberated with the clang of the bell and banging of heavy metal doors slamming shut.

A ship's officer stepped from one of the opposite cabins and said, "Stay calm, ladies."

Muriel asked, "What's going on?"

Turning toward the exit, the officer replied, "I'd advise you two ladies to dress warmly."

Muriel thought for a moment, then said to Agnes, "Oh, let's just go up on deck as we are and see what's happening. If we need something warmer, we can come back for it."

"Muriel," Agnes replied firmly, "the officer said to dress warmly, and that's exactly what we are going to do."

While the women put on slacks, sweaters, and light raincoats, wisps of smoke filtered under the door. Leaving the room, Agnes said, "So there's a little fire somewhere! They have all kinds of foam and chemicals to put it out. We'll be back down in our cabins in no time." Muriel hoped so. Her purse and jewelry were locked in a suitcase, along with her passport, other travel documents, vaccination certificates, and papers containing a summary of her medical history.

Captain Wabeke's assurance that the small fire in the engine room was out instilled such confidence in lecturer John Graham and his daughter Malory that they didn't bring their life jackets. World War II combat veteran Earl Andrews took no chances and appeared on deck with the life jacket on and securely fastened. Retired Colonel Henry Heinichen led his wife Leila onto the deck and exclaimed, "Thank God the rain's stopped."

Oil executive Jack Barclay sniffed the pungent air in the stairway to the Promenade Deck and had no doubt that the problem down in the engine room was a fuel fire. Betty Milborn had yanked a blanket from her bed and wrapped it around her mother's shoulders. Retired insurance man Frazier Reed joked to a young man ahead of him on the steps, "I hope Holland America is up to date on their fire policy." Doctor Stanford Farnsworth worried about senior citizens inhaling smoke out in the cold night.

Alex Composito had been in a hotel in Italy that had a fire. The experience had taught him to wet a towel and hold it against his mouth and nose. Soaking all the towels in the small bathroom, he emerged from his room and found two elderly women already coughing. "Take these," he said, pushing towels at them. "Use 'em like gas masks." Leading them and his mother toward an exit, he chuckled and said, "Since we look like a bunch of bank robbers, maybe we should stick up the purser's office."

The women giggled.

John Courtney was asleep when Edwin Ziegfeld closed the book he had been reading, Agatha Christie's *Surprise Surprise*. He wondered what the ringing meant. Something about bells had been explained during the emergency drill, but he couldn't remember what one long and three short meant. A whiff of the odor of smoke catapulted him out of bed. When the light by his bed didn't work, he shook Courtney and yelled, "Johnny, wake up. We have to get the hell out of here."

Fumbling for clothing in the dark in the nude, David Levin grabbed the first thing that his fingers touched—his purple jogging suit. Ethel and Francis Burrowski of Miami, Florida, were veteran cruise-takers. They had been on one of the *Prinsendam*'s first Indonesian odysseys in 1977. His response to being awakened by the captain's announcement was, "C'mon, honey, let's get dressed."

When the lights went out, Jim Flynn opened the drawer of the bedside table and took out the flashlight he always took on trips. In warm coats over pajamas, he and wife Kitty headed for the Promenade Deck.

Before the captain's announcement, Betsy Price noticed the engines had stopped. Lynn Detroit asked, "Do you smell smoke?" Betsy opened the cabin door to darkness and a stronger odor of something burning. "When you're adrift at sea and there is smoke," she would assert later, "there is *big* trouble." She grabbed a wool skirt and sweater, raincoat, sneakers, and a constant companion when traveling—a flashlight. By its smoky-looking beam Lynn gathered a raincoat, sneakers, and both life jackets. They dressed as they rushed up two decks.

Comedian Roger Ray also noticed that the engines had stopped. Picking up the phone, he called magician Jack Malon's room and blurted, "Jack, the ship's stopped." Malon replied, "Yeah, I noticed." Detecting a "noxious odor," he said to Beatrice, "Let's get out of here." She put on a silk housecoat over her nightgown and high-heeled shoes. Over pajamas Jack donned the long-tailed coat he wore in his act and slipped bare feet into black patent leather shoes.

Wakened by the captain's voice on the loudspeaker, Isabella and Irving Brex got into coats, walked a short distance to the Lido at the rear of the Promenade Deck and found a small cluster of passengers in night clothes. The café's doors were closed.

Reverend Thatcher had put on a bathrobe and slipped her Bible into the pocket. Peter Kapetan had fallen asleep reading *Shogun*. Wide awake now, he left the thick novel behind and headed topside. John Gyorokos tried to call his son and daughter in other rooms, discovered the phone wasn't working, and grabbed the first thing in his closet. He left the room wearing his tuxedo pants and jacket and an undershirt.

Ann Corey and her mother hurriedly dressed in their room on B Deck. When they got to the hallway exit, the watertight door was closed. Fearing being trapped, they were glad to see two crew members. With the door pried open enough for them to squeeze through, they headed to elevators that were not running. Because Mrs. Foster's mobility was restricted, Ann gave her helping pushes up steps. As they stopped several times so her mother could rest, thick, black, choking smoke rose in the stairway.

Richard Steele gripped Louise's arm as they closed their stateroom door and concluded that the situation was not as under control as the captain had said. Crewmen were running up and down the stairs with heavy firefighting equipment. Richard wore a bathrobe. Louise was in a New York couture designer's negligée that was his idea of a Geisha's kimono. Richard started to go back for blankets, but the acrid smoke was too thick. Stepping onto the

Promenade Deck, he thought back to the reception on the first full night on board. Elegant people had been served by crisply uniformed waiters. Gaiety. Laughter. A holiday atmosphere. A Broadway show by handsomely costumed young people. Now, looking round the Promenade Deck, he saw gowns replaced by robes and nighties. Men who'd worn tuxedos to dinner two nights earlier now had on sweaters and windbreakers. Jewels and black ties had been exchanged for orange life jackets.

The Promenade Deck hadn't been so crowded since the departure from Vancouver. That night, Steele had a feeling that came close to enchantment as the *Prinsendam* sparkled with lights like a Christmas tree. Now she was dark. Painfully so. Built for fun, the ship felt as if she were in shock. Except for a slight rocking, she was motionless. The eerie quiet was broken now and then by a laugh, a cough, or a loud remark that seemed as shocking as a fart at a dinner table. The odor of smoke permeated the cold air, but was strongest on the starboard side. None was noticeable at the top of the orange smokestack that ship builders called the funnel. With the electricity off, the radar antenna had stopped turning.

The experiences of a long life, most of it spent in a business based on recording facts and follies of human events, taught Steele the contrast in behavior under stress was fascinating. The best and the worst appeared. He found himself remembering a poem he'd read somewhere, sometime, by Eileen Lynch, to the effect that there was "a strange foreboding in the sea." It crashed hard upon the heart to "stir weakened memories of shipwrecked dreams."

Being aboard a ship in the dead of night that might or might not be, as the navy hymn said, "in peril on the sea," put the world he'd left behind in perspective. Would it really make a difference if

Ronald Reagan succeeded in unseating Jimmy Carter? Did anyone on the *Prinsendam* at that moment care if Holmes beat Ali, or vice-versa? Or what team won the World Series? How many shivering souls on the Promenade Deck gave a hoot about anything but the fact that very young men were scampering here and there with axes and dragging fire hoses that looked like dead snakes?

Could there ever be such a thing as a *small* fire on a cruise ship? Was it, in fact, *out*?

Standing patiently next to the love of his life, and noticing that Louise was as beautiful as the day he married her, Richard Steele contemplated all of this as a man and newspaper editor and left all the questions and answers to the Almighty. As time passed, he wished he'd thought to bring along a cigar, for, as someone advised long ago:

Then smoke away till a golden ray
Lights up the dawn of the morrow
For a cheerful cigar, like a shield will bar
The blows of care and sorrow.

When Muriel and Agnes reached the Promenade Deck, Muriel looked skyward and was glad to see "a beautiful clear night." John Graham saw no moon, but observed a dancing green belt of Northern Lights, "so bright it hides the stars." Jeannie Gilmore gazed at the sky and pondered the fact that the ship was well out to sea. She said to nobody in particular, "I wonder if anyone knows where we are?"

A frail-looking, white-haired woman replied, "Somebody in charge *must* know."

CHAPTER 7

Crowded Hour

The only certainty at one fifteen a.m., Saturday, October 4, 1980, for the master of the motor vessel *Prinsendam* as he stood in the wheelhouse in his gravest crisis in his years as a captain was his ship's location. The course reckoning put her at 53-18 degrees north and 140-25 west. In the less precise calculation and language of landlubbers, the *Prinsendam* was dead in the water about 120 miles southeast of Yakutat. The nearest town on Alaska's southeast coast, a village with a population of no more than four hundred, it reminded Wabeke of his home, Krabbadijke, in the Netherlands, not only because of its seafaring history, but its hardy, self-sufficient residents. Born on April 13, 1928, Cornelius Dirk Wabeke was, in the lingo of sailors, a trim and steady-as-she-goes ship master. He possessed all the capable, reassuring, steadfast qualities of the daring Dutch navigators who for centuries had ventured around the globe to open its oceans to European civilization based on Christianity and commerce. From Henry Hudson exploring the vast river in the New World of America that would be named after him to the wayfarers who claimed the Pacific islands that they called Dutch East Indies, and were now the home waters of Captain Wabeke's endangered ship, sturdy men of Holland had sailed away from home in tiny ships or giants and claimed many of its places for the Netherlands.

One of those who had left the land of tulip fields and windmills, Cornelius Roosevelt, had emigrated to the New Amsterdam that became New York and planted seeds that sprouted into a family tree whose branches eventually yielded two American presidents, Theodore and Franklin. The former had described his heroic leadership of his dismounted Rough Riders' cavalry charge up the San Juan Heights of Cuba in the Spanish-American War by embracing the sentiments of Sir Walter Scott that were recalled by a poet of the American Revolution, Thomas Ushert Mordaunt, in 1791 in *Verses written During the War*:

One crowded hour of glorious life
Is worth an age without a name.

"People at sea," wrote same-name authors of the Holland America Line's centennial book in the year the *Prinsendam* was born. "They all have their own special memories, and often the memories, like the ship, form a bridge across the seas."

Facing a decisive hour in the life of the seven-year-old *Prinsendam*, Captain Wabeke understood that shivering passengers summoned to her Promenade Deck would have plenty of tales to recall and relate to family, friends, and all who would listen of their crowded hour on a once-in-a-lifetime Far East cruise that had been rudely interrupted because their ship was on fire.

Designed for calling at tropical ports and warm seas, the *Prinsendam* now sat immobilized in an area of the world that ranked high in every sailor's log of most dangerous places. The Gulf of Alaska was where tropic and Arctic ocean streams clashed head-on, turning the sea bottom into a graveyard for countless ships. According to depth charts, the ocean floor beneath the *Prinsendam* was marked between 2,500 and 2,600 meters, or roughly 9,000 feet. The weather had quieted. Not much wind or swell. Rain had stopped. The temperature on deck, four degrees centigrade, was not conducive to comfort of passengers rousted from warm beds in sleepwear to stand around the Promenade Deck a minute longer than necessary. But their comfort and convenience had to be secondary to a fire, no matter how small and contained it was reported to be.

Efforts to quell it with equipment at hand by the engine-room watch had failed, forcing Wabeke to issue the order to passengers to leave their rooms. He had hoped to be the voice of calm and appeared to have succeeded. His officers reported an orderly evacuation. A check of staterooms found complete compliance. Rather than encountering panic among the men and women as they made their way to the Promenade Deck and waited to hear further instructions, officers and crew had observed not only restraint and patience, but almost a feeling of frivolity. Whether this was genuine, or a manifestation of "eat, drink and be merry, for tomorrow we die," only the passengers knew. One of them, William Powell, was overheard saying in a tone that could have been interpreted as jocular or fatalistic, "Damn, there goes the trip."

Whether Powell would turn out to be right remained to be determined. Extent of damage to the engines and the engine room was difficult for Wabeke to quickly ascertain. Why there had been a fuel leak, if that's what happened, and what sparked the fire, were all questions for the experts at another time. An investigation by a court of inquiry was inevitable and proper. But this was not the time for hand-wringing hindsight. Wabeke hoped that pumping carbon dioxide would extinguish the fire, permitting, he also hoped, the ship to get underway again with the undamaged engines. If not, she would have to be towed to a port capable of handling her, and the disappointed passengers provided transportation home, or wherever they wished to go.

Then would be the time of lawyers and litigation. Holland America would refund the prices of tickets, of course, but how could anyone place a dollar amount on lost adventures and shattered dreams? The sight of the *Prinsendam* under construction, the thrilling day she had been christened, and taking her to sea for the first time had been proud, priceless moments in the long and distinguished career of Captain Cornelius Wabeke. The mere thought of her being laid up was beyond unsettling. It was depressing. That *Prinsendam* might sink and be left to rot on the floor of the treacherous Gulf of Alaska, with her blue hull and white superstructure battered and beaten to pieces by the tides, and turned into a playground for sea creatures, was horrible to contemplate. But all that, if it happened, was in the future. At the moment, all that mattered was the crisis at hand, what had been done, and what was needed to keep the *Prinsendam* alive.

When the ship was delivered in 1973, she was in accord with the international rules and standards. She had periodic inspections by Netherlands Shipping Inspection and the United States Coast Guard. She was pronounced good and in compliance. Previous cruises had gone well. By all accounts, she was a fine ship, lauded by the passengers and writers for travel magazines and efficiently run. Officers and crew were well trained and understood both their duties and their obligations regarding the safety of ship and passengers. Without confidence in them, no captain could function, especially in an emergency, and certainly not with a fire on board.

What Wabeke knew at a quarter past one in the morning was that the middle watch had commenced at 0040 with Third

Engineer Van Hardeveld and Assistant Engineer Officer Kalf in charge. Greaser Ali was already on duty. The four main engines were at full power, provided by two shaft alternators driven by engines number two and three. Two sea water pumps were functioning, one in the stabilizer room and the other in the auxiliary engine room. They were respectively powered by the shaft alternator of main engines number three and two.

These pumps were designed to supply the water for firefighting and secondary needs, including air conditioning, cooling for a water distilling plant, and a condenser for the steam plant. When deck washing was underway, a second pump always had to be engaged to sustain sufficient pressure.

Following Ali's discovery and report of an oil leakage in the low-pressure oil-supply line near cylinder seven of engine two, measures were taken to turn down the pitch of the port propeller, stop engine two, turn down the pitch of the starboard propeller, disengage the gear of engine three, and sound the engineer's alarm. Stopping the main engine had no effect on the leakage. The booster pump continued to supply pressure, but apparently resulted in a drop in pressure that started a second pump automatically. Stopping engine two resulted in starting the emergency alternator and an interruption in the power supply to the firefighting pump in the auxiliary engine room.

Water for firefighting could then only come from the pump in the stabilizer room that also supplied water for other purposes. This caused a decrease in water pressure. Consequently, when the engineer's alarm was sounded, water for firefighting was unavailable. At this moment, Van Hardeveld resorted to dry extinguishing powder, but at a safe long distance, to no avail. The action taken by Third Engineer Officer Aarnoutse was to connect the starboard auxiliary alternator with a control switchboard. He was followed into the smoky engine room by Electrician ten Voorde, Second Officer Repko, Second Engineer Officer de Boer, Fourth Engineer Dörr, and others. With no one taking command or evaluating the situation, their actions were not as coordinated they ought to have been, with the effect that the fire continued. Ordered to shut down the engine room's ventilation system, the assistant engineer officer was unable to reach the control buttons because of the intensity of the smoke.

Approximately twenty-two minutes passed between Ali's report of a blue flash and spurting oil and the bridge being informed of the fire. Captain Wabeke was alerted by telephone from the wheelhouse. At 1:15 a.m., he was told that it was "a large and serious fire," with a plea that CO_2 be authorized. After ascertaining that the engine room was evacuated, Wabeke gave the order at 1:37 a.m., nearly an hour after Ali saw the flash and the oil leak. Required of him now were steps designated in a fire procedure guide known as the "fire station bill." It listed four actions:

1. warn and accompany passengers to safety
2. render assistance to engine room personnel as needed
3. prevent the fire from spreading outside the engine room by checking and, where needed, spraying water on bulkheads and closing ventilation openings to prevent smoke from spreading
4. prepare life saving appliances.

Except for some confusion on the part of passengers when they encountered closed fire doors that crewmen quickly opened, the first step had been accomplished with satisfying speed and efficiency, although uncomfortably for many of the elderly men and women who had been roused from their sleep and found themselves suddenly outside on a cold night wearing garments unsuited for the purpose.

With the engine room evacuated and filled with carbon dioxide, the danger existed that the immediate area around the engine room would become overheated and even combust. Spreading of smoke was also an urgent problem. To keep it contained, the ship's ventilation had to be shut down by closing intake and exhaust mechanisms. These procedures were the duty of the officers and crew.

After assuring himself that all the emergency actions were being carried out, Captain Wabeke's primary responsibility, after informing passengers through the ship's public address system of the problem, was reaching out for possible assistance from ships that might be nearby and the U.S. Coast Guard's Rescue Coordination Center (RCC) in Juneau, Alaska. He had done this in the XXX transmission that went out from the wireless room shortly after he came to the bridge and conferred with his officers.

Like a general after the order was given to begin an attack, Wabeke had no control over the outcome. He had read that an historian had written that after General Dwight Eisenhower gave the word to his commanders to launch the D-day invasion, Ike had quipped that a second ago he'd been the world's most powerful person, but now he was as useless as tits on a man. The same was true for Admiral George Dewey once he turned to his skipper of the battleship *Olympia* to commence the decisive Battle of Manila on May 1, 1898, and said, "You may fire when ready, Mr. Gridley." From those moments on, Ike's and Dewey's victory and reputations depended on the performance of others. So it would be for Captain Cornelius Wabeke in his crowded hour on the bridge of his beloved but crippled *Prinsendam.*

CHAPTER 8

If This Were a Movie

Nearly an hour had passed since the captain's announcement that a small fire had been brought under control and that, strictly for the sake of prudence, everyone should go up or down to the Promenade Deck. During that time, Richard Steele had observed the crew running up and down the stairs with firefighting gear. When he started back to his cabin for blankets, he had been thwarted by smoke that seemed too thick and plentiful to be from a small fire in an engine room several decks below.

Some passengers brought their orange life jackets. A few had put them on. The majority had come on deck without them. Except for the wide variety of mostly hastily donned clothing, Steele thought that the men and women on the Promenade Deck resembled an audience of a play mingling in the lobby during the intermission. If the scenario in which he and Louise were part were in a Hollywood movie, he imagined, the camera would scan the crowd and zoom slowly in to find the picture's star, or whatever actor or action had been scripted to begin the story. If the director were known for making romantic films, it would become a love story. An action film director would have people in peril on a ship saved by a dynamic star that audiences expected to be heroic.

Could anyone who had seen *The Poseidon Adventure*, Steele wondered, board any cruise ship eight years later without remembering the towering, terrifying wave flipping that huge, beautiful ship upside down as if it were a toy in a bathtub? Because the *Prinsendam* was upright and afloat, he saw a better cinematic parallel in Alfred Hitchcock's *Lifeboat*. Without showing a throng of unsuspecting passengers on a doomed ship the director immediately put his cast of disparate characters into a lifeboat. He brilliantly overcame the cinematic challenge of keeping the audience that had become accustomed to action and movement on screen interested in a story that depended entirely on dialogue, characterization, and psychological complexities and human interaction in a crisis.

The moment Edwin Ziegfeld stepped onto the Promenade Deck he regretted that as he and John Courtney vacated their cabin he didn't think to grab his new camera. He saw at once that he could have gotten great pictures of people on the deck who looked as if they were at a pajama party. With the long-range lens fixed he could have tried to capture an amazing display of northern lights. As he chastised himself for his oversight, earthly bursts of white light from a flash camera farther ahead on the deck indicated the presence of someone more nimbly witted.

Muriel Marvinney said to Agnes Lilard that it was a "weird circumstance" to be "drifting in such a vast blackness with only the stars and the brilliant northern lights overhead."

"You know, Muriel," said Agnes, supposing that by now their clothing in the cabin was smoke-damaged, "they'll have to turn back. I just wish they'd tell us more."

Still in a tuxedo, former New Jersey State Senator Fairleigh Dickinson shared Agnes' dismay at the lack of information. Although he was no longer serving in government, as a lawmaker he was accustomed to demanding answers from bureaucrats, elected officials, and citizens and getting them. He had tried to question a scurrying crewman. The harried Indonesian youth blurted, "No worry. Everything in control." When all this mess was over with, Dickinson vowed as he turned away in frustration and mounting anger, the people in charge of Holland America Cruises and those who worked for them on the *Prinsendam* would have to be called to account.

Now that the sea was calmer, Betty Milborn was feeling better. Wearing a blue sweater and skirt, she stayed close to her seventy-eight-year-old aunt and namesake. Mrs. Clapp was beginning to accept that they would probably not realize their plan to celebrate her birthday in Peking, China. Despite being huddled on the deck, Betty recalled the captain's announcement and was certain the situation was not serious. "It was actually a lovely night," she would recall. "It was not really cold, and nobody seemed to worry."

Louise Peyrot of Lake West, Florida, had been brushing her teeth when the water shut off. Hearing a commotion in the hallway, she went to investigate and met an officer who told her there was a small fire. Advised to put on a coat and go to the Promenade Deck, she donned a raincoat over her nightgown, confident that soon she would again be snug and warm.

People who had come on board a ship of strangers became instant friends to whoever stood next to them. Impromptu conversations were often startlingly intimate. One old man said to a woman he'd never seen before, "I got out of my room so damn fast that I forgot to put in my dentures and had to go back and get them." This discomfort, he would learn later, was minor if compared to a man who'd rushed from his room and left behind his glass eye. A regal-looking woman revealed hearing the captain's announcement seated on the toilet. Leila Heinichen had almost forgotten large eyeglasses with the corners of the rims resembling the wings of an exotic bird. Jeannie Gilmore decided they were the gaudiest eyewear she'd ever seen.

If the plight of the *Prinsendam* were the fruit of the imagination of a screenwriter, at this point in the drama the script might call for cutting away from the passengers to the bridge and a closeup of the ship's skipper. In Hollywood's golden age from the 1930s until the advent of the demon small screen called television that Richard Steele knew best, Captain Wabeke might be portrayed by Spencer Tracy, Gary Cooper, William Holden, or even John Wayne, but he was too tall and decidedly Nordic in appearance for the role to be filled by James Cagney. The captain was closer to a Humphrey Bogart type. To play the officer in charge of the *Prinsendam*'s engine room, the choice of character actors in the old Hollywood would be almost unlimited, from the rugged-looking William Bendix and Paul Douglas to crusty Walter Brennan and, one of Richard Steele's favorite he-man actors, Edmund O'Brien. To play himself, Steele imagined steady and reliable Frederick March. Louise would be Ingrid Bergman or Grace Kelly.

As he momentarily indulged his imagination under the northern lights, his concern that the ship was in a more serious condition than the captain said deepened. As a newspaperman he had learned enough about fires to know that black smoke was the sure sign a fire was not under control. When a blaze had been knocked down, smoke turned white. More than an hour after the captain's "small fire" announcement, if the blaze in the engine room had been put out, ship's staff with responsibilities to look after passengers would be on the decks to provide assurances that they would soon be allowed to return to their cabins. He also wondered why passengers had not been admitted to the lounge, Lido Restaurant, Prinsen Club, and theater. If fire doors had been shut and secured, they and the walls (bulkheads) ought to have prevented the spread of smoke from the engine-room deck, yet the acrid odor had risen the four levels from the engine room to permeate the ship.

CHAPTER 9

Command Decisions

Forty-five minutes after fire was reported in the engine room, hoses had been unrolled at fire stations and snaked across the Promenade, Bridge, and Sun decks for the purpose of playing water on the *Prinsendam*'s funnel. Resembling a slightly flattened, tall, and inverted cone, the stack was located toward the rear of the ship at roughly three-fourths of the distance from the bow to stern. It rose from the Sun Deck to form an outlet of a ventilation shaft that ran through the ship to the engine room on the bottom deck. On B Deck this shaft separated cabins from an aft sports area. On the Promenade Deck it stood at the rear of the lounge and separated it from the Lido Restaurant, with a passageway between them that ran from port to starboard. On the Main Deck the shaft created two wings of the U-shaped two-hundred-place dining room. On A and B decks it formed a longer protuberance and a divider, along with midship rooms, offices, crew quarters, and two parallel passageways. In terms of a home or factory the funnel was the ship's equivalent of the chimney or smokestack. In the era before oil-fueled ships, when ocean liners were powered by coal furnaces that made steam to drive propellers, one, two, three, and sometimes four funnels belched columns of smoke.

Because the *Prinsendam*'s lone funnel served primarily to release the heat from the engine room, with a fire raging it was vital to the safety of the ship that the funnel be kept as cool as possible. If it became excessively hot, there was a danger that any structures around it could reach a temperature to produce spontaneous combustion. This is why fire hoses were deployed and fire crewmen assigned to continually douse it with water. Unfortunately, the ship's watering system failed, leaving the hoses useless. Following Captain Wabeke's order to flood the engine room with carbon dioxide, the heat flow through the funnel supposedly would be decreased, as would the heat stresses upon the walls (casings) of the engine room.

A slight cooling appeared to validate the belief that the CO_2 had either extinguished the fire or would in time put it out, reducing the heating of engine-room bulkheads. The thermal insulation material within the room's metal casing had been designed to prevent the heat from escaping. These control elements together would deny the fire oxygen and contain the heat. In planning and building the *Prinsendam,* the engine-room bulkheads were constructed and insulated to meet specifications requiring an A-type bulkhead to retard smoke and flames in a "standard" fire test of one hour. This meant that after sixty minutes, at gradually increasing temperatures up to 927 degrees Celsius, the average temperatures of the exposed outside would not rise more than 180 degrees above the temperature before the fire. Burning oil produced temperatures in excess of 1,200 degrees Celsius.

When Wabeke approved carbon dioxide around two a.m., the fire had been raging for more than an hour. Having given the CO_2 command, he again turned his attention to passengers. Satisfied that his order that they go to the Promenade Deck had been heeded and with only a few minor complications, he listened to a request by Hotel Manager Zeller that doors to the lounge and Lido Restaurant that had been closed and locked be opened to allow passengers to get in out of the cold. Chief Officer H. E. Valk and Chief Engineer Boot endorsed the suggestion, not only for the comfort of passengers, but to dissipate any smoke that might have seeped up into public spaces. There was an indication that this had occurred in the dining room. Foreman Zaini Abidin had reported seeing wisps of smoke. To ventilate the dining room the officers also recommended opening two doors at the aft end that flanked the funnel's air shaft.

Believing that the fire was either out or rapidly would be, Wabeke saw no reason why he should not accept proposals that would not only improve the well-being and comfort of people, most of them elderly, who had been exposed to the elements for more than an hour, but clear the decks for crewmen and officers. He felt he had done everything expected of the skipper. He had ordered an XXX signal. He consulted with officers he knew well and trusted to give him their assessment of the situation. All that could be done was accomplished. Most importantly, nobody had been injured.

CHAPTER 10

What a Nuisance

When members of the ship's staff appeared on the Promenade Deck, Jeannie Gilmore supposed that the moment she had been anticipating had come at last. From the minute she and her mother left their room, she expected to hear an order for passengers to assemble at appointed lifeboat stations. Theirs was number four on the port side. As the crewmen opened doors to the lounge and Lido Restaurant, she was glad to be getting her mother out of the cold.

Richard Steele again visualized a theater crowd at intermission. As the passengers began moving toward the opened doors, the sudden stir was like the press of people when lobby lights flashed off and on and ushers announced, "Return to your seats, please." Act One of the drama of the good ship *Prinsendam* had certainly reached an exciting conclusion. For nail-biting, edge-of-your-seat tension as the curtain came down it was hard to beat a scene in which the players were huddled half-dressed on a cold night aboard a burning cruise ship a hundred or more miles at sea under a canopy of the aurora borealis. How would Act Two unfold?

Without a wristwatch, left on a bedside table, Elizabeth Price had lost track of the time. Muriel Marvinney was beginning to think that her friend Agnes Lilard was right in believing they would soon be allowed to return to their room, even if they were likely to find that their clothes had been ruined by smoke. Betty Milborn took the hand of her aunt, Betty Clapp, and held it tightly as they joined a line that formed at the starboard door to a passageway between the back of the theater and the inoperable elevators, with a left turn into the front of the lounge. The forward door on the port side required a right turn to the lounge. Other entrances were port and starboard swinging doors into the corridor between the lounge and the Lido Restaurant. Seating in the lounge accommodated a little more than a hundred people. The Lido had about a hundred more places. Men and younger women graciously yielded seats to their elders or remained outside. Both rooms were hazy with gray smoke, but mercifully warm and dry.

With an impressive mustache and a navy blue yachting cap worn squarely on well-trimmed gray hair, Colonel Henry Heinichen not only looked to Richard Steele as though he'd been sent from the central casting office in Hollywood to fill the role of a decisive, take-charge character, but proved that he was one. Grabbing a couple of bottles of whiskey from the shelves behind the lounge bar, he made his way from one chilled person to the next and from table to table telling even non-drinkers that a good stiff shot was just the thing for warming up by getting the blood going. When he thrust a bottle at Jeannie Gilmore, she took a swig, despite a look of disapproval from her abstemious mother, and passed along the bottle.

Demonstrating that there was truth in the timeless theatrical adage that nothing can keep show people down, the girls and boys who had been hired to provide the musical entertainment during the cruise decided that what was needed to boost everyone's morale was a lively songfest. While Colonel Heinichen circulated whiskey bottles and the young troupers offered tunes from their Rodgers and Hammerstein repertoire, a man in a corner of the lounge shouted, "Go to it, kids! They had music on the *Titanic* when it was sinking, so why not us?"

A remark that may have been meant to be bitterly macabre and fatalistic, noted Richard Steele, was accepted by the passengers as funny. It was the same floor show they had all seen, the same entertainers, he would recall and record, "But the effort is directed toward lifting spirits drooping with fear and apprehension."

Suddenly, the people crowded into the *Prinsendam* lounge who didn't like or understand rock-and-roll and probably never would found themselves transported to a long-ago Oklahoma and singing along with a lovesick cowpoke named Curly, loping along on his trusty horse in a field where the corn was as high as an elephant's eye. The wind came sweeping down the plain, a weepin' willow was laughing, and a little old maverick was winkin' its eye. Next, they were the raucous sailors on an island in the South Pacific on the subject of there being nothing like a dame and then they were navy nurse Ensign Nellie Forbush, as corny as Kansas in August and in love with a wonderful guy, vowing to wash that man right out of her hair.

Jim Flynn decided the people in the lounge resembled the audience for television's venerable repository of musical nostalgia, *The Lawrence Welk Show*. In the parlance of rock-and-rollers they were "oldies but goodies." John Graham had described women that he danced with on such cruises as "waltzing widows with blue hair." Most had the gray of lengthy lives of raising their kids and spoiling grandchildren. The majority were from the West Coast, but the passenger manifest listed All-American-sounding

Worcester, Cleveland, Miami, Detroit, North Carolina, Maryland, New Jersey, New York City, Arizona, Vermont, and Connecticut. There were also Canadians and Australians. Travelers with disparate experiences and reasons for being on the *Prinsendam* were now more than names on a list. If time permitted, each one could tell a good story. Whether it was a former state senator from New Jersey with tales of lawmaking, a Massachusetts newspaper publisher with insights into the Kennedys, a pair of widows excited about seeing the Orient, a comedian, a guy with a magic act, a singer of show tunes, or a schoolteacher and her mom, they were people worth hearing and caring about. But suddenly they were forced to ponder what they once considered a distant concern. As Jeannie Gilmore had told the preacher on the airplane, thinking about meeting your maker wasn't on the *Prinsendam*'s itinerary.

Leaning against the wall at the rear of the lounge that separated it from the ventilation shaft, which culminated in the orange funnel two decks above, Richard Steele felt heat against his back and thought that the smoke in the lounge was getting denser. While the sing-along continued, he was also aware of heat under the soles of his shoes. Familiar with the layout of the ship, he knew the dining room was directly below. If the lounge floor was becoming warmer, the only conclusion to be drawn was that the dining room ceiling was also heating up.

The puzzling aspect of this was that the dining room was *three* decks above the engine room. If the fire there had been extinguished, as the captain had said, and thick steel doors had been shut throughout the ship, how could the dining room ceiling have become so heated that warmth was felt through the floor of the lounge? And what accounted for the increasing density of the smoke in the lounge more than an hour after the captain's announcement?

Confident that appropriate fire-extinguishing actions had been taken, including the use of carbon dioxide, Captain Wabeke had to deal with the simultaneous problems of widespread smoke in public areas and the comfort of the more than three hundred passengers he had ordered to vacate their rooms. By acceding to the request of the hotel manager, supported by his chief officers, he had ordered doors of the lounge and the Lido Restaurant opened, allowing venting of smoke and relief of the passengers. His ventilation order also authorized opening two doors to the kitchen area (galley) aft of the dining room and the forward dining room entrance from the main foyer. This created a wind-tunnel between the galley/dining room service doors and the dining room entrance. The surge of air led to a phenomenon popularly called self-combustion and "auto-ignition" by chemists and physicists.

While the *Prinsendam*'s chefs and food-service staff thought of their Sterno heaters and cognac and liqueurs as essentials of meals, their common chemical component, ethyl alcohol, had an auto-ignition temperature of 425 degrees Celsius. This means that a vapor-air mixture of 3.5 to 15 percent volume of alcohol to air can be ignited by a hot surface with that temperature or higher. Table linens, menus, and wine lists can also be ignited without a flame. When they are heated, a form of decomposition occurs. This produces a distillation of components in which vaporous and gaseous elements are released. When they contact a surface of 600 degrees Celsius, they explode. Because the outer walls of the funnel shaft within the ship had not and could not have been cooled as a result of lack of water, the sudden and continuous draft of opened doors and radiating heat converted ordinary materials that contributed to memorable dinners and midnight suppers into torches that set tables, chairs, and other décor afire, creating a potential inferno.

Alerted to the fire in the dining room, Captain Wabeke ordered closing of all the doors that he had recently allowed to be opened. An attempt to shut all the dining room doors was thwarted by the fire and smoke that prevented access to the main entrance. Learning of this, he ordered that his passengers be directed to immediately leave the lounge and Lido Restaurant.

Faced with standing in the cold night, passengers grabbed tablecloths and tore drapes from walls to use as wraps. On Captain Wabeke's order, the shopping area was opened so that sweaters and other outerwear could be distributed. His wife and members of the housekeeping staff handed out blankets. For anyone desiring fortification with drinks, the Prinsen Club bar was opened to serve them without charge. Some passengers sought refuge in the relatively smoke-free theater, well forward of the Main Deck dining room. The frivolity that marked the almost hour and a half since Wabeke reported a small fire in the engine room, noted Richard Steele, was abruptly gone.

At 2:25 in the morning, somewhere off the coast of Alaska, there was silence, broken now and then by a whisper.

CHAPTER 11

A Dark Jest

"Excuse me," boomed a male voice from somewhere in the throng of quiet passengers, "but would anyone care to play a little shuffleboard?"

There was a smattering of nervous giggles.

It was a well-intentioned dark jest meant to lighten a dark night, thought Alex Composito with an arm around his mother's shivering shoulder. But no one seemed in the mood for a joke. Told to get out of the Lido Restaurant, he and his mother exited onto the Lido Terrace and stood under the roof formed by the Bridge Deck's sports area. Between them and the back end of the ship was the swimming pool that he had planned to try out when the *Prinsendam* reached the warmer climes of Pacific isles. Now that idea had gone up in smoke, along with everything else he'd been anticipating as a way of putting his wrecked marriage behind him, at least temporarily. As to his grieving mother's plan to scatter his father's ashen remains on the waters of Yokohama Bay, it seemed likely that the urn would either be returned home or emptied into the Gulf of Alaska. Assuming, Alex thought in his own dark joke, that the ship didn't sink and take it, him, his mother, and everyone else down with it.

The Reverend Joan Thatcher believed that if perishing at sea were God's will, then his will would be done. He was, after all, the

God who had made the waters, brought the land out of them, and created man and woman to have dominion over both. Where anyone met death and slept until the great awakening of the resurrection was irrelevant. Should she and the souls around her be confined to the depths, they had been mercifully granted the time to prepare for it, to pray, and repent of their sins. If any or all survived, she hoped and prayed they would have confronted mortality and recognized they'd been granted continued life not by chance, but by his grace.

Senator Dickinson considered the fact that lifeboats hadn't been deployed and found this somewhat reassuring. He took this as evidence that the ship wasn't in imminent danger of going down. She appeared to him to be at even keel. He detected no listing, indicating she was not taking on water. As a former Coast Guardsman, he also felt confident that by now U.S. Coast Guard and Canadian rescue units had been informed of the *Prinsendam*'s situation, along with ships in the immediate vicinity. Living in New Jersey, he had learned that when a vessel was in dire distress, whether a passenger ship, yacht, fishing craft, or a rowboat, the U.S. Coast Guard was, as the service's motto *semper paratus* promised, always ready. Standing with his wife in the slightly smoky Prinsen Club and looking out at the Gulf of Alaska, he had no doubt that he would soon see the white shape of a Coast Guard cutter slicing through the dark.

Leila Heinichen let go of Colonel Heinichen's hand to adjust the eyeglasses that Jeannie Gilmore deemed ostentatious in the extreme and tried not to think about the fate of $15,000 in jewelry and clothing, including a mink coat and fifteen formal gowns, in the cabin deluxe they had booked for $4,000 each a year in advance. Not once in their previous two *Prinsendam* cruises had they ever experienced trouble. If the smoke had ruined everything in the cabin, she would be left with what she'd put on after being ordered to the Promenade Deck–a skirt, two blouses, and a raincoat. Wishing she'd thought to wrap herself in the mink, she had the consolation of knowing it was adequately insured.

A seasoned traveler and frequent Holland America Line passenger, Leila was by now an expert on what ship operators called the "terms and conditions of contract" that a passenger accepted when booking a trip. Holland America Cruises Inc.'s contract specified that it and the passenger "mutually agreed that the value of the passenger's money, jewelry or other valuables, whether or not deposited in the vessel's safe deposit box or safe, and the value of all property and luggage of the passenger (including all articles acquired during the voyage) do not exceed a total of U.S. $500, unless a higher value is declared to the Shipowner and extra payment made at the rate of one percent of such excess," the line was not liable. If the shipowner should be found responsible for any loss or damage, the amount "shall not exceed U.S. $500," with the proviso that the value of the item(s) had not been "willfully misrepresented."

The contract also held the company not responsible for "injury, death or delay of or to the passenger or for loss, damage or delay of or to his baggage or other property," nor for the non-performance of any provision of this contract due to any cause beyond the Shipowner's control." Nor did the shipowner guarantee the time of arrival at any port.

For $2,876 dollars each, reflecting a deduction from $3,625 of an air allowance of $754 each, Jeannie Gilmore had booked a Main Deck FF room (204) through Riordan-Winnett Travel of Santa Cruz, California, on September 2. Thirty-two nights later, they were out of the room and one deck higher not knowing if they would ever see their family and friends again. Although Jeannie had never been superstitious, she couldn't help recalling that she had made a joke of James Flynn's reluctance to tell strangers that he was a mortician. And that she'd been asked by the preacher on the airplane to Vancouver if she were prepared to meet her maker. And that she'd told her mother that if the ship sank, she'd go with it wearing her pearl necklace. Her innate optimism that everything would work out fine was evidenced by the fact that she made sure when she and her mother left their room that she had the room key.

Betsy Price took the edge off the situation by taking advantage of the Prinsen Club's free drinks by having a brandy and munching handfuls of peanuts. The only annoyances were lack of information from the ship's staff, and first being allowed into the lounge and not long after being abruptly ordered out. She again wished she'd brought her watch. Beyond the big forward-facing window of the Prinsen Club lay the bow and the seemingly limitless expanse of the Gulf of Alaska. She understood enough about the ship's course to know that the *Prinsendam* could not be too far at sea or distant from the coast to be beyond a timely response by rescuers, should they be necessary.

Directly north was the port of Valdez. The terminus of the eight-hundred-mile trans-Alaska oil pipeline, the town attributed its settlement and growth to fur trading, salmon canning, and mining. The sea abounded with sea otters, Dall porpoise, harbor seals, Stellar sea lions, and Humpback and Orca whales. Coastal mountain cliffs were home to mountain goats, black and brown bears, and bald eagles. During the Klondike Gold Rush (1897–1898), prospectors came in droves in the belief that the Copper River and Valdez

Glacier were pathways to the interior gold fields. Copper and gold mining flourished in the early years of the twentieth century, but in the 1970s, it was black gold that fostered wealth through the Valdez Marine Terminal to receive and ship petroleum to the gas-guzzling lower 48.

Several hours before the *Prinsendam* entered the Gulf of Alaska, the biggest supertanker ever built in the United States, the *Williamsburgh*, along with the tanker *Greatland*, had departed with a full load of 1.5 million barrels of crude for Corpus Christi, Texas. The *Williamsburgh*'s life had begun in 1969, when Seatrain Shipbuilding Corp., a wholly owned subsidiary of Seatrain Lines, Inc., announced it would build four oil-transporting supertankers bearing New York City names. The *Brooklyn, Stuyvesant, Bay Ridge,* and *Williamsburgh* were constructed pursuant to a contract with another Seatrain subsidiary for design, manufacture, and installation of turbines that would be the main propulsion units for the 225,000-ton supertankers. When each ship was completed, the ownership title was transferred from the contracting firm to a trust company. It chartered the *Williamsburgh* to Kingsway Tankers, Inc. In what was known in the shipping trade as a "bareboat charter" it assumed full control of the ship for twenty years as though it owned it, with the obligation that after expiration of the charter the ship reverted to Seatrain. Put into service in 1974, the 1,099-foot ship had two helicopter landing pads and facilities for five hundred people.

On October 4, 1980, the *Williamsburgh* carried a crew of only twenty-seven. The skipper was Arthur Fertig. Radio operator Jim Pfister had picked up the XXX signal and reported it to Fertig. While maintaining course, the captain alerted the men on the bridge and the engine room's crew that it might have to be altered.

Hoping the fire on the *Prinsendam* had been brought under control and he would not have to give the order, he located the position given by the *Prinsendam* on his Gulf of Alaska chart. Calculating the distance, he estimated that to turn the supertanker and reach the cruise ship would take about six hours.

Also at sea due south of Valdez, on the way from San Francisco, the 850-foot oil tanker SOHIO *Intrepid* was empty. The freighter *Portland* was bound for Anchorage. They'd also heard the XXX and kept radio rooms alert for any follow-up distress reports while keeping on course and hoping that their assistance would not be required. Although the XXX was less urgent than an SOS, the message from the *Prinsendam* was awesome and horrifying. Since men first set out to sea in wooden ships under sail, fire had been a mariner's constant dread. Even in the age of high-tech shipboard fire equipment, instant communication, response by planes and helicopters, and fast steel ships racing to the rescue, a fire on a ship with more than five hundred passengers and crew was a terrible thing to contemplate.

CHAPTER 12

Always Ready

No one can say with certainty when the Latin phrase *semper paratus*, meaning "always ready," became the watchword of the United States Coast Guard. It was made the official motto in 1910. Twelve years later on board the Coast Guard cutter *Yumacraw* in the port of Savannah, Georgia, Captain Francis S. Van Bosekerck decided that his branch of the armed services deserved a song that would rival the navy's "Anchors Aweigh" and the army's "Caisson Song." He wrote the music to go with the words in 1927 while stationed in the Aleutian Islands. Titled "Semper Paratus," the song began, "From Aztec shore to Arctic Zone. . . ."

By then, the Coast Guard was officially 180 years old, but it had been plying the coastal waters of the United States and beyond them seven years earlier. When the First Congress of the United States authorized a "system of cutters" to enforce tariff laws, the service drew its men from the disbanded U.S. Navy (abolished in 1785). The "Act of 4 August 1790" provided that the commander of a cutter be paid the same as a captain in the army, while other officers be given the "subsistence" of a lieutenant. Enlisted men were equivalent to soldiers. The service's first captain commissioned by President George Washington was Hopley Yeaton of New Hampshire. Three years later, the cutter *Diligence* drove a pirate ship ashore in Chesapeake Bay. The next year (1794) the cutter *Virginia* "arrested" the privateer *Unicorn* as it was being outfitted by supporters of the French Republic.

During Washington's two terms, Congress authorized the president at his discretion to place the cutter service under control of "the naval establishment, and employ accordingly, all or any of the vessels, which as revenue cutters have been increased in force and employed in the defense of the sea coasts." Presidents did so between 1797 and 1814. Following the War of 1812, the cutters chased and captured pirates and supported navy and army operations in the Seminole Wars (1836–1842) and the War with Mexico (1846–1848).

Throughout the Civil War, cutters patrolled for commerce raiders and often provided fire support for troops. When the cutter *Harriet Lane* encountered Confederate steamer *Nashville* in the harbor of Charleston, South Carolina, the shot she fired across the ship's bow was the first Union naval action of the war. The cutter *Miami* carried Abraham Lincoln and his party to Fort Monroe, Virginia, in May 1862 preparatory to the Peninsular Campaign. When the United States declared war on Spain in 1898, eight cutters, carrying forty-three guns, joined Admiral William Sampson's fleet in blockading Havana, Cuba. To protect U.S. shores from the Spanish fleet, the navy assigned coast watching to its new Life-Saving Service.

On January 28, 1915, the Congress combined the Life-Saving Service and Revenue Cutter Service to form the United States Coast Guard. The law stated that the Coast Guard was "an armed service" at all times and made provisions for its transfer to the navy when needed. This occurred in both world wars, Korea, and Vietnam. On April 1, 1967, primarily for administrative purposes, the Coast Guard was transferred from the Treasury Department to the newly created Department of Transportation.

While Coast Guard personnel, known to themselves as Coasties, performed heroically in combat in wartime and played a major role in drug interdiction in the post-Vietnam decades, to the American people the Coast Guard would always be known and revered for its search-and-rescue missions. This aspect of the original cutter service had been added to its responsibilities in 1833 when Congress authorized the president of the United States to "cause" the government's vessels "to cruise upon the coast, in the severe portion of the season," and to afford "such aid to distressed navigators as their circumstance and necessities may require." The cutters were also authorized to "go to sea prepared fully to render such assistance."

Many of the rescues were spectacular. When the immigrant ship *Ayrshire* grounded at Squan Beach, New Jersey, in 1850, all but one of the 202 people on board were saved. After the Life-Saving Service was revitalized in 1871 under the leadership of Sumner L. Kimball and the former commander of the history-making cutter *Harriet Lane*, Revenue Marine Captain John Faunce, a service that had depended on civilian volunteers was federalized. Equipment and life-saving techniques developed in the mid-1880s continued in use for a century. They included the Lyle gun (named for the army captain who developed it) that shot a line to secure a distressed ship. Rescuers trained for night operations. From 1871 to 1914, nearly one hundred eighty thousand lives were saved.

In the 1930s, amphibious aircraft were added to the Blue Water rescue service. Ocean stations were created after World War II, first in the Atlantic and then the Gulf of Mexico and the Pacific. Cutters stationed in mid-ocean provided rescue sites and weather-condition reports. Helicopters that had been developed by the Coast Guard for anti-submarine warfare in World War II were adapted for search and rescue.

Successful negotiations for the purchase of Alaska from Russia in 1867 by Secretary of State William Seward, derided at the time as "Seward's Folly," resulted in a widening of the scope of the cutter service that became the Coast Guard. The first cutter to venture into the Gulf of Alaska, the 165-foot *Lincoln,* under the command of Captain W. A. Howard in 1867, had orders to locate potential spots to build coaling stations and lighthouses, as well as customs houses. The cruise lasted four months. Later in 1867 and over the next two years, the cutter *Wayando* made a coastal survey from the Alaska Panhandle to the Aleutians and into the Bering Sea. In 1895, the Bering Sea Patrol Fleet was formed and based at Unalaska. Its duties ranged from coast patrols to blocking illegal traffic in firearms and liquor to assisting in the introduction of reindeer from Siberia to northern Alaska and exploration of the Kowak and Noatak rivers, then maintaining law and order on the Yukon River during the gold rush.

On October 4, 1980, headquarters of the Coast Guard Rescue Coordination Center (RCC) for the Coast Guard's Seventeenth District (covering Alaska) was at Juneau. Its chief was Commander Richard Schoel. Born in Seattle, Washington, he'd spent much of his career in Northwest posts. When the *Prinsendam* sent its XXX, he was at home and had just gone to bed. Schoel went to bed late because he had attended the centennial celebrations of the founding of the port city set against the mountains of the Gastineau Channel. Awakened by a call from the RCC informing him of the *Prinsendam*'s XXX, Schoel knew that in every rescue the critical factor was always time.

He remembered thinking that whether the good lord would grant the Coast Guard's always-ready crews, ships, and planes enough of it remained to be seen.

CHAPTER 13

God and Proportionality

One and a half hours after Captain Wabeke revealed there was a small fire in the engine room, Richard Steele supposed that news wire association members among Alaska's newspapers had sent bulletins to newsrooms all over the United States and on to the rest of the world that the cruise ship *Prinsendam* was in trouble. He imagined the editor of his own *Telegram-Gazette* of Worcester, Massachusetts, deciding to compose a front page banner headline that would bring the story dramatically home:

WORCESTER PUBLISHER AND WIFE ON BURNING CRUISE SHIP, FATE OF 500 OTHERS IN GULF OF ALASKA BLAZE ALSO UNKNOWN

A cynical journalistic wag who understood that news, like politics, was always local had once created what he'd titled "Newsworthiness Proportionality Chart" that listed:

250,000 Bangladeshis drowned in a typhoon =

100,000 Turks buried in Ankara earthquake =

5,000 Italians left homeless by volcano eruption =

500 Englishmen dead in collapse of Grand Derby grandstand =

25 gamblers killed in bus accident on the way to Las Vegas =

4 New Jersey high school kids die in after-prom car crash =
1 Three-year-old local girl rescued after falling into
   abandoned well.

Recalling the callous but funny truth about news evaluations
and decision making by news editors, Steele found himself
remembering the 1940s movie *The Naked City*. About New York
City detectives looking for a killer, the film inspired one of the
first series about cops on television. Produced and narrated by
ex–newspaper columnist Mark Hellinger, the film offered a last
line that proved more indelible in most memories than the movie:
"There are eight million stories in the naked city; this has been
one of them."

If there were time to sit down and talk with each of the
passengers, officers, and crewmen aboard the *Prinsendam*, Steele
ruminated, their stories probably wouldn't rise to the standards of
great moviemaking or even a weekly TV show. But that didn't
mean they weren't important to them and to someone else. He'd
listen to love stories and some that were funny, embarrassing,
heartbreaking, uplifting and inspiring, and humdrum. But should
the worst happen, if the ship were to sink on this cold October
night in the Gulf of Alaska under the glow of the northern lights,
hundreds of hometown newspapers would have to pay attention.
Lives that were unremarkable and worth no more than a
paragraph, if that, in the obituaries on the back page would at
least for a day rise in newsworthiness to the level of a front-page
story with a big bold headline and an accompanying photograph
of the deceased.

Strangers plunged into trouble had been a theme of
countless writers. The Italian official of the Wagon Lit Company

that operated the European railroad in Agatha Christie's classic detective story had exclaimed to Hercule Poirot in the dining car, "Ah! If I had the pen of a Balzac! I would depict this scene." It lent itself to romance. All around him and the famous Belgian-born detective sat people of all classes, nationalities, and ages. They would sleep and eat under one roof, unable to get away from each other for three days.

The *Prinsendam* had attracted more than three hundred people to a journey nine times as long. Each had come on board in giddy expectation of a leisurely delight-filled cruise to exotic places. Now the dream trip had become a nightmare. Rousted from their warm rooms to the Promenade Deck with the assurance that the engine-room fire was under control, some were mildly annoyed, but most were in good sprits that were rooted in confidence that they would be okay. So far, they were right. If the ship were in danger of sinking, the lifeboats would have been made ready. The officers and crew would have been sure everyone had a life jacket, yet many of the people on the Promenade Deck were still without them. Wrapped in blankets, tablecloths, and drapes ripped from walls, some resembled war refugees. A few women in sweaters over nightgowns looked as if they'd stepped outdoors on a chilly morning to bring in the morning paper. A dapper man in a tuxedo looked like a befuddled partygoer wondering where he'd parked the car.

If the captain decided to issue an order to the crew to lower lifeboats, the 320 passengers would be directed to get into six with rowing equipment and space for 99. Two had motors and one was equipped with a radio transmitter. A dozen inflatable rafts were made to accommodate twenty-five crew members each. The pair of covered motorized tenders could be employed to tow any of the lifeboats requiring assistance in moving them clear of the ship.

Reviewing all that he had learned about the *Prinsendam* before booking passage for him and Louise, as well as what he'd been told during the first day's emergency drill, Steele became aware of an elderly woman by his side.

She asked, "Do you think it's going to turn out all right?"

Steele smiled. "I'm sure it will."

The woman chatted as if they were old friends, telling him her name was Elsa Hutson and that she was an octogenarian. She recalled childhood mornings as her devout mother sent her off to school with the blessing, "May the spirit of the Lord go with you and protect you and make your path easier. The Lord is our shepherd."

Squeezing Steele's hand, she said, "It always made me feel better. I hope it does the same for you."

Were there any nonbelievers on the ship, Steele mused, or did an announcement of a fire in the *Prinsendam*'s engine room produce the same effect observed by an army chaplain? He had famously said, "There are no atheists on a battlefield."

Some people who had never tasted a spirited drink found some solace, if not the comfort of Biblical quotations, among lifelong imbibing enthusiasts at the Prinsen Club bar. The ex-GI Earl Andrews and sporting-goods purveyor Herman Solomon lamented the fact that the Los Angeles and San Francisco baseball teams had fallen out of the running and debated whether the Phillies or the Royals would win the World Series, and in how many games. Former state senator Dickinson in conversation with former Jersey State College art professor Courtney predicted that Jimmy Carter would beat Ronald

Reagan. Australian Len Bennett's down-under accent seemed to enthrall Edna Marcus of Cleveland, Ohio.

Lecturer John Graham assumed that this crisis, like all the others in his life, might take him to the brink of terror, but not over it. The difference between now and other times was that he had time to think about it. "All those other near misses," he recalled, "whether a bullet or an avalanche or a climbing fall, had been sudden and swiftly over." He had never thought of himself as particularly religious. "But let me tell you," he said, "in circumstances like these, one is led to prayer." His was unusual. "My dying is idiotic," he said. "I've left the Foreign Service so I can devote everything I have to this new life of making the world a better place, which I'd assumed would be doing your work. So how is it now, just as I'm beginning, I'm being wiped out? It doesn't make one damn bit of sense. I can accept dying, Promising young people die every day. But at least I deserve to know why. I've always assumed there's an order and logic to the universe. My death now seems so illogical. I have a right to know what's going on."

Still unwilling to meet her maker just yet, Jeannie Gilmore was increasingly concerned about so much thick, black, acrid smoke. Why was there no sprinkler system? Had the ship been constructed with the devices, they would have quelled most of it. She decided that this puzzle would have to be explained by Holland America, but if no one else raised the issue she would do so at the first opportunity. Meanwhile, she was confident that she, her mother, and all on board the ship would get through all of this and, God willing, have plenty of years in which to talk about the night their cruise ship had a fire.

Eighty-year-old Mildred Griber from Ocilla, Georgia, was old enough to recall reading newspaper accounts of the sinking of the *Titanic* in 1912. Six decades later on a trip to New York City, she'd gone to the theater to see a musical about the *Titanic*. Based on the life of one of the ship's passengers, *The Unsinkable Molly Brown* had a number that expressed Mildred's present attitude. In the musical's title role, the delightfully rambunctious, gravelly voiced singer and actress Tammy Grimes had defiantly belted out "I Ain't Down Yet." The loss of 1,503 lives on an ocean liner that White Star Line had claimed was unsinkable had provided not only the framework for the musical comedy, but inspiration for Walter Lord's best-selling book, *A Night to Remember,* and a 1958 British film adaptation that Mildred considered a better telling of the story than 1953's *Titanic,* starring Barbara Stanwyck and Clifton Webb. As these memories of a doomed ship stirred, Mildred wondered how many of her fellow passengers on the *Prinsendam* had thought at least for a moment, or were thinking now, about the *Titanic*.

Differences in circumstances and proportionality made the *Prinsendam*'s plight to the *Titanic*'s like comparing apples and oranges. The gigantic *Titanic* had carried five times as many passengers as the *Prinsendam*. Most people on the *Titanic* were in a class known as "steerage" that in the history of international travel had been replaced by three-across "tourist" seating on jet planes. The tragedy and scandal of the *Titanic,* aside from the arrogance of believing anything man-made could trump an ocean, was that the *Titanic* had gone to sea without a sufficient number of lifeboats. The *Prinsendam* had plenty. The *Titanic*'s orchestra played the hymn "Nearer My God to Thee." The band on the *Prinsendam* had offered diverting songs by Rodgers and Hammerstein.

In the sixty-eight years between the *Titanic*'s collision with an iceberg and the *Prinsendam*'s engine-room fire, advances in communication and navigational technology had provided the cruise ship with equipment that could have saved the *Titanic*. The *Prinsendam* had the public address system to alert passengers, telephones, radiotelephony, radiotelegraphy, VHF radio direction finder, radar, echo sounding, automatic pilot and gyro compass. Although walkie-talkies were not required, the ship's crew and officers had several. Its course was within the scope of AMVER. And she was within range of the cutters and helicopters of the United States Coast Guard.

CHAPTER 14

Notifications

Rushing to the USCG RCC headquarters in the seven-story federal building in downtown Juneau, Commander Richard Schoel reviewed assets available for a rescue operation. Luckily, the cutter *Boutwell*, usually stationed in Seattle, had been sent to Juneau to take part in the one-hundredth anniversary commemoration. Schoel reckoned the distance between the capital and the cruise ship's stated position at about 300 miles. The cutter *Woodrush* was at Sitka. The cutter *Mellon*, also based in Seattle, was on patrol near Vancouver, approximately 550 miles. The RCC base at Kodiak, 250 miles from the *Prinsendam*, had two HH-3 helicopters and two Hercules HC-130 cargo planes. The Alaskan Air Command RCC at Elmendorf Air Base at Anchorage could send out an HH-3 chopper and a Hercules. The Canadian Air Force in British Columbia also had a pair of CH-46 choppers, but they were more than 600 miles away.

The night watch had located the *Prinsendam*'s position and marked it on a wall map of the Gulf of Alaska with a small magnetized metal silhouette of a ship. Arrows showed locations of the *Williamsburgh*, *Greatland*, SOHIO *Intrepid*, and the *Portland*. Schoel was told that there had been no further word from the cruise ship. No one said aloud what was on everyone's mind. Fire might have spread so fast that the *Prinsendam* could not transmit an SOS. Whether she was at the bottom, a burned-out hulk, or an adrift derelict, the Coast Guard had to respond as quickly as possible to either assist in firefighting or get people still on the ship off, rescue anyone in the lifeboats or in the water, and ultimately recover any bodies.

Standard operating procedure required notifications of Coast Guard responses to every emergency be sent to USCG Commandant John B. Hayes in Washington, D.C., and the Pacific Coast Area commander, James S. Gracey, in Seattle. In 1961, Hayes had been the secretary of a committee that was set up at the direction of President John Kennedy's Secretary of the Treasury (and the civilian head of the Coast Guard), C. Douglas Dillon, to review the service's needs following the loss of three Coast Guard boats and seven lives (three Coast Guardsmen and two crab fishermen) in a rescue effort in the Gulf of Alaska "graveyard of the North Pacific." The worst Coast Guard loss in more than a decade, it was attributed to obsolete equipment and insufficient training of personnel. The result of the review was Congressional passage and the president's signing of the Act to Increase the Efficiency of the Organization of the Coast Guard. The law strengthened the position of the office that Admiral Hayes assumed in 1978 and held to 1982, to be succeeded by Admiral Gracey (1982–1986).

The oldest of Schoel's ships, the 180-foot seagoing tender *Woodrush*, built in 1944, had participated in a vast rescue operation involving a famous Great Lakes shipwreck in 1975 that was memorialized in a hit song by Gordon Lightfoot, "The Wreck of the Edmund Fitzgerald." As described by Jenny Nolan in *The Detroit News*, "on November 8, 1975, a storm born in the Oklahoma panhandle" picked up force and moved through Iowa and Wisconsin. The next day, gale warnings were issued for Lake Superior. The giant Great Lakes freighter *Edmund Fitzgerald* was carrying 26,116 tons of taconite pellets from Superior, Wisconsin, to Detroit. At 729 feet, it was at that time the largest freighter on the Great Lakes. With a seventy-five-foot beam and a depth of thirty-nine feet, it had a load capacity of almost 30,000 tons, weighed 13,632 tons, and cost more than eight million dollars. The furnishings and design of the staterooms and dining room were the height of nautical fashion, with a down-cushioned sofa sectional, linen drapes, and panoramic windows in the lounge. The windows overlooked nearly two city blocks of cargo hatches to the stern.

When the *Fitzgerald* came within twenty miles of the vessel *Arthur Anderson*, under the helm of Captain Jessie B. Cooper, near Two Harbors, Minnesota, Nolan wrote, "The captains commiserated by radio over the storm's increasing intensity, and at two o'clock a.m. on Monday the 10th, they decided to change course and take the northern route along Superior's north shore. This would put them in the lee of the Canadian shoreline, which hopefully would protect them from the gale force winds which were whipping up the seas."

At seven a.m. McSorley contacted his company to report that weather would delay his arrival at the Soo Locks. The *Anderson* was following the *Fitzgerald* at a distance of nearly sixteen miles and keeping in contact. Winds were high, and getting worse. Waves were eight to ten feet in the early afternoon and increasing in power and size as the day wore on. At 7:10 p.m., the *Anderson* radioed the *Fitzgerald* to warn of another vessel nine miles ahead, but assured McSorley that on present course the ship would pass by to the west. The first mate of the *Anderson* asked, "How are you making out with your problem?" The *Fitzgerald* replied. "We are holding our own." It was the last contact with the ship.

A search was launched with aircraft and patrol boats crisscrossing the area. The *Arthur Anderson* discovered a piece of a lifeboat. Also found were a life preserver, another lifeboat, a raft, and a stepladder, but neither bodies nor any trace of the huge ore carrier. The search went on for three days. Recalling being on board the *Woodrush*, Coast Guardsman Robert Ravenna wrote, "We were on six-hour standby and were underway in two and a half hours. A 180-foot buoy tender and twenty-five-foot seas don't mix all that well." He added, "The [Coast Guard] blue book says we've got to go out. It doesn't say a damn about having to come back!"

The *Woodrush* was home-ported in Duluth until transferred to the northwest in 1978.

In a Coast Guard tradition that honored secretaries of the Treasury by naming cutters for them, the 378-foot *Boutwell* took its name from the Treasury secretary in the Grant administration, George S. Boutwell. Built in New Orleans, the cutter was commissioned in 1968. The *Mellon* was named for Andrew William Mellon, head of the Treasury Department in both the Coolidge and Hoover years. In June 1976 she towed the disabled cutter *Polar Star* from Hawaii to home port in Seattle. On November 8 of that year, at the end of an Alaskan patrol, the *Mellon* rushed to the aid of motor vessel the *Carnelian I.* In terrible weather with low visibility and high winds a hundred miles north of Oahu, Hawaii, the *Mellon* recovered sixteen of thirty-three crewmen who clung to logs and debris. Awarded the Meritorious Unit Commendation for operations between June 1975 and February 1976, the cutter was featured in the movie *The Last Flight of Noah's Ark.* On October 11, 1976, the ship participated in

Alaska Day festivities, with the crew taking part in a parade, and was toured by two thousand people.

Almost exactly four years later, while Commander Schoel assessed his assets, it was the *Boutwell* that was the center of attraction during the city's one-hundredth birthday party. In a history of the city for *The Juneau Empire* Ann Chandonett noted that in October 1880, two prospectors beached their canoe near the mouth of Gold Creek and struggled among slippery rocks and dripping moss, through alders, berry canes, and devil's club to reach an area local Tlingits called Bear's Nest. Following the gulch down from the summit of the mountain into the basin, Richard Harris and Joe Juneau were guided by Chief Kowee. " It was a beautiful sight to see the large pieces of quartz, of black sulfite and galena," Harris wrote of that day, "all spangled over with gold."

The day after the discovery, Chandonett wrote, Harris drew up a code of laws for the new mining district. On October 18, he and Juneau established a 160-acre town site on a beach named Harrisburgh. "Having founded what was to become Juneau," said Chandonett's account, "they returned to Sitka with a thousand pounds of ore."

"When the people of Sitka saw the quartz," Harris recorded, "they were half crazy to get over here and locate claims, and set sail on all kinds of rigs, but finally reached here." One of the first men to arrive was William H. Pierce. He wrote, "We all camped on the beach, about forty miners all told, and started a new town."

It was the beginning of the Alaska gold rush. After beginning as Harrisburgh or Harrisburg, the growing mining town was known as Pilsbury, Fliptown, and Rockwell. Juneau was chosen in 1881, reportedly after Joe Juneau bought the naming committee round after round of drinks.

Southeast Alaska's worst maritime disaster occurred on October 24, 1918, when the *Princess Sophia*, a 245-foot Canadian ship southbound from Skagway, struck Vanderbilt Reef thirty miles north of the town. "At first the ship merely seemed to be lodged on the rocks," wrote Chandonett, "and the captain hoped the next high tide would float it free. Several rescue ships waited overnight in the area." The following day, the weather worsened and forced the rescue ships to take shelter. At about five p.m., the *Sophia* signaled, "Taking water and foundering, for *God*'s sake come and save us." The storm prevented the only vessel that heard the message from approaching. The next morning, rescue ships arrived to find only the blue above the water. None of the 353 passengers survived. Many were suffocated by bunker oil that coated the water. Juneau and residents of nearby Douglas faced the burden of recovering, cleaning, and sending the victims' bodies home.

When the U.S. Navy arrived in Juneau during World War II, the town gained a reputation for being as rough and ready as cow towns of the Old West. "There were the biggest fights you ever saw," said John Dapcevich, who worked at Percy's Café as a teenager. "Fights were going on from Percy's on Front Street to the end of South Franklin. The police just disappeared, there was nothing they could do."

The Coast Guard intervened. Quartermaster Red Holloway was ordered to take a seven-member shore patrol team from Ketchikan to Juneau. "It was a wild town and the admiral wanted law and order," Holloway noted. "During the first three months we just cleaned it up." Holloway would later own several Juneau cab companies and the Prospector Hotel, but on that day his patrol teams moved up and down the street from the Baranof

Hotel to the City Café to round up drunks. To handle the rowdies and miscreants, the Coast Guard opened a jail on South Franklin with cots and buckets for drunken soldiers who felt sick.

"They could be belligerent as hell going in but nice on their way out," said Holloway. After the soldiers sobered up, Holloway prepared a "skin sheet" that detailed why the men were thrown in jail. After they slept it off, they were taken back to their ship. It was then up to the commander to throw away the skin sheet or punish them.

The center of this activity, South Franklin Street, was lined with bars offering colorful names, including the Bloody Bucket and Blacky's Bar. The street was also a red light district with houses of prostitution operating between the bars. Following Holloway's arrival, navy and Coast Guard personnel were barred from the red light district, but army troops were allowed into the area, with orders to stay away from the prostitutes. Bawdiness remained legal until the early 1950s. After two decades of economic struggle, the city and state revived on the crest of a flood of oil created by the trans-Alaska pipeline. Newcomers heard residents joke, "An Alaskan is anyone who had a chance to leave but didn't, but they were the smartest, toughest, funniest, best-looking, friendliest people in the whole world. If you don't believe it, ask one."

With the trans-Alaska pipeline gushing dollars, the city named after Joe Juneau kicked off its centennial celebration in 1980 with fireworks, art exhibitions, and a New Century Ball featuring live music and prizes for the best historical attire. The arrival of the *Boutwell* for the big party meant that scores of Coasties on shore leave would flood into town in dress uniforms they called "Bender Blues." The name remembered that Rear Admiral Chester R. Bender had in 1968 recommended that the service adopt a uniform to distinguish the Coast Guard from the Navy. The result was a deep-blue, single-breasted jacket for all ranks.

Five years later, the uniform became standard for a new kind of Coastie as the service's officer training academy was opened to women. Four-year sign-ups in the enlisted ranks were also offered. In 1977, women went to sea as crew members on cutters *Gallatin* and *Morgenthau.* On July 4, 1979, Lieutenant j.g. (junior grade) Beverly Kelly became the first woman to take command of an American warship, the ninety-five-foot *Cape Newagen,* at Honolulu. On the same day, Lieutenant Susan I. Moritz was aboard the *Cape Current* when it seized the cabin cruiser *David* and three thousand pounds of marijuana seventy-five miles southeast of Miami. In June 1980, Cadet First Class Linda Johansen was the first woman to head the cadet corps at the Coast Guard Academy as she and several classmates became the Academy's first women graduates.

Six months after graduating with the class of 1980, Lieutenant j.g. Monyee Wright was serving in the engine room of the *Boutwell.* Born in Japan because her navy father married a Japanese woman, she grew up in California. In high school she had her heart set on joining the navy. When her school counselor told her that military academies were being opened to women, she replied that she preferred to get into the service "on my own merits," rather than being appointed to a service academy by her congressman. The counselor suggested that she look into joining the Coast Guard.

"I knew a lot about the navy," she recalled, "but almost nothing about the Coast Guard. It sounded like a great organization. So I applied for admission to the Coast Guard Academy."

The *Boutwell* was her first duty. Her husband, Richard (Rick) Wright, was serving on the *Mellon.* They'd met at the Coast Guard

Academy and married the day after graduation. Rick was tall and Monyee was five feet four. Because Rick's nickname was "Moose," she became "Mrs. Moose" and then "Moose." The first woman to report to the ship, she learned that she would share quarters with Lieutenant (junior grade) L. E. Burgess. Divorced with a young son who was cared for by her mother, she wanted to be called "L. E." so Monyee never learned her first name.

"We were so different," she remembered. "Her soap dish had a bar of Dove. Mine had a bar of black Lava because I needed a coarse soap to get the engine grease and oil off my hands. She wore perfume and smelled great. I smelled like diesel fuel."

While Commander Schoel was reviewing the locations of ships and aircraft, Monyee and many of the *Boutwell's* officers and crew were ashore. Most, including Monyee, had headed for Juneau's most famous drinking establishment, the Red Dog Saloon. At the corner of Franklin Street, it was described by one patron as "raucous and real crowded." Deep sawdust covered the floor and giant stuffed bears and moose heads contributed to the rustic décor. Beneath an open staircase, an industrial-size vacuum cleaner evidently had not been used in years. Coasties who couldn't squeeze into the Red Dog patronized more than two dozen other bars, taverns, and saloons.

Consequently, the order from Schoel at RCC notifying the *Boutwell* that it had to sail immediately meant that Captain Leroy Krumm had to send out patrols and seek the assistance of the Juneau police department to round up most of the officers and crew.

Remembering that night and the *Boutwell's* skipper in an interview nearly a quarter of a century later, Monyee laughed affectionately as she said, "Captain Leroy Krumm was a character. He came on duty on the *Boutwell* at Seattle around the time I did. He used to be on buoy tenders up in Alaska. He was very familiar with the waters up there. He had been in some really tight situations. He was fun. I remember my roommate and I having a Halloween party at our house. He came near the end of the party wearing a serape and sombrero. He used to wear them and smoke cigars at poker parties that he gave."

Recalling that prior to Krumm taking command of the *Boutwell* the ship had a reputation for a lack of discipline and as a dumping ground for the hopeless and misfits, Boatswain Mate Pete Marcucci credited Krumm with restoring discipline, self-respect, and pride while forging a bond with the crew. It began on the day he took command at Anchorage. Immediately after the end of the formalities, he turned to the assembled crew and said, "Ship dismissed." The order gave them twenty-four-hour liberty. Said Pete a quarter of a century later, "I'd sail with him anywhere."

Admittedly having been a hard-drinking, carousing, and "skirt-chasing youth from a dysfunctional family in New Jersey," Pete had enlisted in the Coast Guard on an impulse in 1979 at age nineteen. "I was kind of surprised myself," he said, "because I always thought the Coast Guard was a bunch of pussies." After getting into trouble while serving in Alaska, he recalled, he found himself "booted" to the *Boutwell,* which was "like a prison ship, with lots of guys who were on restriction." Deciding that he was not going "on that ship," he "took off for a month." When he returned, he was punished with four hours extra duty every day.

"One of the hardest things was fitting in on a headquarters unit ship that's like an honor guard with Academy people," Marcucci recalled. "Here I come out of Alaska where guys have beards down to their bellies. We're catching fish with our hands and chasing native women and in the hardest core sailing unit. It was shitty duty and that's why there were personnel problems."

During the roundup of crew and officers, he and several others from the deck department were in the bar of the Baranof Hotel. He recalled, "They stopped the band and announced that *Boutwell* crew members had to go back to the ship. I and Fernando Martinez, who was out of the barrio in Los Angeles and was afraid of water and didn't swim, set up firefighting equipment on the helicopter flight deck, but after awhile we stood down from that. It was a beautiful night. There was an aurora borealis."

Although Monyee Wright's degree from the Academy was in marine science, her place in the graduating class left her few choices in duty assignments. Preferring a job "not all spit and polish," she settled on engineering and learned on the job. "I was so ignorant," she said, "that I knew next to nothing." Changed into work shirt, dungarees, and steel-toed boots as *Boutwell* made ready, she imagined the fire in the *Prinsendam* engine room with horror.

CHAPTER 15

Three O'clock Call

"In a real dark night of the soul," wrote novelist F. Scott Fitzgerald, "it is always three o'clock in the morning." It was at a quarter to three in the Frank Sinatra song that the bartender named Joe was told by a downbeat lone drinker to "set 'em up" and listen to a little story about the end of a brief episode that required one more for the road. "Three o'clock in the morning courage," said President Teddy Roosevelt, "is the most desirable kind."

A few minutes after three in the morning on Saturday, October 4, 1980, at Elmendorf Air Force Base at Anchorage, two time zones west of Juneau, Captain John Walters of the Alaskan Air Command answered his bedside telephone expecting to hear that someone was in trouble.

"Captain, have we got a mission for you," said a male voice in the RCC at Juneau with barely restrained excitement. "There are 520 people in the Gulf of Alaska."

Absorbing the scant facts of the situation, Walters was heir to an air force tradition that went back four decades to the creation of the Alaskan Air Force in 1942 as part of the World War II Western Defense Command. With its name changed in February 1942 to the Eleventh Air Force, the unit was responsible for the air defense of Alaska, with bases at Umnak (Fort Glenn), Adak, Cold Bay (Thornbrough Army Airfield), Attu, Kiska, and Anchorage. The Air

Command divided Alaska into two air defense sectors. The one headquartered at Elmendorf Air Base was responsible for the southern half and Ladd AFB had the northern half. The Alaskan Command's (ALCOM) base for the Eleventh Air Force at Anchorage opened on June 8, 1940. First personnel arrived on August 12. Three months later, the Department of War formally designated what had been popularly referred to as Elmendorf Field as Fort Richardson. The air facilities on the post were named Elmendorf Field in honor of Captain Hugh M. Elmendorf, killed in 1933 while flight testing an experimental fighter near Wright Field in Ohio. After World War II, the army moved its operations to the new Fort Richardson and the air force assumed control of the air field and renamed it Elmendorf Air Force Base.

The first air force unit assigned to Alaska, the 18th Pursuit Squadron, arrived in early 1941. Other air force units poured into Alaska in the face of a threat from the Japanese and the field played a vital role as the main air logistics center and staging area during the Aleutian Campaign. After the war, Elmendorf assumed an increasingly important role in the defense of North America in the Cold War. The 11th Air Force was re-designated as Alaskan Air Command (AAC) to provide communications to the isolated and often rugged region. Regional Operations Control Center (ROCC) for North American Air Defense (NORAD) at Elmendorf served as the nerve center for all operations in Alaska and earned the name "Top Cover for North America."

A turning point in Elmendorf's history in 1970 was the arrival of the 43d Tactical Fighter Squadron from MacDill AFB, Florida. The squadron gave the AAC an air-to-ground capability that was further enhanced with activation of the 18th Tactical Fighter Squadron at Elmendorf in October 1977. The base's strategic location made it an ideal deployment center not only for military operations, but search and rescue involving civilian aircraft and ships.

Captain Walters was the pilot of a Sikorsky HH-3E helicopter. Known as the "Pelican," it carried a crew of pilot, copilot, flight mechanic, and navigator, with room for twenty passengers. Its cruising speed was 120 knots and the maximum 142. A side hoist had a lift limit of six hundred pounds. A nimble air platform, the Pelican was a proven asset for missions at sea in all types of weather and had been widely used in the Vietnam War. Troops in battle in Vietnam had named those used as gunships the "Jolly Green Giant."

Also based at Elmendorf, the versatile Lockheed C-130 Hercules cargo plane had been designed as an assault transport. Adapted for a variety of missions, including low-level attack, close air support and air interdiction, midair space capsule recovery, weather mapping and reconnaissance, electronic surveillance, firefighting, aerial spraying, and disaster relief, the plane was ideal for search and rescue (SAR). With a wing span of 132 feet and powered by four Allison T56-A15 Turboprop engines, the Hercules had joined the U.S. Coast Guard's inventory because it was large, rugged, and extremely reliable with the ability to fly on two of its engines to greatly extend its range. Maximum speed at high altitude was 290 knots. Low-altitude cruise speed was 210 to 250 knots. The plane also provided in-air refueling.

While Walters was being briefed, a call to action from RCC in Juneau went to the Coast Guard RCC at Sitka. Its primary aircraft was the Boeing CH-46 helicopter. Known as the Sea Knight, it was procured in 1964 to meet medium-lift requirements of the U.S. Marine Corps in Vietnam. The aircraft served in combat and peacetime environments. Unique twin-rotor design, with propellers at the front and rear, provided increased agility and superior handling in strong winds, allowing rapid direction changes during low airspeed maneuvering. One of the largest helicopters in the American inventory, the Sea Knight was sixteen feet, eight inches tall. Six rotor blades measured twenty-five and a half feet. With a maximum lift capability of six thousand pounds, it could carry twenty-five combat-loaded troops with a fuel endurance to stay airborne for approximately two hours. Able to land and taxi in the water in case of emergency and stay afloat for up to two hours in two-foot seas, it excelled in rearward and sideward flight. Sitka's RCC had two Sea Knights. Fueled to their limit, they waited for word that a Hercules from Elmendorf had found the *Prinsendam* and provided its location coordinates. Also waiting were two HH-3 choppers and two HC-130s at the CG RCC in Kodiak and two CH-46s of the Canadians at Comox, British Columbia.

Less than half an hour after the calls went out from Juneau, with only the data provided by the XXX signal in a briefing by Walters, the Pelican and C-130 personnel at Elmendorf, including five pararescue jumpers (PJs) and a flight surgeon, Captain Donald Hudson, boarded their aircraft to launch the biggest peacetime air-sea rescue mission in American history.

CHAPTER 16

Butterflies and Optimists

As nineteen-year-old Seaman Apprentice David Hughes and his buddies Bill Thibodeaux of Texas and Arthur Garcia of New Mexico exchanged work uniforms for civilian clothes at the end of their work shifts to join most of the *Boutwell*'s crew of 150 who had gone on liberty for Juneau's centennial celebration, a blast of the cutter's horn signaled the end of plans to party and the start of a hasty roundup ashore of officers and crew on orders from Captain Leroy Krumm.

When Dave thought about what to do with his life after high school, he'd entertained the idea of a religious life as a youth minister. Born in Illinois, he grew up in Albia, Iowa. After a semester in college, he decided to review his choice and take some time off to see the world that lay beyond the rolling cornfields of the Hawkeye state west of Ottumwa. Although the largest body of water he'd ever seen was nearby lake Rathbone, the possibility of joining the U.S. Coast Guard was suggested by a great uncle who served in World War II. Enlisted in Des Moines in March 1980 with his friend Paul Van Klaven and trained at the U.S. Coast Guard boot camp in Alameda, California, he and Paul received orders to report to pier 39 in Seattle, Washington, for assignment to the *Boutwell*.

Rousted out of the Red Dog Saloon, Seaman Apprentice Thomas Ice and a couple of his buddies made it back to the ship just in time. From Akron, Ohio, he'd joined the Coast Guard at age seventeen "to get out of Ohio and have some adventure."

Of the roundup of the cutter's officers and crew in the bars of Juneau early on October 4, Dave Hughes recalled, "Some of the guys who made it back to the ship were not exactly in sea-ready shape. We were told there was a ship in distress and it was going to be a long evening. We also heard that there were storms coming in. As we were steaming out, I had butterflies in my belly. I was the guy at the bottom of the totem pole, a lowly deck hand. My job normally was to break loose the lines. Because the report was that a few hundred people were in big trouble about 150 miles at sea, we were in a hurry to get underway. I saw a few guys who just missed the ship and were left stranded on the dock with looks of amazement on their faces, but there was no way that we could turn back to pick them up."

Among the fifteen left behind were Lieutenant (junior grade) L. E. Burgess and the Executive Officer, T. D. Smith. They'd been dining at a restaurant. When they learned of the recall, they were unable to return to the ship in time. On duty that night as Yeoman, seventeen-year-old Seattle native Chris Macneith had the responsibility for noting the names of those who were on board, retrieved, or left ashore. He had joined the Coast Guard after dropping out of school and at the suggestion of his mother that he ought to seriously think about what he was going to do with his future, other than "sitting around the house." When she pointed out that a friend of his brother was in a similar situation and joined the Coast Guard, Chris looked into it and signed up. After training he learned that a billet (job) was available on the Seattle-based *Boutwell.*

"It was the first time we'd been called in the middle of the night," Chris recalled in an interview at his post with the Pacific

Northwest command after twenty-three years of Coast Guard service. "My function ended up being in the combat information center, helping get out of port. A lot of us were trying to get some rest because we figured we were going to have to do some heavy-duty work. No one actually told us what was going on, except that a cruise ship was in distress. It was estimated that it was going to take us about twelve hours to get on the scene."

In the *Boutwell's* engine room Lieutenant j.g. Monyee Wright knew that the ship had gotten an urgent order to get underway. The destination was not her concern. "My duty was to make sure we got there," she recalled. "I didn't know exactly where we were going, but I knew there was a cruise liner that was on fire, that we were to assist and several units were heading out there, and that some commercial ships were around to assist." She did not know that among the Coast Guard units was her husband Mike's cutter, *Mellon*, ordered to cease its patrolling near Vancouver and head for the *Prinsendam*.

At the helm of the *Williamsburgh*, Captain Arthur Fertig had informed his company's office in Valdez of the crisis and that he was changing course to assist and proceeding at seventeen knots. By agreement with the skipper of the *Eastland*, that tanker would remain on standby status in the region. The SOHIO *Intrepid* and the *Portland* were also altering course. Crews on all these ships were on alert to receive and help any passengers that might be taken on board.

Supervising the organization of the rescue force in the Juneau RCC, Commander School was satisfied that everything available was on the move. While he did not describe his feelings as a belly full of butterflies, he knew the situation was a challenge involving moving aircraft and cutters long distances rapidly at night in worsening weather to reach a burning ship carrying more than five hundred souls. His hope was that the RCC would receive a message from the *Prinsendam* advising that the fire was out and the ship was again underway without loss of life and injury. Until such an all-clear signal was received, the choppers, planes, and cutters would continue toward the coordinates given in the XXX. If the *Prinsendam*'s next message reported that the conditions on the ship had worsened, the crews of the first helicopters to arrive on scene would rapidly assess and report the condition of the ship and look for lifeboats, rafts, and people who might be in the water. If the ship had been abandoned, hundreds of passengers and crew would find themselves caught in the worst possible position in terrible and worsening weather in frigid waters of North America's most perilous and unforgiving sea.

Were the choppers to report that *Prinsendam* was afloat and everyone was still on board, the task of the aircraft and ships would be challenging, but not as daunting as plucking scared and desperate human beings out of lifeboats in darkness. Should they find people in the water, the likelihood of locating them alive rapidly diminished. If the XXX message that had been sent a few minutes after one o'clock were followed by an order to abandon ship, chances of survival by anyone who had plunged into the cold water of the Gulf of Alaska until choppers arrived were slim to none. If that were the case, the mission of the aircraft and ships would eventually shift from search and rescue to finding and recovering bodies.

Against strong headwinds encountered soon after leaving the Coast Guard's Sitka air station, Lieutenant Commander Joel Thuma's HH-3 had to cover 429 miles, with time of arrival estimated around four a.m. His plan was to first locate the

Prinsendam, eyeball its condition, and contact it by radio. He would then ascertain the location of the supertanker *Williamsburgh* and assess its capability for landing a helicopter, should it be necessary to establish an airlift of the passengers and crew, either from the ship or out of lifeboats. In the air in support of the effort, including Thuma's chopper, were twelve helicopters and an HC-130 to provide in-air refueling for the helicopters and serve as on-scene coordinator of rescue operations. On a helicopter on a southern course from Elmendorf Air Force Base, flight surgeon Captain Donald Hudson was worried about passengers who might suffer from hypothermia. When body temperature dropped, and all vital signs slowed down, the heart was subjected to irregularities. This was especially dangerous in the elderly. If there were one cardiac arrest, he speculated, the sight of efforts to resuscitate could arouse fear among other passengers and result in several heart attacks.

Also on board a helicopter were five pararescue specialists (PJs), including José Rios and John Cassidy. Born in the Bronx, Cassidy had spent his formative years in a rural county located about fifty-five miles northwest of New York City in his large family's 250-year-old house surrounded by the fields and woods belonging to two operating dairy farms. As a teenager he sold furs of muskrats he had trapped and skinned, caddied at the local golf course, and threw clay pigeons for trap and skeet shooters at a local gun club. At age fourteen he took a summer job working washers and dryers in a commercial laundry and the following summer worked for a sanitation company. He also pumped gas. Enlisted in the air force on the day he graduated from Monroe Woodbury Central High School, he earned an Associate Degree at the Community College of the Air Force and a Bachelor of Science

Degree at Southern Illinois University. He, Rios, and the others were trained to drop from the plane to the ship. If the *Prinsendam* had been abandoned or was too dangerous to board, they would jump into the sea as close as possible to the lifeboats–assuming there were any to be found in the vicinity of the ship.

That the passengers had not been alerted to the possibility of being ordered into the six lifeboats did not concern Richard Steele. He appreciated that such a step might, and probably would, engender a feeling of imminent doom among the passengers who thus far had been an orderly and even light-hearted bunch. Fearing that the effect of lowering the lifeboats from the Main to the Promenade Deck could result in a wave of panic, he tried to imagine what was going on in the wheelhouse. The worst thing a ship's captain could face as his crew battled a fire and sought assistance from the Coast Guard and nearby ships was three-hundred-plus out of control passengers.

Although they were quieter as they milled or wandered the Promenade Deck, Steele saw no evidence that anyone was on the verge of panic. One man seemed so relaxed that he had gone about the deck proposing a betting pool in which participants ventured what time they would be ordered to get into lifeboats. Although such macabre guesses were common in newsrooms if a famous person had been reported close to death, Steele chose not to participate. The proposition could have been even more cynical, he mused, if the man who offered it had asked him to make book on which of the male passengers could be expected to reject the tradition of women and children first and let nobody stand in his way of getting into a boat ahead of everyone, as one man was alleged to have done on the *Titanic* by putting on a woman's coat and head scarf.

If the *Prinsendam*'s lifeboats were somehow unable to accommodate all the passengers, Steele decided, and Louise emulated Mrs. Nathan Straus, wife of the owner of Macy's department store, by refusing to abandon her husband on the *Titanic*, they would go down together without regret, remembering the fabulous and fulfilling life they'd shared.

Senator Fairleigh Dickinson assured everyone he encountered that if they had to abandon ship they could count on his former service to uphold the Coast Guard's *semper paratus* motto by coming to their rescue. "They'll be here," he said, "before anybody's feet get wet."

Jeannie Gilmore heard music in her head. "There are some songs that once they get into your brain keep coming back until they almost drive you crazy," she said as she thought back almost a quarter of a century to the early hours of October 4, 1980. "The one that was presented by the *Prinsendam*'s gallant troupe of stalwart performers to bolster the spirits of the people on the Promenade Deck that I couldn't get out of my head was 'Cockeyed Optimist' from *South Pacific*. That's probably because I've been an optimist all my life. I guess that's the explanation for my absolute, constant belief that I was going to get through the crisis."

Reasoning that she and her mother would be warmer sitting rather than standing in the biting wind, she found a place for them on the port side of the deck by their lifeboat and adjacent to the entrance to the smoke-filled lounge. "I was content to wait for an announcement from the captain or one of the officers that the fire was out and that soon Mother and I could either return to the lounge or go back to our rooms," she recalled. "Then I heard a *whoosh*."

Feeling a hot blast of air on her hand, she looked down and saw flames sticking out like tongues under the door of the lounge.

CHAPTER 17

The Sun at Night

To all who knew Cornelius Wabeke as a man and were familiar with the great literature of the sea, the captain of the *Prinsendam* seemed to be straight out of the Herman Melville novel *White Jacket*. Born for "the rover's life," he yearned "to snuff thee up, sea breeze! and whinny in thy spray." Those who sailed with him might quote another passage: "In time of peril, like the needle to the lodestone, obedience, irrespective of rank, generally flies to him who is best fitted to command."

As a sailor, Wabeke appreciated the power of the eternal sea and had acknowledged it by ordering the XXX. As a Christian believing in the sustaining power of hope, he was not ready to give up his ship. The XXX was not surrender, but an alert that help might be needed. Confident that the fire could be brought under control and ultimately vanquished, he'd ordered no letup in fighting it. While the electrical system between the generators and the emergency pump below the engine room had been knocked out, an emergency generator on the Bridge Deck was working and providing light in the wheelhouse and power to the radio room. Dawn was five hours away. If they could hold out until daylight, Wabeke believed, with help from the Coast Guard and the *Williamsburgh* at hand the odds would favor saving the ship.

The first Coast Guard aircraft was expected to be overhead soon. The supertanker had estimated its arrival at around eight o'clock. At that time, the lifeboats would be lowered and passengers loaded. The *Prinsendam*'s pair of motorized tenders would tow them one at a time to the tanker–*if necessary*. Meanwhile, to avoid panic among the passengers, and to assure that hundreds of people would not be crammed into lifeboats, possibly for hours, he ordered that the boats be held on the Bridge Deck.

Like a coach or team manager in sports, Wabeke had what a report on the subsequent investigation called "an all-embracing task." He had to see that the right measures were taken to fight the fire and at the same time care for more than five hundred people on board, while maintaining communications with the Coast Guard and nearby ships. He had a further duty to the Holland America Line to do everything possible to save the $27-million ship and minimize the firm's legal liability in the event of death or injury. Also weighing on him were the timeless maritime tradition of a captain not giving up the ship and a reputation for reliability as a captain that he'd built and nurtured over three decades.

In this situation, the skipper of the *Prinsendam* embodied another observation by Herman Melville. "Familiarity with danger makes a brave man braver, but less daring," he'd written in *White Jacket*. "Thus with seamen: he who goes the oftenest round Cape Horn goes the most circumspectly."

As the seagoing equivalent of a coach or manager in sports, Wabeke could be only as good as his team. In this athletics analogy, his team's leader was Chief Officer Hendrik Egbert Valk. Born on May 9, 1927, he was a resident of Haarlem. His functions were foremost adviser to the captain and supervisor of the deck department, hotel operations, catering and firefighting on deck and in passenger accommodations. He was assisted by Second Officers P. W. Schol and M. J. H. M. Oosterwijk and third and fourth officers Paul Welling and S. L. Douwes. The Chief Engineer Officer, Albertus Marinus Boot, was forty-four and made his home in St. Annaland. He was second in responsibility to Valk. The Assistant Engineer Officer, Robert Kalf, was twenty-four and lived in Purmerand. Second Engineer Officer John Frederick Repko resided in Oost-Souburg. The Third Engineer Officer, Jacob Jan Cornelis van Hardeveld, was from Veenendaal. They shared supervision of engine room personnel on alternate watches.

Continuously on the bridge since the first report of the engine room fire just before one o'clock, Wabeke was painfully aware that in roughly ninety minutes the smoke from the blaze he'd believed was under control had spread to the Main Deck. Opening doors to vent it had resulted in a draft that evidently contributed to spontaneous combustion of objects in the dining room and smoke in the lounge above it, resulting in an order to passengers who had just been allowed to enter it to go back onto the open deck. Through all of this, there had been no reports of injuries.

As Wabeke reviewed the situation at four a.m., he heard a distant but fast-approaching fluttering noise that made "chopper" a synonym for helicopter. Stepping out onto the starboard wing of the bridge and searching the starry sky, he saw a winking red light that grew larger and larger as the helicopter sped toward him. At its controls, Lieutenant Commander Thuma and copilot Lieutenant Bruce Melnick peered across the black water and saw a wisp of gray smoke on the starboard side of the motionless white ship, but no flames. While it circled the ship, Melnick switched on a floodlight that Jeannie Gilmore would describe as "the sun at night." Scanning the ship and seeing nothing alarming, Thuma established radio contact with the wheelhouse.

Informing Thuma that there were no injuries and no need for evacuation of passengers and crew, Wabeke reported the failure of the water supply system and requested firefighting equipment. With none on the helicopter, but aware of the location of the *Williamsburgh*, about fifty miles away, Thuma banked the chopper and headed in that direction while Melnick radioed the supertanker that the chopper was en route and to have firefighting equipment ready to be picked up at its helicopter landing pad.

As the Coast Guard helicopter disappeared into the blackness, Wabeke was confident that with the airlifted firefighting gear his crew would be able to bring the fire under control without further assistance. But within minutes of the chopper's departure, he was told that the fire had spread into the lounge. This left Wabeke with no recourse but to order chief radio officer Van der Zee to flash a shipmaster's most dreaded signal.

By radio, Telex, VHF radio, and satellite the *Prinsendam* sent SOS.

CHAPTER 18

"I'm Sorry."

Informed of the *Prinsendam*'s SOS, Commander Richard Schoel looked at tiny symbols representing aircraft and ships on the giant map on the wall in the command center of the U.S. Coast Guard's North Pacific Rescue and Coordination Center in downtown Juneau and reviewed the decisions he had made. In the most challenging crisis of his career, he had been in constant touch with his assets by telephone and radio. The Coast Guard air stations at Kodiak and Sitka, along with the air force at Elmendorf and the Canadians at Comox, British Columbia, had sent out a baker's dozen of choppers and fixed-wing aircraft. The AMVER system had located ships within three hundred miles of the *Prinsendam* and all of those with the capability to respond were doing so. The *Williamsburgh* reported a speed of seventeen knots and an estimated arrival time of five hours. To prepare for reception of the rescued men and women, should it come to that, the air force was flying medical supplies to Yakutat, along with medical personnel. A chopper carried a doctor, Captain Don Hudson, and a team of parajumper rescuers (PJs). The *Mellon* and the *Woodrush* were underway, but had a long distance to travel. The *Boutwell*, with orders to "proceed and assist at best speed," reported nearly all its officers and crew who'd been exploring Juneau's streets and bars were back on board.

Once the *Boutwell* was clear of numerous channels and into open sea, Captain Leroy Krumm reported, it would rev up its speed to twenty-seven knots. A *Hamilton*-class cutter, the ship was 378 feet long with a displacement of 3,250 tons. Powered by two Fairbanks-Morse diesel engines that delivered 7,000 horsepower, it also had two Pratt-Whitney gas turbine engines providing a total of 36,000 horsepower and speeds up to twenty-nine knots. With two controllable pitch screws and a bow propulsion unit, it was maneuverable in tight situations and equipped with a helicopter flight deck, retractable hangar, and able to support helicopter deployment. Twelve of these cutters were introduced to the Coast Guard inventory in the 1960s in a class of ship named for the first Secretary of the Treasury, Alexander Hamilton. Built at a cost of $16 million to $20 million and originally designed to be 350 feet in length, they were stretched to 378. With a bow that Coast Guard historian Robert Erwin Johnson called "sharply raked," the cutters became known to their officers and crews and throughout the Coast Guard as "three-seventy-eights." In the years of the Cold War, *Hamilton*-class cutters on the West Coast were frequently the only regular military presence in the Bering Sea and Gulf of Alaska. Classified high-endurance (WHEC), they were designed for use in law enforcement, coastal defense, and oceanographic research, but the primary mission was protecting the safety of life and property at sea. With a flight deck capable of landing helicopters, a WHEC was equipped to serve as a command center, coordinating ships and aircraft in search-and-rescue operations.

Three years before Monyee Wright reported for duty in the engine room of the *Boutwell*, CGC *Morgenthau* (WHEC 722) became the first cutter to have women permanently assigned. Because Lieutenant (junior grade) L. E. Burgess had been left in Juneau, when the *Boutwell* headed out to sea Monyee had by chance attained the distinction of being the only woman among hundreds of Coasties and air force personnel in ships and aircraft represented in miniature on the wall map in Commander Schoel's coordination center. Although Monyee's work did not require her to know either the ship's destination or how long it would be until it arrived, Captain Krumm had given Schoel's RCC an estimate of ten hours. If this calculation held, the cutter would not arrive on scene before one o'clock in the afternoon. The *Mellon* and *Woodrush* were unlikely to be on hand until near nightfall. This meant that if *Prinsendam's* passengers and crew were forced to abandon ship in the interim, helicopters would have to hoist them out of the lifeboats one at a time in steel lift-baskets and body slings, then fly them in small groups either to the tanker or Yakutat and Sitka. Even if the vast rescue operation went without a hitch, plucking five hundred people from lifeboats and airlifting them to the supertanker or land would require numerous shuttles and several hours. Complicating the problem was that most of the passengers were elderly.

Although Captain Wabeke had reported fair weather and moderate sea conditions, the forecast provided by meteorologists indicated the presence of a storm front approaching rapidly from the west with strong winds, a drop in temperature to at least thirty-two degrees, rain and waves of at least five to ten feet, but possibly higher. In such conditions, a lifeboat with frightened senior citizens might capsize. This gloomy assessment portended not only rough conditions for those in lifeboats, but difficulties for helicopters hovering above them, in flights to the supertanker and bases on land, and meeting the C-130 Hercules for air refueling. The maximum flying time for a fully fueled Jolly Green Giant was six hours.

An even more unsettling scenario that Schoel had to contemplate was one in which the fire swept through the ship so quickly that there was no time to deploy the lifeboats, requiring removal of passengers and crew by choppers from burning decks in thick clouds of black smoke. Captain Wabeke had reported that a decision to launch the lifeboats had not been made. Another skipper might have chosen to do otherwise, but second-guessing Wabeke's decision to keep the passengers on board was not a step that Commander Schoel was prepared to take from a distance of three hundred miles. Because the *Prinsendam* was not an American-flag ship, but had been registered in the Netherlands Antilles and flew the Dutch flag, the Coast Guard's only legal responsibility was to assist, if and when it was asked. Investigation of what the maritime lawyers called "the casualty" would be a matter for the government of the Netherlands. As captain of a ship on the high seas that was far outside the jurisdiction of the United States Coast Guard, Cornelius Wabeke was not only the unquestionable master of the *Prinsendam*, but validated by international law and maritime custom as the man best suited to evaluate what was required to preserve her and the lives of the passengers and crew.

For nearly five hours, Wabeke's decisions, after consultation with his officers, had been made calmly and given clearly. He had followed established procedures for fighting a fire in the engine room, but efforts to quell the flames had failed. The fire had climbed upward to the Main Deck dining room and was now at the Promenade Deck and blazing in the lounge. Noting the time in the official log book as 0454 on 4 October 1980, he recorded the most painful decision of his oceangoing lifetime. Using loudspeakers powered by a back-up generator, he announced to the passengers, "I'm sorry. The fire is completely out of control. We have to abandon ship."

CHAPTER 19

God and Lifeboat Number Four

Three miles from setting his HH-3 down on the *Williamsburgh*'s chopper landing pad to take on fire-fighting gear, Lieutenant Commander Joel Thuma was informed by radio from the RCC in Juneau at five o'clock that the *Prinsendam* had signaled that orders had been given to abandon the ship. Reversing course, Thuma had to get his helicopter back to the scene—a fifty-mile flight—as quickly as possible to begin a rescue operation involving more than five hundred people crammed into six lifeboats, assuming everything went well and all boats had been launched.

The evacuation plan called for the cruise ship's pair of motorized tenders to be put into the water first so they could be used to tow lifeboats away from the ship. Lowering number two on the port side with the fourth mate and fourth engineer on board proceeded flawlessly, but number one on the starboard side, as the report of the investigation would note, "got fouled due to a hitch in a lashing." With a potential capacity of forty-six passengers and operating officers, it would dangle on its davits at midship uselessly at a forty-five-degree angle.

As specified in the emergency plan, officers designated as the lifeboat commanders had reported to the bridge to obtain passenger muster lists. These were organized in expectation that the passengers had been informed during the second-day emergency drill where to go and to be wearing their life jackets. For the most part, they had followed the directions after being rousted from their rooms around one o'clock. But in the intervening four hours, they'd spread throughout the Promenade Deck. They'd been allowed into the lounge and then ordered out, resulting in a disorganized crowd. Instead of orderly and disciplined groups at lifeboat assembly stations, they were now scattered over the Promenade Deck from the Lido Terrace at the stern to the Prinsen Club overlooking the bow, with many having sought rest and refuge from the cold and smoke by crowding into the darkened theater.

Jeannie Gilmore and her mother had stayed close to their lifeboat station, number four. "Nobody was panicking," she recalled. "We were just wondering how long it would be until someone told us to get into the lifeboats."

When the order came, she waited for the boat to be lowered from the Bridge Deck and was gratified that nobody was trampling others to get in. "There was no injustice of any kind," she observed, "but members of the crew were throwing wheelchairs overboard. They just wanted everyone to get into the boat as fast as possible."

Seated in the middle of the boat, Jeannie looked up with horror to find another lifeboat lowering toward hers. Only shouts to the Indonesian crewmen on the Bridge Deck and wildly waving arms prevented it from descending onto number four and crushing it. "I wasn't really scared as the boat was lowered," she remembered, "but when we were in the water, the waves shoved it against the side of the ship repeatedly. I got really angry. I thought, 'I'm not going to die being slammed into the side of a ship.' I didn't know where its fuel tanks were and I had a horrible image of them exploding, the ship rolling over, and dragging us down with it, like the people in the *Poseidon* movie."

Helping his wife into lifeboat number four, Richard Steele observed no panic. He recalled, "There was a bit of shoving and some squirming for priority position in the lifeboat–inevitable when ninety persons occupy sixty seats. Two ladies in wheelchairs were handled tenderly. One by one, the lifeboats struggled to free themselves from the mother ship. She is reluctant to sever the umbilical cord. Our boat swings on its davits and crashes, time and again, against the hull, up and down in crazy fashion. There was no place to sit and no one was in charge. We were let down to about thirty feet above the water and then the cables jammed. We went up and down like a yo-yo until we dropped some twenty feet straight down in a free fall and crashed into the Gulf of Alaska–free at last from the clinging parent."

Elizabeth Price was glad she'd paid attention during the lifeboat drill and stated later that it was "the most thorough and informative I've ever seen on a ship." Moments after the order to abandon ship, she saw "a burst of flame" at the aft end of the ship. In an account in the Spring 1981 issue of the magazine *Steamboat Bill,* she wrote, "Entry into lifeboats was swift, but no pushing–everyone waited his turn. Some Indonesian crew members did jump over the rail and preceded passengers into the boat. William, the maître d', was in charge of our boat–a veteran Dutch sailor. We were in good hands. Our boat was overloaded since ours was the last to be lowered into the water. William ordered thirty-five people out, the crew first. Only twenty-three left, leaving about eighty. I sat along the aft side of the lifeboat, so I had back support, with Lynn across from me."

Noting "quite an impact as we struck the water," she continued, "but the most terrifying moments came immediately. Our lifeboat could not break away from the ship. The wave action and wind forced us into the hull. We would crash into the ship with great force, then be tossed away from it, almost tipping over. This happened repeatedly, crushing the side of the fiberglass lifeboat and breaking the overhead supports."

When Captain Wabeke announced that the ship must be abandoned, Muriel Marvinney turned to traveling companion Agnes Lilard and said, "This is it, Ag."

Shaking her head, Agnes muttered, "I don't believe this!"

"Suddenly, people were five-deep at the railing to get into lifeboat number four," Muriel would remember in an article for a religious magazine. "There was no panic, except for a bit of shoving as crew members asked us to move back so they could open the railing."

An officer shouted, "Passengers only! Passengers only!"

Muriel watched two crewmen press forward and leap over the railing. She assumed they were going to assist passengers into the boat. "Instead," she recalled, "they disappeared under the blankets. I felt anger and disgust, but in a moment it melted into pity for their cowardice."

Canadian oil company executive Jack Barclay wasn't so forgiving. He would later tell a reporter for the Anchorage *Times* of the behavior of some of the young Indonesian crewmen, "They were pushing elderly women out of the way in order to get into the lifeboats. It just made me sick to see that."

Muriel's account continued, "The passengers pouring from the direction of the theater and lounge were opposite our boat station. Instead of going to their assigned stations, they were crowded at ours. In a short while our boat was jammed with a mass of humanity. Agnes had a seat, but I was standing. Between us, a big, heavy-set girl was wedged, leaning all over Agnes."

Agnes said, "Could you move a little?"

"I can't budge," replied the girl.

In a less perilous situation, Muriel thought, it would be funny, but no one laughed.

"Suddenly with a groan," she wrote, "the lifeboat tilted at a crazy angle, leaning toward the ship. Looking straight down, we could see the waves slapping the hull. Some people began screaming. There was no time to think, no time to pray! Instinctively everyone leaned in the opposite direction. The lifeboat righted itself."

An officer on deck yelled, "Twenty people will have to leave this boat. We have other lifeboats! Please!"

Although some passengers reluctantly obeyed, Muriel still had nowhere to sit. Jammed into the thirty- by ten-foot boat, she estimated, were eighty-five scared, confused people. "But," she wrote, "at least we could breathe."

When an officer pressed a button to activate the lowering mechanism, nothing happened. Without electrical power, the system was useless. As the officer frantically worked to lower the boat manually, pulleys holding it slipped, plunging it seventy feet into the water. Had it tilted toward the ship's hull, everyone on board would have tumbled into the sea and possibly been crushed between lifeboat and ship.

"It struck the water hard with a tremendous splash," Muriel noted. "My eyes locked with Ag's. We could hardly believe we were still in the boat. Then the waves began bashing the boat against the steel hull of the ship—once, twice, three times. The boat was sturdy, but how much pounding could it take before it began to crack?"

Muriel prayed, "Dear God! Please get us safely beyond the ship."

To retired Army Colonel Henry Heinichen, every moment from the captain's attempt to allay fears by announcing that a fire in the engine room was "small" and had been extinguished to the order to abandon ship had an air of fantasy. On the dance floor of the Prinsen Club a few hours ago he and his wife Leila had felt as carefree and graceful as Fred Astaire and Ginger Rogers whirling across the silver screen of the movie theater in San Carlos, California. As they waited to climb into motor launch number two, he recalled his previous *Prinsendam* cruises and found it hard to believe that on this one he witnessed behavior by members of the crew that was incompetent, unprofessional, and insensitive.

In his opinion, the lifeboat drill had been so lackadaisical that it bordered on becoming a French farce. Incredibly, as hundreds of thinly clad passengers who had been rousted from their beds shivered on the Promenade Deck, a few members of the crew went around offering dishes of ice cream! His suggestion to a steward that the door to the lounge bar be opened had drawn the ludicrous reply, "It's locked up, sir, and I don't have a key." Only when told to smash the glass or get out of the way did the steward reluctantly comply.

With little assistance from officers and crew, Heinichen had organized a group of men to set up deck chairs and distribute blankets. Observing the chaotic scene of people getting into the lifeboats and shocked to see some crew members pushing passengers aside to scramble into the boats, he said to Leila, "If they were soldiers in my command, their asses would be mine."

Adjusting her large eyeglasses, Leila teased, "How does that old army motto go? 'Once a Colonel, always a Colonel.'"

"Emergency or not," said Heinichen, "the way this situation has been handled from the start does not conform to the standards I expected of the Holland America Line. Outrageous!"

Among the first into number two, Alex Composito helped his mother to the rear with the idea of being available to help the operating officers. Seated close to his mother, he felt the launch rocking as if it were a hammock. As passengers climbed in and tried to find steady footing while looking for a place to sit, the pulleys at each end creaked. Thick ropes holding the boat looked as taut as violin strings. He calculated that at the rate the quiet and frightened men and women boarded, the boat would quickly reach its capacity. Peering down at the water seventy feet below, he hoped that the lowering apparatus had the kind of fail-safe system that prevented overloaded elevators from plummeting. If the ropes holding the launch snapped, it would hit the water with the force of an object felling from a ten-story building. Should one pulley give way, tipping the boat, people could spill into the sea. If the impact didn't kill them, they would either drown or slowly die of exposure in the frigid water. Contemplating these horrible possibilities, he felt a surge of respect for the seafaring father whose ashes were in a bronze urn in a suitcase in the room he and his mother had been forced to abandon and that now seemed destined by an out-of-control fire to find rest not in Yokohama Bay, but on the floor of the Gulf of Alaska.

Separated from Edwin Ziegfeld, John Courtney looked ruefully around the launch and thought about the dramatic pictures his friend could be taking if he hadn't left his camera in their room. In countless conversations about the lectures he had given at Columbia, Edwin had spoken of trying to impress upon students who were enamored of modern art and impressionistic landscapes the nobility of the human face. Picasso and his successors and emulators were great artists in their way, but only time would tell if they would be enshrined with Michelangelo, Rembrandt, DaVinci and those who earned immortality by depicting the glories they'd found in the human form. If any of them could somehow be in the launch they would see masterpiece paintings, drawings, sculptures, and photographs in the old, middle-aged, and young faces in a time of crisis and stress. It was easy to imagine a silver-haired woman seated opposite him with a lifetime of joys and sorrows etched into the deep lines of her face as the aged Mother of Christ. A young man next to her could be the model for her son before he set out on the path that led to the cross. A girl with him had a quiet beauty worthy of the brush of a Renaissance master.

Parted from their parents in the confusion on the port side of the Promenade Deck after the order to get into the lifeboats, nineteen-year-old Sandra Gyorokos and her eighteen-year-old brother, Gene, had been swept up in the rush toward the launch. As their children boarded the launch, Mr. and Mrs. Gyorokos were sandwiched between comedian Roger Ray and magician Jack Malon and his wife in lifeboat number three. Eighty-two-year-old Elsa Hutson, who had spoken to Richard Steele about her mother's daily prayer, remained calm by repeating it silently. In number four, Reverend Joan Hatcher was also silently praying. Betty Milborn gripped her aunt's cold hand. John and Malory Graham, ex–insurance man Frazier Reed, his wife Susan and former state senator and ex–Coast Guardsman Fairleigh Dickinson and his wife were in number two.

For World War II vet Earl Andrews, the tableau at portside boat station number six stirred memories of troop ships and young, mostly untested warriors waiting to board landing craft to assault a beach that until that moment had been a mark on a map or a place on a sand table model. Many of the passengers had shocked, unbelieving expressions. Except for clothing and age, they seemed like those soldiers who had never really accepted that they would actually be ordered to get into small boats and go into an actual war. The passengers had been instructed during the lifeboat drill about what to do if the ship had to be abandoned, but blithely dismissed such a dire scenario as highly unlikely. Now that it had happened, the people waited their turn to climb into a lifeboat with the same quietly eerie resignation as the thousands of men on the troop ships four decades ago. Of course, Andrews thought when his turn came to get into number six, no one was shooting at them.

When an officer told the boat's occupants that it had reached its capacity, Audrey Goral volunteered to board one of the rafts. She thought the covered inflated rubber craft resembled an igloo with an opening at each end. She recalled, "I took off my shoes so the high heels wouldn't puncture it, but I was wearing a coat, sweater, slacks and gloves. I thought that with a roof over my head, I'd be nice and dry. I sat at the bottom, surrounded by about twenty crewmen. We were lowered and hit the water hard. No one had secured the two openings and water came pouring in. Suddenly I was sitting in seven or eight inches of water. At one point, I found a repair kit with rubber patches and a tube of glue like the ones that used to be in every car trunk to fix a flat tire. When I read instructions on the side of the kit, I had to laugh. It said, 'Caution: Before applying a patch, be certain the area to be repaired is completely dry.'"

CHAPTER 20

What a Mess

As Lieutenant Bruce Melnick's helicopter approached the *Prinsendam* about two hours before dawn on October 4, 1980, flight mechanic Petty Officer Michael Oliverson looked down at efforts to cram people into lifeboats and rubber rafts and exclaimed, "What a mess!"

Horrified at seeing one of the boats being lowering directly toward another, he grabbed an Aldis lamp and frantically blinked the brilliant "night sun" to alert the crew of the danger. Sweeping the beam over the starboard side of the ship and observing a dangling motor launch, plumes of black smoke and bursts of flames from the midship portholes, he recognized that in undertaking the biggest personal challenge in his years of rushing to aid mariners he had become part of the largest effort at air-sea rescue in the history of the Coast Guard.

Procedures of air-sea rescue to be followed by Petty Officer Oliverson and others speeding to save the *Prinsendam* dated back to a manual devised by the same man whose name had been become a description of their uniforms' shade of dark blue. In 1944, Lieutenant Commander Chester R. Bender was ordered to prepare a manual of operations for a proposed Office of Air-Sea Rescue. He was the right man for the job. Born on March 19, 1914, at Burnsville, West Virginia, he'd entered the Coast Guard

Academy in New London, Connecticut, in 1932, earning a bachelor of science degree and a commission as Ensign in 1936. His initial duty was as line officer aboard the cutters *Mendioa* and *Bibb,* both on Atlantic patrol. Transferred to the cutter *Ossippee* in 1938, operating in the Great Lakes, he was selected for flight school in 1939 and began training at the U.S. Naval Air Station at Pensacola, Florida. A year later he received his aviator's wings and was assigned to flight duty at the Coast Guard Air Station at Elizabeth City, North Carolina. At the start of World War II, he flew anti-submarine patrols out of Elizabeth City.

Promoted to lieutenant commander, he served as the commander of an air-sea rescue squadron at the Coast Guard Air Station at San Diego, California (June 1943–December 1944). Raised to the rank of commander halfway through that tour of duty, he served as air-sea rescue advisor and liaison officer at the Far East Air Force Headquarters, Philippines, for the remainder of the war. Awarded the Bronze Star for this service, he was assigned to USCG Headquarters, Washington, D.C., as executive officer of the Air-Sea Rescue Agency. The following September he became pilot and personal aide to the commandant. In June 1950, he became the executive officer of the Coast Guard Air Station at St. Petersburg, Florida. Three years later, he went to Traverse City, Missouri, to command its air station, then returned to headquarters in June 1955 to head the War Plans Division. Promoted to Captain in 1958, he took command of the Coast Guard Air Detachment at Barbers Point, Hawaii. The following year, after twenty years in aviation, he returned to sea in command of the 311-foot cutter *Bering Strait,* operating on ocean station duty out of Honolulu. In July 1961, he undertook a one-year assignment as the mobilization and readiness officer on the staff of the Western Area Commander in San Francisco, then returned to the nation's capital as Chief of the Administrative Management Division and later Chief of the Program Analysis Division at Coast Guard Headquarters. Elevated to Rear Admiral, he assumed command of the Ninth Coast Guard District headquartered in Cleveland, Ohio, and a year later was named Superintendent of the Coast Guard Academy, where he established the Coast Guard Museum to preserve and display artifacts of the early Coast Guard. In June 1967, he was named commander of the Twelfth Coast Guard District and the Coast Guard Western Area, with offices in San Francisco, with responsibility for all the Coast Guard units in Northern California, most of Utah and Nevada, and areas in the Pacific. On April 16, 1970, President Richard M. Nixon appointed him Commandant of the Coast Guard with the four-star rank of Admiral. Retired after four years, he was lauded for outstanding contributions to the control of marine pollution in his role as delegate and alternate chairman of the United States Delegation to the Marine Pollution Conference in 1973 and cited for his work in marine safety, environmental protection, and law enforcement, but he was best known to Coasties for their "Bender Blues."

When Bender drew up the air-sea rescue manual in 1944, the Coast Guard had two kinds of airplanes, the Catalina PBY-5A and the Martin PBM-56 Mariner "flying boats," and a handful of helicopters, transferred from the army primarily for anti-submarine operations. Effectiveness of the helicopter became apparent in 1945. After the crash of a Royal Canadian Air Force plane in a remote region of Labrador and the failure of fixed-wing planes to rescue its crew, a small Coast Guard HNS-1 based at Brooklyn Air Station, New York, was disassembled and loaded on a C-54 transport plane to be flown to Goose Bay, Labrador. Reassembled, the helicopter lifted nine men to safety, one at a time over two days. Although early helicopters were difficult to fly, the chief of the Brooklyn Air Station, Lieutenant Commander Frank Erickson, predicted that one day the helicopter would be recognized as "the most versatile item of rescue equipment operated by the Coast Guard."

Formed at San Diego in 1943, the first Air-Sea Rescue Squadron had been organized to deal with an increasing number of offshore crashes by student pilots that were a result of rapid expansion of military aviation during the war. By 1945 Air-Sea Rescue was responsible for 165 aircraft and nine air stations. During that year, it responded to 686 crashes. With an explosion in the number of recreational boats after the war, the helicopter was deemed ideally suited because of its ability to react swiftly, lift entire pleasure boat crews from impending disaster, and deliver water pumps and fuel. During the Korean War, the service established Sea-Air Rescue units in the Pacific to safeguard tens of thousands of airlifted United Nations troops. Helicopter crews were among the seven thousand Coasties who served in Vietnam. By 1965, the service had fifty-seven choppers in an air fleet that included 153 fixed-wing planes.

Use of helicopters with a range of hundreds of miles resulted in a decrease in the number of lifeboat stations, while development of cutters that were large enough to have landing pads extended their reach. Advances in the design, technology, size, and operating procedures, along with midair refueling, made it possible for helicopters to not only be first on the scene in a high-seas emergency and carry out rescues, but remain on location in a coordination role until the arrival of cutters.

Six months before the *Prinsendam's* distress call, as more than a hundred thousand Cubans fled the Communist island and risked their lives in unsafe craft to cross the Straits of Florida, an HH-52 helicopter from the cutter *Courageous* aided the refugees after the overloaded boat sank in rough seas. It hoisted eleven people aboard. Other USCG choppers and the *Courageous* rescued thirty-eight more.

In the lifeboats and on the cruise ship below Petty Officer Oliverson on October 4, 1980, while he leaned out of an HH-3 above the frigid Gulf of Alaska to shine his Aldis lamp were half a dozen lifeboats, four rafts, and a tender. He had no information on how many people were in them or the number of people still on the cruise ship. While the tender had a roof and the rafts were covered, the people in open lifeboats were not only exposed to the cold air, but subjected to the waves dashing against the sides and spilling into the boats. Even more alarming, the boats were slamming against the ship's hull. Until they moved farther away, bringing the chopper lower in order to deploy a rescue basket to lift out passengers and hoist them into the chopper was a risk to the chopper and for the people in boats that could not be taken.

Although the evacuation protocol called for the motorized tenders to tow the lifeboats, number one had been rendered useless by fouled lowering lines and hung from its davits like a dead seabird. Successfully deployed, number two was left impotent as a towboat because the failure of the *Prinsendam's* water-fed cooling system left one of its two engines inoperable and the tender unsuitable for work in a high sea. When it attempted to tow one of the lifeboats, the ropes that should have been routinely tested for strength proved so old that they came apart. Remembering lifeboat number four a quarter of a century later, Jeannie Gilmore explained, "The ship was on fire, and here we are in an overloaded boat. It's bobbing up and down and banging against the side of the ship. We're packed in like sardines in a can. No one has a clue what to do to get the boat away from the ship. We'd been told during the drill where to go and what people went into which of the boats, but nobody had told us what to do after that. There were no oars, and even if there had been, we were so tightly jammed together that there was no room for anybody to move. To say that I was angry is an understatement, but I was determined that I was *not going to die*. I was going to get through this so that someday I could tell my grandchildren about the night their grandma was in a lifeboat in the middle of the Gulf of Alaska."

Curious about a metal bar above her head that was one of several that ran from one side of the boat to the other and connected to a pole at each end and supposing they were supports for some kind of covering for the lifeboat that no one had taken the time during the drill to point out, she touched it and felt a slight movement. "Like a kid who discovers a loose tooth," she recalled, "I started jiggling that bar and it suddenly occurred to me that maybe it wasn't meant to hold up a covering, but might be some kind of mechanism. The action reminded me of what I had to do when I was working one summer to earn money for college. I'd taken a job at a nearby army post, driving one-and-a-half-ton trucks. To put them in gear, they had to be double-clutched. To test my idea, I yanked the bar toward me and then shoved it away. At the risk of making a fool of myself, I told a young man next to me that I thought the bars were for rowing. After he gave it a try and said he believed I was right, we passed the word that if everyone who was able to do so coordinated their actions, we might be able to row the lifeboat away from the burning ship."

As the space between the lifeboat and the *Prinsendam* widened a little with each push and pull, Jeannie began singing "Row, Row, Row Your Boat." While most joined a chorus, Muriel Marvinney was seized with a feeling of utter loneliness. "Even though pressed in on all sides by a mass of humanity," she recalled, "and although the ship was ablaze, it was big and stable and felt safe. But now we were adrift in the night in a little cockleshell of a lifeboat."

When the song ended, Jeannie exclaimed, "Well, that was fun. Does anyone remember the words to 'I'd Like to Get You on a Slow Boat to China'?"

Muriel's impression of the officer assigned to command number four, second maître d' William Dansberg, contrasted with Jeannie Gilmore's. Muriel praised him. Jeannie recalled, "If anybody said anything to him, he turned around and looked at the water as if he expected the fish to give him an answer."

Assessing the performance of officers assigned to lifeboats, the report of the investigators stated, "From statements made by passengers and crew members it appears that the atmosphere in a lifeboat depends to a large extent on the personality of the commander." Those who had mastered the English language were able to "carry through and maintain their leadership with their English-speaking occupants more easily."

The investigation found that lifeboats carried an inventory of supplies, including food, water, and canopies, but these materials were not within easy reach "due to the large number of shipwrecked passengers, who were mostly elderly and benumbed."

Monitoring radio communications between the RCC at Juneau and resources of the Coast Guard and those of the U.S. Air

Force at Elmendorf and the Canadians at Comox that he had deployed, Commander Richard Schoel found himself presented with the worse possible combination of impediments in executing an air-sea rescue operation.

He had a ship on fire in the dead of night. It lay 150 miles from the nearest land in the most perilous stretch of ocean in the Northern Hemisphere.

Weather conditions were expected to rapidly deteriorate.

The nearest commercial ships were two supertankers and a pair of smaller cargo vessels, none of which was suitable for the task of search and rescue.

The estimated time of arrival on the scene of the closest cutter, the *Boutwell,* making way from Juneau, was at least ten hours.

An unknown number of people were adrift in open lifeboats and the majority of them, according to the captain of the *Prinsendam*, were over the age of sixty-five. Many were much older.

These elements added up to a daunting challenge for the only assets that were on hand.

In a race against time and weather, helicopters operating in strong winds would have to hover above lifeboats in a tumultuous ocean and lift terrified, elderly occupants to safety one at a time, fly them in small groups to Sitka or Yakutat, unload, return to the scene and repeat the process as often as necessary.

Gazing at the map on the wall of the RCC and listening to radio transmissions from the scene, Schoel knew of no air-sea rescue in Coast Guard history, and probably in the annals of the sea, to equal the drama unfolding at that moment in the Gulf of Alaska. The lives of nearly five hundred shipwrecked souls depended on the valor, audacity, ingenuity, and the professionalism of a few daring young airmen in a handful of helicopters.

CHAPTER 21

Impressions in a False Dawn

If Captain Dave Briski didn't know the time and that his C-130 Hercules was heading west from Sitka Air Station in search of a burning cruise ship, the sliver of reddish sky on the rim of the distant, cloudy horizon could have been mistaken for the first glimmer of a new day. With dawn at least three hours away, the plane arrived above the *Prinsendam* at approximately four a.m. The most successful airplane built by the Lockheed Corporation since its graceful, triple-rudder, four-engine Constellation airliner prior to World War II, the rakish, twin-fuselage P-38 fighter that saw action in both the European and the Pacific theaters, and the popular post-war Electra, the C-130 was designed to be a short field takeoff cargo aircraft after the Korean War. First flown in August 1954, the Hercules quickly caught the eye of the army, marines, army and air force reserves, the National Guard, and eventually the Coast Guard. The plane's pilots and crews gave it the nickname "Herky."

Powered by four Allison AE 21 00D3 turboprops, it carried a crew of two, with provision for a third, and up to ninety-two troops, sixty-four parachutists, seventy-four litter patients plus attendants, fifty-four passengers, or five freight pallets. Its maximum payload was 41,790 pounds, with a maximum cruising speed of four hundred miles per hour and range of 3,262 miles.

These factors were ideal for carrying fuel tanks to provide other aircraft an in-air "filling station" and for functioning as a flying command post, whether it was directing action on a battlefield or guiding an air-sea rescue mission by the Coast Guard.

According to standard operating procedure, Briski's C-130 would be the on- scene commander until the arrival of the *Boutwell* and would coordinate a series of helicopter airlifts of the passengers and crew from the lifeboats to Yakutat. Following medical checkups, they would travel overland to the Sheffield House Hotel in Sitka where the Holland America Line would take over the responsibility for their care and well-being. The supertanker *Williamsburgh* and other ships would stand by to render whatever assistance might be needed. If required, the choppers would convey firefighting equipment and specialists to the decks of the *Prinsendam*. The *Boutwell*, *Mellon*, and *Woodrush* were to continue at top speed, with the *Boutwell* expected to arrive in the late morning or early afternoon and assume command.

All this depended on weather conditions. If the weather remained relatively calm, the intention was that the operation would be completed by nightfall. Otherwise, the guiding principle would be found in the meaning of the Coast Guard's motto. Every Coastie in Bender Blues or everyday denims and work shirt understood that the motto Always Ready left room to follow the tried-and-true Coast Guard maxim that said, "If the plan goes haywire, fuck it and improvise."

Bringing the C-130 to a low altitude and cutting back the engines to the minimum rpm to stay aloft, Briski peered down at the white cruise ship in the center of a patch of fiery glow on a seemingly endless gray sea. Because the ship lay motionless, it left no wake. A stream of billowing grayish smoke on the starboard

Holland America Cruises' postcards featured a photo of the *Prinsendam*
(top) and an artist's rendering. *Author collection*

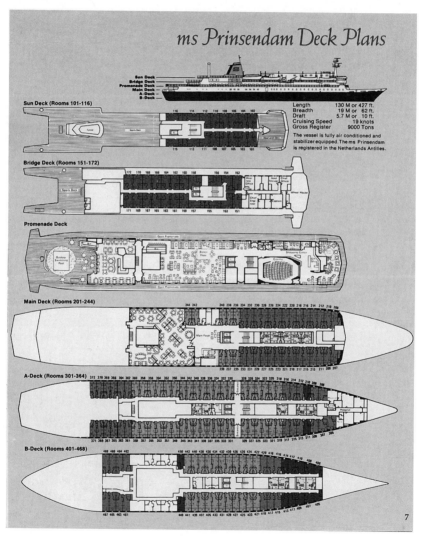

ms Prinsendam Deck Plans

Sun Deck (Rooms 101-116)

Length	130 M or 427 ft.
Breadth	19 M or 62 ft.
Draft	5.7 M or 10 ft.
Cruising Speed	19 knots
Gross Register	9000 Tons

The vessel is fully air conditioned and stabilizer equipped. The ms Prinsendam is registered in the Netherlands Antilles.

Bridge Deck (Rooms 151-172)

Promenade Deck

Main Deck (Rooms 201-244)

A-Deck (Rooms 301-364)

B-Deck (Rooms 401-468)

7

The Promenade Deck contained only public rooms, no staterooms. The 200-place dining room on the Main Deck had two seatings (early and late). *Holland America Cruises brochure*

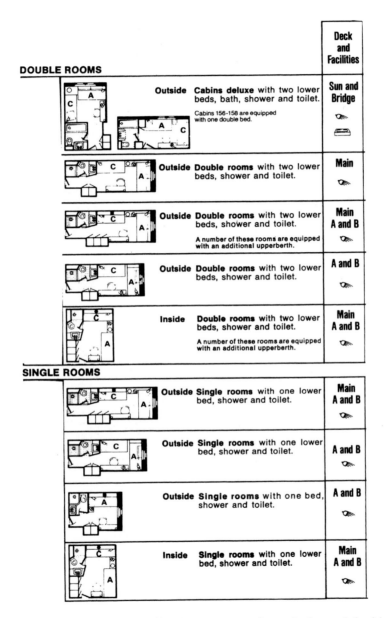

		Deck and Facilities
DOUBLE ROOMS		
	Outside **Cabins deluxe** with two lower beds, bath, shower and toilet. Cabins 156-158 are equipped with one double bed.	**Sun and Bridge**
	Outside **Double rooms** with two lower beds, shower and toilet.	**Main**
	Outside **Double rooms** with two lower beds, shower and toilet. A number of these rooms are equipped with an additional upperberth.	**Main A and B**
	Outside **Double rooms** with two lower beds, shower and toilet.	**A and B**
	Inside **Double rooms** with two lower beds, shower and toilet. A number of these rooms are equipped with an additional upperberth.	**Main A and B**
SINGLE ROOMS		
	Outside **Single rooms** with one lower bed, shower and toilet.	**Main A and B**
	Outside **Single rooms** with one lower bed, shower and toilet.	**A and B**
	Outside **Single rooms** with one bed, shower and toilet.	**A and B**
	Inside **Single rooms** with one lower bed, shower and toilet.	**Main A and B**

Five of the ship's six decks offered staterooms, from singles and doubles to the deluxe cabins on the Sun and Bridge decks.

Holland America Cruises brochure

The outdoor swimming pool at the stern of the Promenade Deck.
Holland America Cruises brochure

The Main Lounge, located amidships on the Promenade Deck.
Holland America Cruises brochure

The Promenade Deck's Lido Terrace bar, portside between the Lido Restaurant and the swimming pool. *Holland America Cruises brochure*

Travel writer Morgan Lawrence relaxed on the port side (left, while facing the front) of the Promenade Deck during the *Prinsendam*'s first cruise to Indonesia in 1973. *Morgan Lawrence*

The *Prinsendam* carried six lifeboats and two motor launches (tenders). *Author collection*

Ten hours after fire broke out in the engine room, the ship had little visible damage. *U.S. Coast Guard*

Note the scorching around the portholes and the billowing smoke. *U.S. Coast Guard*

The U.S. Coast Guard cutter *Boutwell* was usually stationed in Seattle, Washington, but had been sent to Juneau, Alaska, to take part in the city's centennial celebration. *U.S. Coast Guard*

The U.S. Coast Guard cutter *Mellon* and a USCG helicopter in a publicity picture. *U.S. Coast Guard*

Because the supertanker *Williamsburgh* had two helicopter landing pads, it became the primary receiver of passengers who were airlifted from lifeboats by helicopters. Note the small covered motor launch; it took some passengers to the tanker, but was unable to tow other boats. *U.S. Coast Guard*

Rescue 303, a Canadian Air Force CH-113 Labrador helicopter of the 442 Squadron, hoisted passengers from lifeboats three times and flew them to the supertanker *Williamsburgh*. Note the U.S. Coast Guard "surf boat" assisting. *David Hughes*

A lift basket lowered into an overcrowded *Prinsendam* lifeboat. Note the four "rowing" mechanisms that passengers pulled and pushed to turn the boat's propeller. *U.S. Coast Guard*

The crew of the cutter *Boutwell* making sure no one was left in lifeboat No. 4. They marked the lifeboats to show that they had been emptied. *David Hughes*

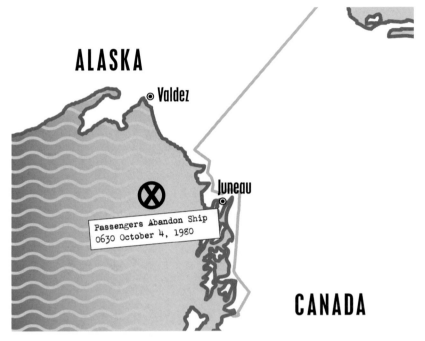

ALASKA

◉ Valdez

☒

Juneau ◉

Passengers Abandon Ship
0630 October 4, 1980

CANADA

The Gulf of Alaska–a cold grave for the burning ship. *Otto M. Vondrak*

After sixteen hours and having been forgotten in the search for lifeboats,
No. 6 was the last to be located. *David Hughes*

Cutter *Boutwell* rescuers
(top) and a helicopter
landing on its "helo"
pad. *David Hughes*

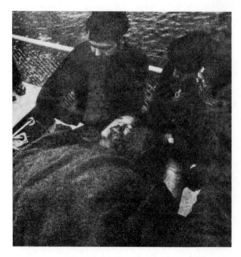

Insulin-dependent passenger
Irving Brex after being rescued
from lifeboat No. 6.
U.S. Coast Guard

Seaman Apprentice Dave Hughes in dress uniform, known as Bender Blues. *David Hughes*

Captain Leroy Krumm, skipper of the *Boutwell*, after the cutter took rescued passengers, crew members, the *Prinsendam*'s captain, and two Air Force pararescuers to Sitka, Alaska. *David Hughes*

A happy reunion of unidentified passengers on the deck of the *Boutwell. U.S. Coast Guard*

Hughes (second from right, in his work clothes and watch cap) among *Prinsendam* survivors as they arrive at Sitka aboard the *Boutwell. U.S. Coast Guard*

Elizabeth "Betsy" Price at Sitka. *U.S. Coast Guard*

Other survivors at Sitka.
U.S. Coast Guard

Photographed on the
Holland American cruise
ship SS *Norrendam* ten years
after they survived the
sinking of the *Prinsendam*,
Jim and Kitty Flynn were
still devoted seafarers.
Colin Flynn

Jeannie Gilmore in 2004 with
her only souvenir of the
Prinsendam–her room key.
Author photo

While the *Prinsendam* continued to burn, the Coast Guard surveyed the ship to see if she could be saved. *U.S. Coast Guard*

HOW WE SURVIVED LOVE BOAT INFERNO

FOR 320 elderly Americans, a dream cruise to the Orient turned into a grim struggle for survival when the luxury liner Prinsendam caught fire in the Gulf of Alaska.

Husbands thought they'd never see their wives again

The Steeles said they were embarrassed by being featured in a "Love Boat" article in the tabloid magazine the *Globe*. *Author collection*

Richard and Louise Steele on the first anniversary of their rescue. *Author collection*

When a tow line to a salvage tug failed, the cruise ship was abandoned.
U.S. Coast Guard

Aerial view of the abandoned *Prinsendam*'s burned-out bridge and wheel
house. *U.S. Coast Guard*

The *Prinsendam* just before she rolled over and sank. *U.S. Coast Guard*

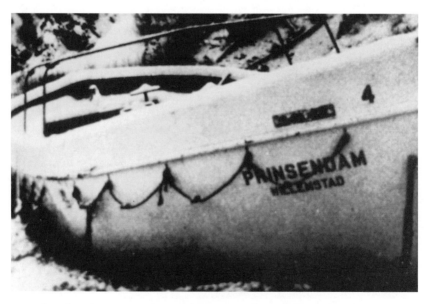

Months after the *Prinsendam* sank, snow-covered lifeboat No. 4 was found washed ashore more than a hundred miles from where the cruise ship went down. *U.S. Coast Guard*

side stretched behind her like a long furry tail. White lifeboats close to the dark blue hull resembled flecks of sea foam. A few that had made their way farther from the ship looked like paper cutouts. Dots of yellowish light indicated that some of the passengers or crewmen had flashlights. Brighter flashes blinked off and on from a nearby tender. Hovering above the ship, a Pelican chopper swept the brilliant Aldis beam from one crowded lifeboat to another like a theatrical spotlight.

The sea appeared calm. How long this would last was anybody's guess. Meteorologists warned of a rapidly moving cold front from the west and predicted plummeting temperatures, strong winds, and rough seas that would make picking people out of wildly rocking and rolling lifeboats dicey at best. The closest ship was the *Williamsburgh*. In the last report forwarded to Captain Briski from Juneau, the supertanker had advised that it was five hours south of the *Prinsendam* and that Captain Arthur Fertig advised he was changing course and would proceed at its top speed of seventeen knots. In constant communication with RCC Juneau, the *Williamsburgh*'s radio operators, James Pfister and David Ring, had estimated that the time of arrival on scene was no earlier than 7:30, about an hour past dawn. Giving continuous updates, they noted that if it were necessary, the thousand-foot tanker had ample living quarters, food, water, and blankets to accommodate hundreds of people. They could be taken aboard either by rope ladders from cutters or by way of the ship's two helicopter landing pads.

Recognizing that removing occupants from lifeboats at night was risky, and with assurances that all the passengers had been evacuated from the ship, leaving fifty officers and crewmen who volunteered to stay on board for firefighting, Captain Briski advised, and Commander Schoel agreed, that a rescue operation should not commence until daylight. Meanwhile, a Coast Guard specialist in shipboard firefighting, Chief Warrant Officer Kenneth Matz, was to be lowered at first light by a chopper from Sitka onto the *Prinsendam* with a pump capable of providing 250 pounds of water a minute, extra lengths of fire hose, and 500 pounds of firefighting gear.

Forty-one years of age, Kenneth Edward Matz Sr. had become a legendary figure in the Coast Guard. In twenty-six years of duty, his skills in battling blazes at sea would be honored with the Meritorious Service, Humanitarian Service, and Coast Guard Achievement medals. Aboard the HH-3 helicopter piloted by Commander Tom Morgan out of Sitka on October 4, 1980, due on scene shortly after four a.m., he prepared equipment that would be lowered onto the ship with him at daybreak.

In the lifeboats, the reaction of passengers to seeing the winking white, red, and green lights of the C-130 and a helicopter was as varied as the observers. Jeannie Gilmore looked up and said to her mother, "That's an airplane. Everything's going to be just fine." Fairleigh Dickinson saw it and identified it as a Hercules. For the Reverend Thatcher, the radiance of the Aldis light evoked the soul-redeeming image of the Star of Bethlehem. "I think it would be a good idea," she said, "if we all prayed."

Richard Steele exclaimed, "Amen to that."

"Lord God," Thatcher said, "we ask you to be with us in our hours of peril, Lord, calm the raging sea, as you calmed the wave of Galilee. Preserve us, your children. Our Father, who art in Heaven . . ."

"From all over the boat," Muriel Marvinney would remember and write, "voices joined in repeating the prayer Jesus had taught us. In spite of the Babel of so many languages–English, Dutch, French, German–we were all one at that moment. Never before had I prayed the words of the Lord's Prayer with such need, with such faith."

Since the struggle to move away from the ship there had been only the sounds of waves bashing the sides of lifeboats, and now and then the unsettling groan of someone vomiting over the side, or someone shouting, "Look out, your boat's getting too close." At one point came the urgent cry, "Oh, sweet Jesus." Now the Gulf of Alaska suddenly was alive with the welcome and heartening drone of engines and the whop-whop-whopping of a helicopter overhead that looked like a giant water bug.

The cruise ship that only a few nights ago seemed to Richard Steele to be a bejeweled beauty, sparkling with lights hung from her masts and bathed in floodlit brilliance, had become a floating torch that reflected off the sea and cast a dull glow on a sky grown overcast. Obscuring the northern lights, the dark gray clouds were like the sky that Shakespeare described in *Hamlet* as "this majestical roof fretted with golden fire." The smoke rising from the *Prinsendam* was, in Shakespeare's words, "a foul and pestilent congregation of vapors." But in the flying machines dancing beneath those clouds, men who dared sky and sea and fire and smoke were proof that the Bard of Avon was right when he wrote in the same play, "What a piece of work is man! How noble in reason! How infinite in faculty! in form, in moving, how express and admirable! in action how like an angel."

Senator Fairleigh Dickinson was not recalling Shakespeare, but Alfred Hitchcock's film *Lifeboat*. "The only person missing," he would tell a reporter for a New Jersey newspaper, "was Tallulah Bankhead." Motivated by instinct and Coast Guard training, he had taken charge of his boat and quickly earned from grateful passengers the nickname "Captain." Although he'd found some food stowed in the lifeboat, he discovered it had "all the features of military K-rations gone bad" and "elected to go without."

Wrapped in a curtain from the lounge and huddled next to her niece Betty Milborn, with the dream of celebrating her seventy-ninth birthday in the People's Republic of China going up in smoke, Betty Clapp found being in a lifeboat nothing like the scenes from the movie *The Unsinkable Molly Brown*, with everyone on the screen "nice and neat in rows." In lifeboat number three the people were "jammed in like cattle." She recalled, "You couldn't move your hands, your body. We were supposed to row but there was no way to move at all."

The people behind them, Betty Milborn remembered, "looked as if they were going to dinner at the Ritz. Evening clothes, kid gloves and all. But also behind us was a man in red silk pajamas–he was old, too–and with nothing on his head. It was freezing cold and before long there was high wind and water. There were no provisions, no water. We couldn't find flares."

In number four, a young Indonesian kitchen helper located a box containing several. Instructions on their use were in English, with illustrative photographs. When the C-130 appeared on the horizon, he decided to attempt to signal it. Standing and holding the flare perpendicular to his chest, he studied the first picture and pulled a paper tab that ignited it. Instead of rocketing up, the flare zoomed forward to flash within an inch of Jeannie Gilmore's head. Watching it streak past others' heads and onward parallel to the water until it burned out, and unable to turn to see who fired the missile, she said calmly but loudly, "Whoever did that, please don't try it again."

A few minutes later, Jeannie again had to restrain herself when a man seated behind her asked, "Would anyone mind if I lit up a cigarette?"

Holding back anger, she blurted, "I'm sorry, sir, but under the international law of the sea, smoking is *not permitted* in lifeboats."

The young man seated beside her asked, "Is that true?"

"If it isn't," Jeannie whispered, "it should be!"

Chuckling, the youth said, "So you made it up!"

Although huddling together might have added warmth, Jeannie noted, "the crowded conditions of the lifeboat actually kept people off balance, with alternate limbs going numb. Arms and legs were pinioned into positions that were immovable because of the pressure of other bodies. The constant rocking and swaying motions caused most of us to be seasick. The sight of those dear sweet senior citizens, so cold and tired and wedged in on all sides, waiting silently without complaint, was an unforgettable sight. It became apparent, without water and in the open ocean, our only hope was to be rescued quickly."

CHAPTER 22

Saturday Morning in the Lower 48

Readers of Saturday morning newspapers in the United States that had gone to press several hours before press associations sent bulletins about the evacuation of the burning cruise ship *Prinsendam* found no stories concerning the drama unfolding in the Gulf of Alaska, but radio networks headlined the story. Newsrooms of radio and TV stations on the West Coast had provided sketchy accounts throughout the night. The *Prinsendam* replaced stories that had been at the top of earlier newscasts that ranged from the 96th Congress calling a recess until after the November elections to Ronald Reagan appealing to Christian fundamentalists in a campaign speech. In other news, as broadcasters liked to say when switching topics, Iran's Prime Minister Mohammad Rajai had told the Swiss ambassador in Teheran that the American hostage situation would not be resolved until after Iran's war with Iraq and had warned other Arab nations not to lend aid to the regime of Saddam Hussein. Polish workers were staging a strike despite warnings from Warsaw's communist government. Washington, D.C., was buzzing about the arraignment of the three-term Maryland Republican Congressman Robert Bauman on charges that he'd molested a teenage boy. Neo-Nazis claimed responsibility for bombing a Paris synagogue.

In the newsroom of Richard Steele's Worcester, Massachusetts, *Telegram-Gazette,* the possibility had to be considered that for its next edition his obituary that had been in the files for years would have to be set in type, updated with details of his death at sea. Newspapers in New Jersey and New York City that knew former Senator Fairleigh Dickinson and his wife were on the stricken ship faced the same possibility. The prominence of *Prinsendam* stories in papers across the country would vary according to the location of the city or town, dictated primarily by whether someone local was involved, but in almost every instance it would make the front page. Placement and sizes of headlines would depend on the numbers of lives lost. Another variable would be the availability of pictures of the burning and/or sinking ship provided by wire service photographers in airplanes or helicopters.

In the newsrooms of television networks that had no newscasts scheduled before early in the evening, depending on when college football games ended, assignment editors were already arranging for freelance cameramen or those employed by their affiliates on the West Coast and chartering planes to carry them to the scene. As ABC, CBS, and NBC scrambled to cover the story, they had a competitor that had been founded by Georgia businessman Ted Turner. Taking advantage of the increasing availability of communications satellites, he'd acquired Atlanta's Channel 17 in 1970 and renamed it "WTBS, the SuperStation," to reflect the name of its owner, Turner Broadcasting System. It began broadcasting nationally via satellite to cable systems. As cable expanded across the nation, new ventures, such as Home Box Office (HBO) began to show the feasibility of niche programming. Seeking to create an all-news cable network, Turner worked with Reese Schonfeld, a former manager for UPI Television News and the founder of the Independent Television

News Association, and planned to launch Cable News Network (CNN) in June 1980. With a bravado that was one of his personal trademarks as owner of an America's Cup yacht, earning him the nicknames "Captain America" and the "Mouth from the South," he predicted that the channel would be "the greatest achievement in the history of journalism." Veteran CBS journalist Daniel Schorr added credibility to the venture as its main anchorman.

Doubters at the three major broadcast networks joked that CNN stood for "Chicken Noodle News." Despite organizational and technical obstacles, including the loss of SATCOM III, a satellite originally scheduled to carry the network's signal, CNN met the June 1 deadline with an estimated 1.7 million cable television subscribers. "Although the first day did not go without a hitch," noted the *Georgia Encyclopedia*, "CNN did get its first 'scoop' only minutes into its inaugural broadcast, cutting away from its first commercial break to bring viewers live coverage of U.S. president Jimmy Carter's visit to the Fort Wayne, Indiana, hospital room of civil rights leader Vernon Jordan, who had been wounded in an assassination attempt."

The concept of CNN was that the news, not the anchorman, would be the star. New items were added to the mix periodically, with emphasis on presenting exactly the kind of "breaking news" afforded by the plight of the *Prinsendam*. For news veterans such as Schorr and colleagues of his age and older at the networks, with little data on the burning cruise ship and no pictures immediately available, an easy comparison to be made to the drama in the Gulf of Alaska was the first sea disaster to be covered by television. In 1956, the Italian ocean liner *Andrea Doria* and the Swedish passenger ship *Stockholm* collided in dense fog about forty-five miles off Nantucket Island. Heroic efforts by other ships, including the French liner *Ile de France*, that rushed to the scene combined with evacuation of passengers in lifeboats, resulted in the rescue of all but forty-seven passengers and five crewmen before the *Andrea Doria* sank ten hours later.

Because of fog that grounded aircraft and the distance from stations in Massachusetts, Rhode Island, and New York, none of ten Coast Guard cutters were able to reach the scene in time to take part in the rescue, but they conducted a fruitless search for survivors, marked the place where the *Andrea Doria* sank and cleared the sea of flotsam that was a threat to shipping.

Serving under Coast Guard Commandant John B. Hayes when he was informed that the 17th District was responding to a fire on a cruise ship in the Gulf of Alaska were 6,463 officers and 32,041 enlisted personnel, with 877 cadets in training at the Coast Guard Academy. As he heard the report on the location and status of a crippled ship with an out-of-control fire, that the majority of the passengers were elderly and many infirm, details of the response set in motion by the RCC at Juneau, and challenges of distance, time, and deteriorating weather, the situation had the ingredients for a maritime disaster of historic dimension.

For three years before becoming the Coast Guard's sixteenth commandant, Hayes had been commander of the 17th District. In an oral history interview conducted after his retirement in 1982 he recalled, "That was one of the most exciting experiences of my career." When he arrived in Alaska (1975), the Coast Guard's principal duties were offshore fisheries patrol, aids to navigation (ATON), and search and rescue. The Coast Guard was also substantially involved in Arctic operations using the Coast Guard's major icebreakers in the Bering and Chukchi Seas at a time when commercial vessel safety and environmental protection programs arose with the construction of the Trans-Alaska Pipeline System.

Hayes recalled, "Implementing two very significant laws occupied the greatest portion of my time as District Commander. One was the Trans-Alaska Pipeline Safety Act (TAPS) which authorized construction of that pipeline and the Valdez terminal and directed the Coast Guard to prepare to handle the subsequent oil tanker traffic. The second major piece of legislation was the passage of the Fisheries Conservation and Management Act in 1976 which established a national legal responsibility for controlling waters out to two hundred nautical miles for the purposes of fisheries conservation. Each significantly expanded the Coast Guard's involvement in Alaskan affairs."

It was "a really exciting place to be," he continued. "Because Alaskan statehood had only occurred in January 1959, it was still a very young state with a relatively small budget, not too much government, and legislators who still showed up in the chambers with suspenders and Alaska shirts when I arrived as District Commander. It was a very, very interesting time to live there. It was a time of transition and we were in the thick of things. We made extensive plans and preparations for the completion of the pipeline and beginning tanker traffic, such as establishing a captain of the port and a marine safety office in Valdez for pipeline terminal oversight. To participate and watch was to enjoy a fascinating microcosm of the environmental processes that our country had established. In retrospect, we made some mistakes, but for the most part a fine District 17 staff developed many new approaches to deal with a host of environmental and safety problems."

The greatest difficulty faced in the transition from a district commander to commandant of the Coast Guard, Hayes said, was loss of the camaraderie that he enjoyed as an operational commander. "The head of any organization, public or private," he explained, "is, by its very nature, a lonely job. In the Coast Guard, there is only one four-star admiral, and all others are subordinate. In the other armed services, that's not quite true, even though it's recognized that the top guy is still the top guy. The second most difficult thing was greater emphasis and awareness of political matters required by the Commandant's role as a service chief."

One of the great things about the Coast Guard, Hayes felt, was that a constant exposure during a career to operational command and the need for time-sensitive, challenging decision making had prepared him for the transition from district commander to commandant. Having been in the position now held by Richard Schoel, he understood that the commander of the 17th District was the only officer in the Coast Guard in a position to make the informed decisions that were required in rescuing the people of the *Prinsendam* and, if possible, in saving the ship.

This was not a time for second-guessing from Washington, but it was a proper time to gather every piece of information in the Coast Guard files on the ship. What was known was that when Holland America had it built seven years earlier, the *Prinsendam* conformed to international fire-protection standards and met U.S. Coast Guard specifications. These incorporated the best fire technology of the time. The ship's structure was designed to minimize the risk of fire, but if a fire did break out, the ship was configured to control it at a predictable rate of spread, even if there were no intervention by the crew or activation of its fire-fighting systems. By all accounts flowing into the RCC in Juneau and relayed to Hayes and others in Coast Guard headquarters in Washington, the *Prinsendam* went to sea with ample lifeboats and properly designated evacuation procedures to be followed by the officers, crew, and passengers. Commander Shoel had ordered choppers into action and they were airborne in under ten minutes. A C-130 was on station as the On-Scene Commander, pending the arrival of the *Boutwell.* Several merchant ships signaled they were responding. Except for Captain Wabeke, officers and crew volunteers who'd stayed on board would go assist in firefighting, and all passengers had been evacuated into boats, evidently without serious injury. There were no fatalities reported.

Offsetting these positives were factors that were always beyond the control of builders of ships, captains, and the United States Coast Guard. The variables in every race to the rescue at sea were the weather, the time available, and human nature. With more than five hundred people at risk, most of them elderly, the climatic conditions were getting worse and the *Boutwell* and other cutters capable of taking people out of lifeboats were still several hours away.

Hungering for more information on breaking news that had suddenly enlivened usually placid and even bored atmospheres of newsrooms on what had begun as a routine and dull news day, editors in radio and television stations in cities and towns from coast to coast called the phone company's information operator seeking the phone numbers of the U.S. Coast Guard in Washington, D.C., and Alaska. Those who got through to Juneau talked to Ray Massey, who would thereafter be identified by the journalistic term "Coast Guard spokesman."

All he could say to them was that the cruise ship *Prinsendam* was reported on fire in the Gulf of Alaska, that the crew had been unable to contain the blaze, passengers were in lifeboats, nearby oil tankers were responding, Coast Guard aircraft were on scene for rescue operations, and that presently a helicopter would air-drop a Coast Guard firefighting specialist onto the cruise ship.

CHAPTER 23

By Dawn's Early Light

For Chief Warrant Officer Kenneth Matz, the first distant view of the cruise ship from Commander Tom Morgan's helicopter out of Sitka stirred an immediate cause of concern that went beyond the plume of thick smoke and occasional tongues of flame. The *Prinsendam* had a forward starboard side list. This came as a surprise. None of the reports on the condition of the ship had advised that she was taking water. Being lowered from a chopper to the deck of a burning ship riding at even keel was one thing; setting down on a pitched deck in a rough and rolling sea was quite another.

With the helicopter circling and illuminating the ship, Matz saw the reason for the list. The intense fire had blown out portholes and the combination of the rolling of the ship and the waves battering the hull sent water surging into those of the lowest decks. The danger was that if the ship dipped lower, there would be an influx through the shattered portholes of the upper decks. Hoping that the ship's watertight doors had been closed and that listing would go no farther, Matz assessed the layout of the ship and decided that the best place for lowering him and his equipment was a wide area behind the swimming pool. It provided outside access by way of open decking on each side of the Promenade Deck, with fire hose connections on both sides, to the forward port and starboard ladders leading up to the Bridge Deck.

Because the ship's electrical supply had been knocked out by the fire, a portable water pump operated by a motor similar to a gasoline-fueled power lawn mower would be lowered, along with fire hosing, couplings for the ship's internal water system and five hundred pounds of various firefighting gear and tools. These items would be distributed to members of the ship's crew.

To prepare for lowering, Matz checked the gear he would carry with him. It consisted of a heat-deflecting hood, breathing apparatus, thick work gloves, walkie-talkie, and fireman's tool belt. Donning fire-fighting clothing over a Coast Guard jump suit, he signaled Morgan and the two crewmen who would hook him to the lowering gear and guide him to the deck of the ship that he was ready. For Morgan, the challenge was maneuvering the chopper to avoid the plume of smoke, maintaining a hover mode in a strong wind and illuminating the deck where Matz would be set down. On his signal, the pump, hose, and other gear would be lowered.

"When you're dangling at the end of a cable unrolling from a winch sticking out the open door in the side of a chopper," Matz explained on the subject of his Coast Guard specialty, "you feel as if you're a spider spinning its web, except that no spider I ever heard of had to do its work being buffeted by the wash of helicopter blades and with quite a few pounds of stuff strapped around its middle. Or you can think of the line you're hanging on as an umbilical cord. But in any case, however you think of it, if something cuts it, you're probably looking at sudden death."

To master his specialty, Matz had trained not only by studying the techniques of fighting ship fires, but the recent history of Coast

Guard involvement in several major blazes at sea since 1954. On December 15 of that year thirty-five miles off the coast of New Jersey, the Coast Guard buoy tender *Gentian* sped to the burning fishing boat *Shannon*. With its five crewmen picked up by a passing trawler, the *Gentian* battled the flames with foam, but was unable to prevent it from burning to the waterline. Four years later, in the worst sea disaster in the northeast since the *Andrea Doria*, the cutter *Laurel* rushed to aid the tankers *Graham* and *Gulfoil* after they collided and exploded in the East Passage of Narragansett Bay off Newport, Rhode Island. The captain of the *Gulfoil* and fifteen crewmen were lost and several remained missing, the *Laurel* saved thirty-four from the ship and the water. When the Panamanian freighter *Beth*'s cargo of lubricating oil and chemicals caught fire ninety miles south of Santo Domingo in March 1964, a Coast Guard Albatross airplane located the ship and dropped a radio to crewmen in a lifeboat and the cutter *Aurora* rescued twenty survivors. In July 1966, the cutter *Spencer* was unable to save the tanker *Alva Cape* after it collided with the tanker *Texaco Massachusetts* 110 miles southeast of New York harbor and had to sink the destroyed *Alva Cape* with the cutter's five-inch guns.

In the year the *Prinsendam* was launched (1973), Coast Guard helicopters joined seven commercial ships in an unsuccessful fight to save the freighter *Key Largo* fifty miles below New Orleans. Fire in midship holds became so intense that the heat melted the entire superstructure. On September 13, 1974, the forty-eight-foot luxury liner *Cunard Ambassador* burned thirty-five miles off Key West, Florida. En route from Miami to New York to pick up passengers for a cruise to Veracruz, Mexico, she carried only officers and crew. All but fifty-three were transferred to a passing tanker. The remainder stayed on board to assist forty Coasties in fighting the fire, unsuccessfully. As in the *Prinsendam*, the *Cunard Ambassador*'s blaze had begun when fuel from a ruptured line spouted onto a hot diesel engine.

Awash in wind churned by whirling blades, Matz stood at the open door on the starboard side of the helicopter with the assurance of the captain of the *Prinsendam* that all passengers had removed from the ship and into lifeboats. Through gusts of gray smoke and between surges of high waves, he could barely discern a few white lifeboats as the rising and falling sea lifted them from deep troughs and lowered them out of sight.

With a nod, he signaled he was ready to descend. After a few snaps of buckles and the testing pulls on straps, he felt a hard slap on his back and stepped out into a blast of chopper-blade wash. Suspended for a moment on a taut cable beneath the winch, he felt as if he were the boy in a production of the musical *Peter Pan*, hooked up to wire controlled from backstage in order to fly out a bedroom window and away to Neverland, with a swoop out over the audience and the exultant cry, "I can fly."

Inching lower, he felt the bite of the harness and heard the rush of wind and the roar of the chopper. Wafted by a moderate wind, smoke from the starboard side of the ship streamed aft, but did not, for the moment, blow over the area surrounding the swimming pool. For him to land on the spot on the Lido Terrace deck behind it, he and Coasties who manned the winch, along with Morgan holding the chopper in hover status, had to negotiate a U-shaped space between wings of the Sun and Bridge decks. This maneuver demanded attention to the roll of the ship and skillful timing. He would also have to avoid a jumble of upturned deck chairs and overturned round tables that bounced around with each roll of the ship as if the Lido deck were a mammoth pinball machine. Beams of brilliant light from the chopper made the wet decking shine like the scrubbed flooring of a cutter at inspection time. In the blaze of the helicopter's Aldis lamp, the stern of the ship was as white as a swan's tail.

As Matz's boots touched the Lido Terrace deck and he unhitched the lowering-harness, the roiling ocean seemed to become even more ferocious and determined to thwart the exertions of the Coast Guard to keep the *Prinsendam* from being dragged into a ships' graveyard. Stepping over and around fire hoses that had proved useless and clearing a way through deck chairs on the Promenade Deck's port side toward the ladder to the Bridge Deck, he saw bursts of flame amid black smoke in the Lido Restaurant and Lounge. Heat radiating through the outer walls turned the white paint into large blisters. Melted sealing tar oozed and bubbled from the cracks between the deck planking. Hurrying under the empty davits of the port lifeboat stations, he came to the ladder to the wing of the wheelhouse. Chief Engineer Albertus Boot waited at the top with an expression that changed from frowning anxiety to nervous relief. In the center of a small group of officers in grease-stained and smoke-smudged white uniforms in the wheelhouse, Captain Wabeke appeared to Matz to be in a state of profound shock. Although he would remain the official skipper of the ship, the SOS and the response in the person of Chief Warrant Officer Matz effectively put the Coast Guard in command of the firefighting, with the officers and crew following his orders. After a brief conference in which he described the equipment that was to be lowered to the ship and explained how he intended to proceed, he led several crewmen to the Lido Terrace and told the chopper crew by walkie-talkie to send down the pump, hose, and other firefighting gear.

Because the ship's firefighting Siamese connection (similar to outside hookups of buildings that are joined to fire engine pumpers) was located on the Main Deck, Matz planned to connect it by hose to the portable pump. Almost immediately, he found it necessary to abandon the plan and improvise a new one. Discovering that the pump and hose couplings didn't marry to those of the ship, he had to cut the Coast Guard hose to force a match. With the pump providing water, he directed members of the crew to try to cool the skin of the ship.

"The effect of this," Matz would report, "was a little like pissing to put out a bonfire."

Discerning that the problem was lack of pressure to pump water from the ocean, Matz decided to move the portable pump down to the lower poop deck (below and aft of the Main Deck). When this failed to draw a sufficient flow of water, he ordered crewmen to find a float and a block and tackle so that the pump could be lowered directly onto the water. With hosing connected to the Siamese of the Main Deck and water flowing at the pump's designed rate of 250 pounds a minute, fire-fighting began and seemed surprisingly effective.

Assured by Matz by walkie-talkie that progress was being made, Commander Morgan radioed the C-130 On Scene Commander that his chopper was low on fuel and requested that an air force Hercules refueling plane at Yakutat be alerted that he was heading there to replenish its supply. The time of departure noted in their logs was 0730.

As the chopper swung east against the slate-gray overcast toward a trace of the pale pink of creeping daybreak on the far horizon, Agnes Lilard kept a tight hold on the hand of the dearest friend of the twilight years of life and said, "Oh, Muriel, the helicopter is leaving. I'm afraid we'll never make it."

For a moment, Muriel Marvinney feared Agnes might be right. It had been awhile since the singing of "Row, Row, Row Your Boat" fizzled out. The people in lifeboat number four sat mute and huddled, some in blankets. One woman with a green drapery from the lounge around her shoulders looked like down-but-never-out Scarlett O'Hara dashing off to Atlanta in a garish emerald gown with gold trim made from curtains to see if she could flirt money out of Rhett Butler to rescue Tara from the tax man in *Gone With the Wind*. A white-haired woman had her bare feet wrapped in a plastic shopping bag from a Ketchikan gift shop. "I was grateful that Agnes and I had dressed warmly," Muriel recalled, "but my heart went out to the half-dressed people huddled under damp blankets."

"If this boat capsizes in this freezing water," said a woman at the rear of the boat, "we'll survive exactly twelve minutes."

The possibility of death swept Muriel back in time and over distance to a hospital room where her husband Louis lay dying, with their children, Sandy, Pam, and Roger, at his bedside at dusk. Months of hospitalization had been a terrible strain on all, but that day, at the very end, an indescribable feeling of peace had filled her. It wasn't merely the emotions of a grieving wife, she recalled in the cramped confines of the lifeboat, but a sense that God was in the hospital room. "In the midst of a raging sea," she would recall about seeing the first feeble light of a Gulf of Alaska dawn on October 4, 1980, "I knew that God was again present and that I should never be afraid of death." As she thought about her baby grandson, she realized that she would not be able to enjoy seeing him wearing the tiny mukluks she'd bought in Ketchikan. If they hadn't been burned up in the fire by now, she thought, they were probably doomed to go to the bottom with the *Prinsendam*.

According to the emergency plan, ship's photographer Terry Allen should have been in lifeboat number three, but in the scramble of people that followed the order to abandon ship very little of what was contemplated had been accomplished. He'd wound up squeezed into the rear of number six between singer Peter Kapetan and Irving Brex. When the fire alarm sounded, he'd been in his tiny darkroom on B Deck, forward of the engine room, developing souvenir pictures of the passengers being greeted by the captain on the first night out. Wearing blue jeans, a white T-shirt, and tennis shoes, he gazed across the watery gap between the bobbing boat and the smoldering, listing cruise ship and regretted not bringing his camera.

Near the bow of number four with Richard's arm tightly around her waist, Louise Steele gazed sadly at the *Prinsendam* billowing smoke, remembered the postcard with its picture that she'd sent from Vancouver to her grandson Jake and pondered the irony of having written, "I hope it doesn't sink!" Her thoughts also turned to their daughter Barbie, looking forward to the arrival of the ship in Hong Kong, scheduled for October 22. With the key to room 324 in his pocket, Richard gazed sadly at the tortured ship and remembered her alight at dockside in Vancouver, beckoning and enticing, with the promise of wondrous sights, enchanted nights at sea, landings in exotic ports and the fulfillment of long-held dreams. Now she was a disaster.

Edwin Ziegfeld had jumped into lifeboat number six without realizing that in the confusion of abandoning ship he'd been separated from John Courtney. That he hadn't observed a trace of panic he attributed to the age of the majority of passengers. "Had the average age been twenty years younger," he would say to a reporter, "you would have seen much more trouble. We'd already lived our lives. We were not worried about children who might need us."

Jeannie Gilmore in number four felt the same. "We'd had a life," she said in an interview twenty-four years later. "I thought that the younger people, who had long lives ahead of them, ought to be the first to be considered."

With confidence inspired by the sight of a circling C-130 and the arrival of the Coast Guard helicopter, she had assured her mother that rescue would soon be at hand. While constant rowing had taken the lifeboat to a point where she could no longer observe the *Prinsendam*, other lifeboats were lifted briefly into view from deep troughs by rising waves. "Everyone was terribly seasick," she recalled, "but we were so tightly packed that the only place for anyone who wasn't at the side of a boat to vomit was in a hand or on the bottom of the boat. Poor souls who had been seasick since the day and night before had nothing to bring up, leaving them with the dry heaves. For anyone who was trying hard not to throw up, the sounds of so many doing so, and the smell, made it impossible not to. And if nature called, it was either do it over the side or in the boat. It was *not* a pretty picture!"

In lifeboat number three, Jack Malon, Roger Ray, and three members of the ship's band had joined in struggling to operate one of the rowing mechanisms. As they labored to move the boat away from the ship while waves repeatedly pushed it back, Ray joked, "I feel as if I'm Charlton Heston in that Roman slave galley in *Ben Hur*. All we need is some brawny guy beating on a drum to set the rhythm." When no one laughed, he exclaimed, "Hey, I'm a comic in a damned lifeboat. I'm not Henny Youngman on the *Ed Sullivan Show* saying 'Take my wife. Please.'"

Several hundred yards away in motor launch number two, Isabella Brex worried about her husband. They'd become parted in the boarding of lifeboats and he was long overdue for an insulin injection. He was jammed between performer Peter Kapetan and Earl Andrews in boat number six. The former soldier had watched in awe as the chopper lowered a man onto the *Prinsendam*'s stern. As the helicopter sped away toward a hint of frail daylight on the distant horizon, he found himself remembering the words "by the dawn's early light." He'd saluted the national anthem almost every day when he was in uniform and had sung it as a civilian before football and baseball games with right hand over his heart, tears in his eyes, lump in throat, and a tingling down his back. In the big war, as men of his age thought of World War II, he'd watched men perform courageous deeds, but being lowered by a cable, or wire, or rope, or whatever it was, from a Coast Guard helicopter onto the deck of a burning ship in the dead of night in a choppy sea was an act of bravery that filled him not only with admiration for that man, but a pride in being an American that not even hearing "The Star Spangled Banner" at a baseball game could match.

The emotion felt by Chief Warrant Officer Matz was not pride, but frustration. He recalled, "The ship was laid out funny." The emergency generator should have been separated from the engine room. The hoses he'd brought on board couldn't be married to the ship's Siamese hookups. The first action in fighting a fire on a ship was the same as battling a blazing building. "You do all you can to vent the fire," Matz explained, "to give it an avenue of escape." In this case, the fire itself had blown out so many portholes that it made controlling the venting impossible and let in so much water that the ship started to list. The fire and the flooding knocked out the electrical supply, shutting down the ship's bilge pumps.

"We tried piling plywood against some of the portholes that had been blown out, but that didn't work, " Matz reported. "The sea was rising, and after about an hour of functioning, the float holding the portable pump was swamped by a wave."

The pump had to be pulled on board to be dried. Returned to the float, it ran for about a half hour before a wave tipped the float, sending the pump sliding into the sea.

"That," said Matz, "was the ballgame for us."

CHAPTER 24

Turn this Boat Around!

To cut hours of flying time off the 350-mile route from Elmendorf Air Force Base to a staging area at Yakutat, Captain John Walters had taken his HH-3 helicopter through Portage Pass. The narrow opening in the mountains was almost always socked in at that time of year, but the weather had lifted enough for the chopper to clear it by about one hundred feet. Over Kayak Island, east of Cordova, an air force Hercules slowed to 130 knots and extended a ninety-foot hose below and slightly ahead of the helicopter. The HH-3 descended to connect its refueling probe to a funnel-shaped nozzle. Coupled, the aircraft flew level at a speed of 110 knots while the cargo plane pumped 1,000 of its 4,500 pounds of fuel per minute. With flight surgeon Captain Don Hudson and pararescue specialists Cassidy and Rios with scuba gear on board, the Hercules was the air force refueling plane for the operation.

After Commander Tom Morgan's chopper's tanks were topped, about an hour after it put Matz onto the *Prinsendam*, Morgan radioed the On-Scene Commander that he was returning and requested orders. The OSC noted that the supertanker *Williamsburgh* had reported that it was approaching the scene. Pending its arrival, Morgan's Pelican was to stand by.

Carrying a full load of crude oil, the mammoth tanker, with a draft of sixty-five feet, rode so low in the water that it resembled a long raft. While the cargo made for slow going, its weight and the ship's broad beam gave the *Williamsburgh* such exceptional stability that it became central to the rescue plan formulated by Commander Schoel at the RCC in Juneau. Because the *Boutwell* would not be on the scene for several hours, Schoel decided that the *Williamsburgh* would be the ideal vessel to receive the people in lifeboats towed to it by the *Prinsendam*'s two motorized tenders. Unfortunately, number one had been hung up on its davits and rendered useless and the tow ropes of number two had failed. This meant that it would have to be used as a ferry, delivering its initial occupants to the tanker, unloading them, and making as many round trips between the tanker and the lifeboats as necessary. Complicating this improvised plan was the grim prospect of shifting mostly elderly people from lifeboats to the tender and from it to the tanker by using rope ladders lowered from the *Williamsburgh*'s deck. All of this would be done in increasingly bad weather and roughening water. Should one of the passengers slip as a wave surged to slam the tender against the tanker's hull, the likelihood was that the passenger would be crushed or plunged into the killing, cold sea.

Rendered unable to tow, tender number two had struggled in vain to keep lifeboats and rafts in sight in a wind-driven strong tide, high and battering waves, and darkness. Because of rowing and drifting, the boats and rafts had become widely scattered. A few had moved out of sight of the *Prinsendam* and other boats. From some, the ship was seen only when a wave lifted them out of deep troughs. For Jeannie Gilmore in number four, the ups and downs were like being on a roller coaster. As occupants of nearby lifeboat number three caught glimpses of number four, she had no way of knowing that her furry white cap had become the means by which people in number three recognized boat number four. One of the women from number three would tell her, "It's a funny thing in retrospect, but we always felt better about our situation whenever your boat popped into view and somebody said, 'Oh, there's the lady in the white hat.' I guess we all felt that as long as we could see that hat, we were all going to survive."

Hopes of the people in lifeboats rose and fell like the waves. Having seen the circling airplanes and a helicopter put a man on the *Prinsendam*, the exhausted rowers had stopped in the expectation that the plane and helicopters were harbingers of a fleet of swift Coast Guard ships that would soon appear on the horizon, like the U.S. Cavalry riding to the rescue of a circle of wagons surrounded by Indians in old cowboy movies. When the boats did not come and one of the helicopters flew away, belief that there would soon be a good old American happy ending turned into bitter disappointment, confusion, and deepening anxiety.

Elizabeth (Betsy) Price recalled, "There was some conversation at first, especially after only being in the water about an hour. Passengers and crew took turns rowing until we were about a mile from the ship. Then we drifted at the mercy of the waves. They had doubled in size and we were being tossed like a cork."

Retired insurance executive Frazier Reed's lifeboat had somehow remained close to the ship. "After we drifted away," he noted, "I could see quite a bit of smoke coming out of the *Prinsendam*. Ninety percent of the people were seasick. The boat was quiet with the exception of people vomiting."

In lifeboat number four, Richard Steele's hands were raw and sore. "With the lifeboat crashing against the hull after it was lowered into the water," he explained, "we really wondered whether we would ever get away from the boat. We scraped our way by hand along the hull and finally got clear of the bow. That was hair-raising."

In tender number two, Herman and Sally Solomon had become surrogate parents to the Gyorokos kids, assuring them that everyone had gotten off the ship and that their father and mother would be just fine and someday they'd be laughing together and swapping tales of being shipwrecked. Seated next to the Solomons, Leila Heinichen gingerly touched a large bruise on her right ankle. In climbing into the boat, she'd slipped and twisted it. Searching the western horizon from the stern of the tender as the sky slowly brightened in the east, her husband observed what appeared to be a streak of smoke many miles away. After a few minutes, he could make out the superstructure at the rear of the long black hull of a supertanker. "Hey, honey," he exclaimed, "there's a ship." Turning to the crewman running the tender, he shouted, "We're going in the wrong direction. Turn this boat around."

Another crewman fired a flare that formed a reddish-yellow streak toward the glowering clouds, then seemed to hang high in the air for a long time. It fell in a twisting arc, leaving a trail of smoke, and continued to glow after hitting the water.

Observing the flare from the prow of lifeboat number three, oil company executive Jack Barclay peered westward. Discerning an unmistakable silhouette, he turned to David Levin, pointed to the ship and said, "That's a supertanker. My guess is that we'll all be on board it by noontime." Levin noted the time. At 7:45 a.m., he'd been in a lifeboat more than an hour. During the five or so hours that began in belief that nothing was seriously wrong, he'd wandered around in the cold in his purple jogging suit with waning confidence as the initial gaiety of the Promenade Deck slowly turned into confusion and uncertainty, without descending into chaos. With a few exceptions in which some young crewmen panicked, the prevailing mood had been one of good manners, perhaps because most of the passengers were of a generation that had not only been told by elders that selflessness and civility were the bedrock of civilization, but believed it.

Like Levin, the majority of the people on the *Prinsendam* who had quietly and calmly gotten into lifeboats had come of age during the Great Depression. They had done their duty in World War II either in uniform or on the home front, then unflinchingly faced the crises of the Cold War and endured the tumultuous 1960s and the excesses of the 1970s Me Generation without losing faith and heart. This did not mean they weren't scared. No one who had been rousted from a snug bed and told that their ship was on fire could help but be frightened at first. What Levin found in the faces and demeanor of the passengers was not fearlessness, but steely resolution and determination in dealing with another messy situation that life had handed them.

Farthest from the supertanker in lifeboat number six, Peter Kapetan was half the age of many of the people he and other singers had tried to divert with a Rodgers and Hammerstein medley while everyone shivered on the Promenade Deck. He felt lucky to have survived waiting for the lifeboat to be lowered. "I was at starboard and standing close to a big window of the lounge," he explained, "when it just burst and exploded in flames." Seated beside Irving Brex in the middle of number six, he'd learned that Brex was an insulin-dependent diabetic who had left his blood-sugar testing kit, vials, and needles in his stateroom. With more than nine hours gone by since the fire alarm sounded, and nearly two hours spent on the water, Kapetan worried that if they weren't picked up soon the old man could go into shock and might not survive.

To Commander Morgan and Lieutenant Bruce Melnick in their hovering helicopters, the distance between the motorized tender and the *Williamsburgh* appeared small, but unlike the pilot of a chopper or C-130 that could be turned on a dime, the skipper of the *Williamsburgh* had to maneuver a fully loaded supertanker that was as long as the Empire State Building was tall, and do it with limited visibility on a rough sea. When the tanker closed to a safe distance from the burning *Prinsendam*, radio operator Jim Pfister reported the *Prinsendam* "listing to starboard and in danger of sinking." Its passengers and crew were "bobbing in lifeboats in the storm."

Captain Fertig and his crew would face the challenge of taking people on board from the tender. Because the ship rode low in the water, the climb up the side on a Jacob's ladder would be about forty feet. If the ship were empty, it would be at least eighty. The people who would have to make an ascent that would be perilous on a calm sea were mostly elderly and had endured the shock of abandoning their ship and hours of seasickness and fright in small bobbing lifeboats.

In radio contact with Commander Morgan's chopper and with Captain Walters in the on-scene commander, Kenneth Matz reported the loss of the pump and the resulting abandonment of efforts to control the fire. He related that he, the ship's captain, officers, and crew who had volunteered to stay aboard as fire fighters were safe in the wheelroom. A decision had been made to shut down the emergency alternator because it was feared the fire would cause a short-circuit in electrical cables and aggravate the situation. Although this left the bridge without power, they agreed there was no immediate need to completely abandon the ship. Wabeke and engineering staff believed that she could be saved and eventually towed to a port by a salvage ship, repaired, refitted, and returned to service. Meanwhile, priority must be given to lifeboats.

Seated in the rear of tender number two in slowly brightening daylight, Alex Composito kept a comforting arm around his mother's shoulder. Confident that they would soon be safely on board the approaching ship, he relaxed for the first time in hours and took in an amazing show that was more thrilling than any movie or television show he'd ever watched. Between the dark overcast sky stretching from horizon to horizon and the angry sea, three helicopters alternately hovered and swooped low like ungainly, wingless sea birds. High up was a huge and slowly circling airplane. In the distance, the *Prinsendam* was a slightly slanting white hulk emitting a plume of dark gray smoke. Massive waves rocked the tender or caused it to buck like a wild horse. Cold sea water splashed over the boat's sides. Everybody was soaked and most were seasick.

Almost two hours after Henry Heinichen sighted black smoke streaking the horizon, the *Williamsburgh*'s captain ordered the ship's giant propellers stopped, slowing the supertanker to a halt a few hundred yards from the tender. Moments later, several crewmen were out on deck to lower a Jacob's ladder at midship. Isabella Brex looked at the massive ship and said to no one in particular, "Oh, it's huge. My, doesn't it look good?" As the tender approached the side of the tanker, she contemplated the forty feet of dangling rope ladder. "I figured I had no choice but to grab and start climbing," she recalled. "There was no way I was going to spend any more time in that disgusting lifeboat."

When she reached the top, she was helped from the ladder by twenty-five-year-old *Williamsburgh* crewman Tim Hagan. Taking her by the hand, he grinned and asked, "What the devil are all you folks doing out here on a night like this?"

Clutching his arm, Isabella merrily replied, "It was such a beautiful night that it seemed like the perfect time to have a rowboat race."

CHAPTER 25

They're Not Hacking It

Two time zones east of the *Williamsburgh* as crewmen assisted the first passengers from the tender in breaking dawn, Commander Richard Schoel and the RCC staff in Juneau were in the eighth hour of a hectic vigil. They'd not only had to keep track of each of the helicopters and airplanes of the Coast Guard, the U.S. and Canadian Air Forces, nearby commercial ships, and cutters *Mellon, Woodrush,* and *Boutwell,* but they had to provide updates to Coast Guard Headquarters in Washington, D.C., as well. They'd been especially tense while monitoring the reports from Commander Morgan's chopper as Kenneth Matz descended to the cruise ship. Disappointed when he related the loss of the pump, they were heartened by the arrival of the supertanker.

After press associations flashed the plight of the *Prinsendam,* the RCC had found itself contending with inquiries from news media in Alaska, the lower 48, Holland, the ship's ultimate ports of call in Asia, and its home base in the Netherlands Antilles. Among these callers was the West Coast producer for NBC television's *Today Show.* Stating that he was planning to arrange for an aircraft to take a camera crew to the scene, he requested the ship's exact location. Other callers wanted to know when and where the rescued passengers would be available to reporters and photographers for interviews and pictures.

Admiral Schoel had become accustomed to the demands of the press for every particle of information when the Coast Guard was called out and lives hung in the balance, but he was also impatient with their expectation that a hunger for news was equal in importance to conducting what was shaping up to be the largest air-sea rescue in Coast Guard history. If he'd had the time, he could have instructed the callers that symbols of ships and aircraft on his wall map did not represent the realities they were facing. The display on his wall represented a passing moment in time. It was the status of the unfolding of a plan that had been devised eight hours earlier, but not a guarantee of inevitable success. No map could show a sudden shift in the wind direction, meaning an abrupt change in the speed and course of choppers, planes, or cutters that were already at their operating limits. The plan envisioned Ken Matz landing on the *Prinsendam* and using a pump to fight the fire. When Matz was compelled by circumstance to improvise, the pump had been lost. Two of the cruise ship's motor launches were to link up with lifeboats and tow them away from the ship. One had gotten fouled on its lines and had been rendered useless. The other's tow ropes had snapped. Three cutters were underway, with projected arrival times, but neither their skippers, Admiral Schoel, nor anyone else could state with certainty that the estimates would hold.

Approximately eighty miles out of Juneau, roughly four hours after shoving off, Captain Leroy Krumm's *Boutwell* was struggling against an increasingly choppy sea to maintain top speed and make its ETA of early afternoon. In Coast Guard parlance, when the cutter was docked in Juneau it had been in "B-24 status" (off duty). The order to sea was the first such emergency order in Seaman Apprentice Dave Hughes' six months of wearing Bender Blues. Now he was working on the cutter's see-sawing deck in dungarees, a dark-blue windbreaker, and a black skull-hugging knit watch cap. Barely six months had passed since he'd received his first order, sent from the U.S. Coast Guard Recruiting Office in room 147 of the Federal Building in Des Moines, Iowa. It directed him and his friend Paul Van Klaven to travel from Albia, Ohio, on a Trailways bus to Omaha, Nebraska. While waiting to be met by a recruiter to go to Des Moines with other recruits, they were lodged at the Paxton Manner Hotel and had their first meals at the expense of the government at the adjacent Olympic Restaurant. Since that initiation into getting orders, almost all the Coast Guard directives he'd received were given verbally by instructors at boot camp and, as the oath taken by everyone in the enlisted ranks of all the U.S. armed services stated, by subsequent "officers and noncommissioned officers" appointed over him. Although he didn't know precisely where the *Boutwell* was heading, except for scuttlebutt that a cruise ship was in trouble, he was glad and excited that he hadn't been left behind in Juneau, standing on the dock with a puzzled look on his face. He knew only that orders from the RCC in Juneau to Captain Krumm stated that the *Boutwell* should proceed at top speed to assist a passenger ship in distress. Krumm did not share the order that the cutter would relieve a C-130 from Kodiak as on-scene commander.

Recalling the voyage twenty-four years later, Hughes said that no one on the ship "got any shuteye because of the anxiety" and "going out there was a kind of blur." As an apprentice seaman, he explained, "I was just doing my job." The "really chilly" weather was "deteriorating rapidly," but the seas "weren't too bad for a three-hundred-seventy-foot cutter."

When the call came from the RCC, Yeoman Chris Macneith knew something serious was up. "It was the first time we'd been activated in the middle of the night," he recalled, "and everybody was pretty high-charged, volunteering to do things they usually didn't handle. Under ordinary circumstances, we did our own work, but on that night everybody seemed a little more excited. It was like that famous line in a mystery novel that's become a cliché, 'It was a dark and stormy night.' But in October in the Gulf of Alaska, nights usually were. It seemed as if we were steaming forever, buffeted by the wind and waves and rain."

Tom Ice recalled, "We tried to grab some rest because we figured we'd have to do some heavy-duty work. Nobody told us what was going on. The only announcement over the intercom was that there was a cruise ship that was signaling distress and they were abandoning ship."

Seven hours after the *Boutwell* began to make way out of Juneau, Richard Steele surveyed an astonishing and thrilling panorama. From lifeboat number four, he saw the thick, gray smoke billowing from the listing *Prinsendam* and held out no hope that she could survive. The surrounding sea was dotted with adrift, overcrowded lifeboats that occasionally popped into and out of his sight. The glowering but slowly lightening sky was dotted with noisy helicopters, alternately hovering and flitting back and forth. Much higher, a large four-engine airplane that circled slowly seemed like a sea bird on the lookout for a movement in the water, signaling an opportunity for breakfast by diving headlong into the sea and grabbing an unwary fish that committed the fatal mistake of swimming just below the surface.

"When you suddenly find yourself in a lifeboat, you can become a little philosophical," Steele would eventually tell a gang of eager reporters. "You also remember the darnedest things, like a prayer I once heard Jack Kennedy quote: 'Oh Lord. Thy sea is so great and my boat is so small.' At some point, I recalled reading about the famous World War I combat ace and aviation pioneer Captain Eddie Rickenbacker being adrift in a lifeboat during the second world war for three weeks after his plane had to ditch in the Pacific. When his plane was reported down, every newspaper in the country gave him up for dead. But the moment I spotted an airplane, I knew that more help would be on the way, so I stopped thinking about the possibility of my newspaper printing my obituary and started composing my own account for the paper of what it's like to be forced to abandon ship."

As the unfolding rescue operation became etched in Richard Steele's memory, Captain Arthur Fertig of the *Williamsburgh* found his supertanker thrust into the center of a drama in which he'd expected, and hoped, the ship would have only a supporting role. The *Prinsendam*'s initial alert had stated that the fire appeared to be successfully contained. The Coast Guard's first communication with the *Williamsburgh,* a request for firefighting equipment to be picked up by a Coast Guard helicopter, had reinforced the impression that the situation could be brought under control without evacuation of passengers. When the *Prinsendam* sent out its SOS, this scenario changed abruptly. The helicopter that was to land on the *Williamsburgh* to pick up the fire gear reversed course. Informed by the Coast Guard Coordination Center by radio that the nearest cutter was hours away, Fertig recognized that his tanker's role shifted from a secondary player to that of primary receiver of people from lifeboats. Rope ladders that were intended to be the means of evacuation for the small number of the supertanker's crew and officers had to be deployed to retrieve scores, if not hundreds, of the stricken cruise ship's passengers. At the same time, preparations had to be made to accommodate, care for, feed, and probably clothe them for a voyage of several hours to the closest port, Valdez.

With the tender aside the *Williamsburgh*, securing lines were dropped. When the boat was firmly tied, a Jacob's ladder was lowered and two of the tanker's crewmen climbed down to the tender's deck to assist passengers in beginning their ascent. When the first got to the top, Fertig chuckled at Isabella Brex's wisecrack response to Tim Hagan about having a lifeboat competition. He admired her pluckiness. Before he could greet her, Isabella said, "I'm a nurse. If there's anything I can do to help at any time, don't hesitate to put me to work."

By the time the third passenger was on board, at least forty waited their turns in the tender. Fertig realized that at such a slow pace it might be well into the night, and perhaps later, before everyone could be brought on board from five more lifeboats and several rafts. Spread widely apart, they would have to be towed over great distances in increasingly rough waters. The wind was picking up and the temperature plummeting, raising the awful specter of hundreds of elderly men and women developing hypothermia.

After nearly two hours of watching passengers struggling from the tender and up the side of the *Williamsburgh*, Commander Morgan was also worried. "The passengers were having a terrible time," he recalled. "It was just too much for those older folks to climb a ladder like that. It was taking too long."

With the Pelican hovering far enough from the supertanker so that its blades would not make a churning sea worse, but still close enough to observe the process, he shook his head in dismay. By radio to the on-scene commander at 9:35 a.m. he said, "They're not hacking it. We have to start hoisting."

CHAPTER 26

Figuring the Variables

Every Coastie who worked with or under Commander Richard Schoel learned that he was not a second-guesser. Like all good leaders, he laid out his plan and left it to those who had to implement it in the heat of action to take it from there. His personal leadership maxim had been expressed by General George S. Patton. "Never tell people *how* to do things," advised "Old Blood and Guts" in a posthumous book, *War As I Knew It.* "Tell them *what* to do and they will surprise you with their ingenuity."

In recommending the hoisting of nearly five hundred occupants of the lifeboats into helicopters, Commander Morgan was calling for the largest, most daring and dangerous air-sea rescue in the annals of the Coast Guard. In doing so he was acting in the great tradition of the service. The first use of a helicopter by the Coast Guard for a lifesaving mission had occurred on January 3, 1944, when a Sikorsky helicopter based in Brooklyn was used to fly blood plasma to an injured crewman of the USS *Turner* after the destroyer exploded off Sandy Hook, New Jersey. Later that year, a helicopter landed on a sandbar in Jamaica Bay, New York, to rescue a teenager who had become marooned. On the other side of the world a chopper was used in combat rescue for the first time when an army lieutenant rescued the pilot and three passengers of a light plane that had been forced down behind enemy lines in Burma. In each case, the helicopter had landed.

Having been created for the purpose of saving the lives of people on water, the Coast Guard recognized that the ability of helicopters to hover had the potential to carry out rescues from the air with a body harness at the end of a cable operated by a winch. In August 1945, a hoist system for rescue was demonstrated at its helicopter facility at Floyd Bennett Field in New York, but not at sea in a real crisis.

Employment of a hovering helicopter to lift a person to safety from trouble on the water took place on November 29, 1945, after an oil barge had run aground on a reef off Fairfield, Connecticut. The barge's captain, Joseph Pawlik, and a crewman, Steven Penninger, signaled for help with flares. Someone in a group of townspeople saw them and noted that Sikorsky Aircraft was located in nearby Bridgeport.

Taking the resulting telephone call was the company's test pilot, Dmitry "Jimmy" Viner. He had followed his uncle, Igor I. Sikorsky, to the United States and had become one of the first employees of the Sikorsky Aero Engineering Corporation on Long Island. Hanging up the phone, Viner summoned a friend, Captain Jackson E. Beighle, an Army Air Force representative at Sikorsky. They took off in one of the firm's helicopters.

Within a few minutes, hovering over the crippled oil barge, they dropped a rope with a weight and a message asking how bad it was "down there." Pulling up a reply, they learned that eight tanks were leaking, the cabin was full of water, and the men aboard feared that the barge would break up.

Recalling the Coast Guard hoist demonstration, Viner and Beighle returned to Sikorsky and switched to an R-5 helicopter. A model that had first flown two years earlier as a rescue-and-observation aircraft, it had recently been equipped with an experimental hydraulic hoist that seemed to be ideal for pulling someone out of danger by a cable fitted with a harness. As noted by a Sikorsky historian, it was "a simple device that looped under the arms. Each man would have to hold on to the cable over his head. Otherwise, he would drop out of the harness."

In one of those coincidences that often occur throughout history, Viner's younger cousin, Sergei Sikorsky, a Coast Guard enlisted man, had participated in the hoist experiments at Floyd Bennett Field. Six years later, the Coast Guard announced that it acquired a new type helicopter, the Sikorsky HO4S-2G, for search and rescue that was equipped with a hydraulic hoist to pick up personnel or equipment weighing up to four hundred pounds. In a series of tests, the harness and several types of slings evolved into a basket-like "Stokes litter" measuring four by two feet and eighteen inches deep that Jeannie Gilmore would describe as looking like "a cut-in-half large supermarket cart."

The decision to save precious time in order to keep exposed occupants of the lifeboats from suffering hypothermia by hoisting them into helicopters and flying them to the deck of the *Williamsburgh* would require coordination between the choppers, the On-Scene Commander, and the supertanker. Each helicopter had space on board for eight to twelve people, depending on their weight. How long it would take to lift one person would certainly vary widely. Elderly people who were already traumatized from the experience of abandoning ship and drifting in cramped conditions for several hours would now be required to deal with being inserted into a basket and lifted, swinging from side to side, between twenty and thirty feet into the air. Once at the open door of the chopper, they would be helped inside in a swift movement that could rightfully be called a yank and a shove.

The operation would initially involve Coast Guard HH-3 Jolly Green Giants out of Sitka, and the air force HH-3 flown by Captain John Walters from the Alaskan Air Command base at Elmendorf. On board Walters' chopper were flight surgeon Don Hudson and the pararescuers. En route were a pair of HH-3s and two Hercules transports from Coast Guard RCC in Kodiak and two Canadian Air Force Labrador choppers of the 442 Squadron based at Comox, British Columbia. With all helicopters operating and each picking up twelve people at a time, each would have to execute eight round trips between the lifeboats and the tanker. Flight times would be variable, according to distances to be covered, weather, sea conditions, and the time required for landings, unloading, and takeoffs on the *Williamsburgh*. Because this unprecedented airlift involved more than five hundred mostly elderly people, there was no guide for estimating how long the process would take. Another variable to be figured in these time calculations was the need for the choppers to leave the scene and fly to the Hercules tanker in the vicinity of Yakutat to refuel and return. The hope was that this massive effort would be accomplished before sunset, giving the operation about nine hours of daylight.

Such a monumental undertaking would be difficult in good weather, but meteorologists reported that with a cold front steadily closing from the west, the already unfavorable conditions were going to rapidly deteriorate. Helicopters and ships should anticipate sustained high winds with strong gusts, heavy rain, and waves of ten to fifteen feet. This raised the horrifying prospect of a lifeboat capsizing and pitching up to ninety people into the water.

Worse to contemplate was two or more, perhaps all, of the lifeboats being overturned, swamped, and sunk. Should that happen, people without life jackets would drown. Among those who had them, hypothermia certainly would claim many, possibly hundreds. The sun would go down with the frigid waters of the Gulf of Alaska littered with floating corpses to be retrieved by the Coast Guard cutters that were heading to the scene at top speed.

CHAPTER 27

A Marvelous Aerial Ballet

All his life, Edwin Ziegfeld had been asked if he were related to the legendary theatrical producer Florenz "Flo" Ziegfeld. The most famous Broadway impresario in the Gay Nineties and through half of the twentieth century, he had presented extravagant variety shows and Follies that featured the world's most beautiful women decked out in lavish and revealing costumes. He had presented the biggest names in show business, from singers Anna Held and Lillian Russell to W. C. Fields, Fanny Brice, Eddie Cantor, Al Jolson, and Will Rogers. Perhaps because of his last name, or as a former patron of New York City's Lincoln Center, the Metropolitan Opera, and stage shows at Radio City Music Hall, Edwin Ziegfeld observed the sudden burst of activity of helicopters from the rear of lifeboat number six and saw a "marvelous aerial ballet."

A low, slowly circling C-130 Hercules operating as the on-scene commander reminded him of a model airplane dangling in a clutter of whimsical and blatantly commercial decorations suspended from the ceiling of the barroom at the rear of an expensive and notoriously exclusive Manhattan restaurant. Named "21" because that was its address, just off Fifth Avenue on West Fifty-second Street, it was close to the Museum of Modern Art, where he and John Courtney had occasionally dined following Sunday afternoons enjoying

MOMA's masterpieces of painting, sculpture, and other works that were featured in their college lectures. Having agreed to retire together in sunny California, they had decided to splurge on a farewell-to-New York "21" dinner. During most of the meal, they'd talked about eventually taking a leisurely cruise to the Far East to acquire works of Oriental art to enhance the stylish décor of their Mount San Antonio Gardens apartment in Claremont. Peering up at the cut-out-like plane and the helicopters' aerial ballet, he felt confident that one of them would swoop down to the rescue and that he and John Courtney would soon be reunited. By the grace of God, and age and health permitting, they would one day resume their Pacific odyssey.

While the helicopters were heard throughout the night, alternately close and far away, they were hard to see, except in the off-and-on glare of Aldis lamps and the small blinking red-and-green running lights. In the light of dawn, flitting here and there, they looked smaller than they'd sounded. Flying low in the full daylight, they had white fuselages and diagonal stripes of Coast Guard red on their noses, and they seemed huge.

In the sudden activity of the helicopters, Richard Steele found another motion picture analogy. "Everyone was looking up," he said of the people in number four. "We were like the war refugees gazing at the plane to Lisbon in *Casablanca,* all wishing they were on it."

Also in number four, Jeannie Gilmore was increasingly worried about her seventy-five-year-old mother. Although Jeannie had fashioned a blanket into a makeshift tent for her, Neva Hall's face was as white as her hair and her hands felt like ice. "When we saw the helicopter," Jeannie recalled, "many of us raised our arms and waved at it. It looked so beautiful, with its twin rotors."

In lifeboat number six, Earl Andrews thought the blades of the propellers whirled so fast that they looked like big horizontal circular saws. Betty Milborn watched from number five and saw haloes of giant descending guardian angels. Senator Dickinson supposed that the flurry of activity in the air was the start of a rescue plan that had been worked out after the helicopters had surveyed the situation and located the lifeboats. He assumed their movements meant the imminent arrival of Coast Guard cutters and that they would make the pickups from the lifeboats. When a door opened on the right side of a helicopter hovering low over number five, he realized that the Coasties had something bolder in mind.

Strapped by a nylon belt in the opened doorway of Lieutenant Melnick's HH-3 Pelican, Petty Officer Michael Oliverson was able to lean out and look down at the lifeboats. He wore a communications headset. Because Melnick would not be able to see what was beneath the chopper as it descended to a hover position, Oliverson, as hoist man, would have to talk the chopper down to between twenty and thirty feet above the ocean. A veteran of numerous rescues of individuals and small groups of people from decks of ships, out of lifeboats, and in the water, he had not dealt with anything near the scope of the scene below that he found during a flyover to survey and assess the situation.

Like daring, fledgling offspring of a swan testing their ability to swim, the white lifeboats had spread from the *Prinsendam* in every direction. They rose and fell on large waves like the horses that bobbed up and down on an amusement park carousel, lurched forward and back like rocking chairs, and rolled violently from side to side. These conditions were more challenging because each of the wildly cavorting boats was so tightly packed from bow to stern that there appeared to be no space to accommodate the hoisting basket. With no way of communicating by radio or walkie-talkie with the lifeboats, and with no one on the Coast Guard choppers equipped with scuba suits and gear who could be lowered to help load the basket, people in the lifeboats would have find a way to do it themselves, assisted only by hand signals from hoist operators.

"It was like fishing," said one hoist man, "except that when you cast your line, you're in a helicopter and you're trying to hook people who are packed like sardines into a bouncing boat. You do this, hopefully, without cracking some elderly gent's noggin with the basket or giving a little old lady who looks like your grandmother a bump that knocks her head over heels into a bath of cold seawater."

As Oliverson anticipated the operation unfolding, the basket would be lowered into the lifeboat, "someone would somehow crawl in, hold on for dear life, and we'd hoist him or her into the copter. Then another crew member would flip the basket over and carry the person back in the copter where we would try to distribute the weight evenly. When we reached our limit, we would hustle over to the *Williamsburgh*, unload, and go back for more."

The plan rested on assumptions by the helicopter crews that the pickups from the boats, shuttling to the supertanker, unloading, and returning for the next load would proceed quickly. With clockwork precision, deliberate speed, and efficiency, the rescue operation would be over well ahead of dusk, before the arrival of the cold front's worsening weather, and possibly before the *Boutwell* showed up. This optimism was the result of the fortuitous presence and response of the *Williamsburgh*. Without its helicopter pads, the choppers would have to make lengthy round trips to Sitka and perhaps other land bases. Instead of flying miles between pickups, the hops to and from the supertanker would take only a few minutes. Less time in the air for choppers meant quicker relief of men and women who'd been suffering in open lifeboats for many hours.

In such conditions, when a few minutes could be the difference between life and death, the first challenge for Captain John Walters in his Air Force HH-3 helicopter was placing flight surgeon Don Hudson onto the *Williamsburgh,* along with blankets and medical supplies. It was Walters' first sea landing. With two chopper pads on a deck that was broader and longer than an aircraft carrier's, and with the guidance of *Williamsburgh* crewmen, Walters set the chopper down as easily as if he were making a routine landing at Elmendorf.

A few minutes after Dr. Hudson and the supplies were off-loaded, the helicopter lifted off and headed out in search of a lifeboat. Farthest from the *Prinsendam,* it was number six. "On the flyover," recalled Walters, "I was struck by the jam-packed conditions and the age of the people. I knew then that we better put our PJs (parajumpers) into the water because those folks would have trouble with the hoist." The type used by the air force, primarily for picking people up on land, had a bullet-shaped casing. Called the forest penetrator, it opened to reveal the lift basket.

As the chopper hovered about ten feet above number six, two PJs in scuba gear and carrying survival equipment, John Cassidy and José Rios, leapt into the sea and swam to the lifeboat.

CHAPTER 28

Daisy Chain

"It seemed like an impossible task," wrote Lois Berk. "At first, there was no space on the lifeboat [number three] where the basket could be lowered because we were so crowded. After a few passes, some people in the stern were able to make room and catch and firmly place the basket in the boat. One at a time, nine persons were raised into the helicopter, and then flown to the *Williamsburgh*. The copter came back five times before I was lucky enough to be helped into the basket, hauled up, and quickly helped out of it on the tanker. I don't know how many more trips the copter made. I heard that the crewman who worked the basket was operating his first real rescue. I was among the first forty-five he plucked from death. We were older people, stiff and frozen, many of them were terribly seasick, and we had to be lifted out of the basket. He must have had extraordinary strength."

Describing the hoisting to *Reader's Digest* writer Joseph Blank, Petty Officer Oliverson noted that once the basket was loaded, he started his winch just as the lifeboat was riding the top of a wave. The account continued, "The survivor suddenly found himself dangling in midair, ascending. Pulled into the aircraft, some passengers were so scared–eyes shut, hands clenched around the edges of the basket–that a third crewman had to work to get them out. It took a helicopter at least thirty minutes to hoist up a load, skip over to the *Williamsburgh* and to unload. It was a daisy-chain operation. As one chopper lifted off the helipad, the command ship overhead gave the next permission to land."

Not all the lifts went as smoothly. As one basket holding an elderly woman rose, it swung out from the side of the boat and suddenly dipped into the icy water. Quickly jerked up, the dripping-wet woman glared toward the helicopter, shook a finger at the hoist operator and yelled, "Young man, don't do that again."

When a helicopter hovered thirty feet over lifeboat number four late in the morning, Marjorie Czeikowitz watched anxiously as the basket slowly descended. Not fully recovered from a stroke, she had difficulty walking and had needed a wheelchair that was left on the ship. As the basket came down, she expressed doubts to her husband Richard about her ability to get into it. "I'm here to help you," he replied. "You'll do fine." As the basket reached the level of the boat, a wave slammed it against her head and knocked her unconscious. The only *Prinsendam* officer in number four, the second maître d'hôtel, assured Richard, "She'll be all right, but you go up in the basket first and tell the helicopter crew what the situation is and to get her to the tanker right away."

In the first hour of hoisting operations, 150 men and women were plucked from lifeboats and transported to the *Williamsburgh*. During the shuttling, the sea had grown rougher, reaching twenty-five-foot swells. The wind had increased to fifty knots. "When the water started washing over the sides of the boat," said John Gyorokos, "the cold was almost unbearable." Lois Berk recalled that the wind was strong, and waves were very high." In the *Williamsburgh*'s wireless room, Jim Pfister radioed, "We have very difficult sea conditions. We have two hundred and fifty survivors on board now but more are still in the water."

Earl Andrews found himself fascinated by the obvious coordination of the helicopters. They circled and made careful approaches to lifeboats at medium altitude. A slow descent had them at hovering level. After completing the hoisting process, they made a fast straight rise and turned to head to the ship. After unloading, they flew back to pick up more passengers.

John Graham watched his daughter Malory "go spinning into space and into a helicopter" and worried about worsening weather. The combination of roughening seas and increasingly strong winds would not only present helicopter pilots and hoist operators with a severe maneuvering challenge, but it would also attack the stability of overloaded lifeboats. Capsizing meant rapid hypothermia and certain death. As Malory's chopper sped away, he wondered if he would ever see her again. With the crests of waves blowing off, the boat was hit with torrents of seawater so cold they took the breath away. As a mountain climber, he knew you didn't have to be in water to develop hypothermia. Looking around the boat, he watched for the symptoms. First, a person felt cold and shivered. When the shaking stopped, there came a feeling of warmth. Then, a sleep from which there is no waking. He figured that if everyone weren't picked up soon, in three to four hours they would die where they sat, or be thrown into the sea and drowned.

Hearing that the people carried to the *Williamsburgh* on helicopters did not report deaths in the lifeboats was little comfort to Dr. Don Hudson. Observing the state of those who stepped from the choppers onto the tanker's deck, he knew that the helicopters were in a race against time and weather. "While obviously relieved to have gotten out of lifeboats," he told magazine writer Josh Eppinger, "the survivors looked grim." They were suffering shock, nausea, and sometimes were unable to control their bladders. The noise of the hovering helicopters made communication almost impossible. He and the makeshift medical team of paramedics, assisted by Isabella Brex, faced "a staggering range of medical problems."

A woman reported that she had a brain tumor. One man had an epileptic seizure, another had terminal cancer, and one suffered from malaria. "Everyone was cold," Hudson noted, "and most were suffering severely from motion sickness. A few were already in advanced stages of hypothermia and I was sure someone was going to die. We had three people that I would say had less than an hour before they were irreversible."

With the help of Isabella Brex and *Williamsburgh* crewmen, he began a triage system to find and separate the most critical cases. They organized a "buddy system" in which each person was told to keep an eye on another. Moving among the rescued on five decks, he examined each person every ten minutes. As more soaked shivering passengers came on board, he said, "I need you." "Watch this guy's eyes." "Take her pulse." "Keep me posted." His purpose was "to get across the feeling that people were going to die" if they didn't help him. Hoping involvement with other passengers would take their minds off themselves, he found the age of many passengers contributed to a smooth and orderly operation. "If I had been dealing with people thirty-five or under," he said, "there would have been more panic."

For skipper Arthur Fertig, a ship on a routine passage from Valdez to Texas with full tanks of crude oil had become an emergency room and makeshift hotel for 250 civilians, with more to come, and a landing pad for the swarming whirly birds. With astonishing speed, his crew had improvised an efficient system of handling the choppers and the dazed figures they brought to the ship. Of the journey from lifeboat to helicopter to supertanker, Betsy Price would write, "The three man crew operating the basket worked so deftly, in no time I was out of the basket and helped to the rear of the helicopter. About three more passengers came aboard, then we were off to the *Williamsburgh*. We had lost sight of the *Prinsendam* hours ago, but when we were in the helicopter we could see three ships in the area waiting to pick up survivors." Noting that the chopper had to make a second approach to the tanker, she continued, "We jumped into the arms of the crew and were ushered the length of the thousand-foot tanker to the quarters and the wheelhouse. We shed our life jackets and were whisked inside to warmth and a reunion with fellow passengers. Immediately, we started swapping tales."

By early afternoon, the crews on helicopters and at the landing pad were near exhaustion. With continuous rubbing against steel cables, leather gloves of the hoist crews wore through. Muscles ached and cramped. Oliverson's chopper, piloted by Bruce Melnick, would eventually carry out dozens of sorties and rescue a hundred people. With the number of helicopters in the air at one time ranging from three to six, the crewman watching the radar screen aboard the on-scene commander C-130 that coordinated their movements also had to keep track of the lifeboats and rafts in what at times seemed more like a videogame than the orchestration of the greatest air-sea operation ever to be carried out by the Coast Guard. In the five-plus hours since the C-130 located the *Prinsendam* around four a.m., the blips representing Coast Guard and USAF aircraft, the cruise ship, and the scattered lifeboats had multiplied to include the tankers *Williamsburgh, Greatland,* and SOHIO *Intrepid* and the freighter

Portland. In time, the screen would mark the presence of the cutters *Boutwell, Mellon,* and *Woodrush,* along with two Canadian Air Force Labrador choppers.

After making two sorties to and from the *Williamsburgh* and lifeboat number four, Jeannie Gilmore's rescuing helicopter appeared in the late afternoon. Approximately twelve hours after she and her mother had wedged themselves into the lifeboat, she feared Neva Hall couldn't last much longer. "Her skin was blue, and she'd been out there a long time, but mother was also a very headstrong lady. When I told her to get in the basket, she said, 'I'm going down with the ship!'"

Jeannie replied, "Mother, there's only so much fuel in these helicopters, and they can't wait. You have to get into the basket right now."

"I'm not going," said Mrs. Hall, removing her rings and handing them to Jeannie, "Give these to my sister Mary Lou."

"Well, I couldn't very well hit her, or use physical force on an old lady," Jeannie recalled with a laugh, "so I got the idea of tricking her by telling her that my son-in-law, John, whom she really loved, was up in the helicopter. I told her, 'He's doing search-and-rescue work and wants you to get into the basket.'"

After thinking a moment, Mrs. Hall threw off her blanket and said, "Well, if that's what John wants, I'll do it."

Relieved that her mother was strapped into the basket and being winched up, and in the expectation that other older passengers would be the next to go, Jeannie sat down to wait her turn. An elderly woman said to her, "You really should go with your mom. She doesn't look very good. I'm sure no one will object."

When no one did, Jeannie reluctantly agreed. Given a farewell kiss on the cheek by the young man who had operated the rowing mechanism with her, she climbed into the lowered basket to be hoisted. As the basket reached the helicopter door, it was caught by a gust of wind. In an interview for this book, Jeannie recalled, "It hit the side of the helicopter and went sailing out like a kite. I found myself seeing more of that ocean than I ever want to see again."

Winched into the chopper and helped out of the basket, she sat on a bench with knees touching those of the woman opposite her. Looking around at "wet and bedraggled people, weak from throwing up and terribly scared," she exclaimed, "We're all going to be fine and you can all come home with me."

Landing on the *Williamsburgh* in heavy rain, they were assisted from the helicopter by Indonesian crewmen of the *Prinsendam* who had been taken from the launch and other lifeboats, then escorted by *Williamsburgh* crew across the deck and into the warm and dry superstructure that rose several stories at the rear end of the ship.

Richard Steele wrote admiringly of the men who carried out the rescue operation, "They fight winds and gigantic waves as they maintain a level course over the lifeboats to complete their death-defying, life-saving mission. After ten hours of drifting in the frigid sea, my wife is hoisted aboard a Coast Guard helicopter. She flashes the 'V' for victory salute."

Because the helicopter Louise boarded was low on fuel, she would be flown to Yakutat. Richard would be picked up by a Canadian Air Force helicopter and flown to the *Williamsburgh*. "Our rescuer is highly skilled and coolly competent," he wrote. "He responds to our effusive thanks with a shrug and a grin and says, 'That's what I'm paid for. Glad you made it.'"

There were flashes of humor. Watching the woman who was briefly dipped in the sea, comedian Roger Ray said to Jack and

Beatrice Malon in lifeboat number three, "What the hell is this, 'Operation Granny Dunk?'" Betty Milborn gasped with horror as an eighty-year-old man who had been lifted from boat number five slipped out of the basket and into the water. When a *Prinsendam* officer grabbed the man's arm and yanked him back into the lifeboat, everyone applauded the quick retrieval. Grinning broadly, the old man shook himself like a wet dog and said, "I'm sure you'll all agree that I really needed that bath! Well, you don't smell like a bunch of fresh-picked daisies, either!" When asked by an interviewer for a Boston television station to describe the experience of being hoisted out of a lifeboat, Steele replied, "I don't know if I can do it justice. It's like the W. C. Fields joke in a movie when he's about to be hanged. When he's asked if he has any last request, he replies, 'I'd like to see Paris before I die, but Philadelphia will do.'"

CHAPTER 29

Make Room for Grandma

"Sooner or later in an operation as big as this," mused Richard Steele during an interview a few days after returning to his desk off the city room of the Worcester *Telegram-Gazette,* "some things were bound to go amiss."

Although it would be more than a year before Dutch government investigators reported findings of fact in the chain of events that began with an engine room fire and abandonment of the ship, resulting in the boldest air-sea rescue in Coast Guard history, reports from the scene to the Coast Guard RCC in Juneau and accounts by passengers provided anecdotal evidence of a series of mishaps, faulty calculations, unexpected consequences, equipment malfunctions, and human failings. They ranged from the lackadaisical attitude of many passengers during the fire drill, the motorized launch hanging up on its davits, failing tow ropes and some of the crewmen pushing aside passengers to get into the overloaded lifeboats to an overall absence of leadership by the ship's officers during and after the order to abandon ship.

While some of these might have been averted, and some were perhaps excusable, other challenges were the result of what Jeannie Gilmore called the "bad luck" of a ship that caught fire more than a hundred miles out in the Gulf of Alaska at night and at the tail end of a typhoon.

"Considering the horrible weather and the very long distance the rescuers had to cover," she said in retrospect, "it's amazing that we weren't all dead before they got there."

A Coastie who took part in the race to save the *Prinsendam* offered a philosophical view. "The Coast Guard lives up to its motto, 'Always Ready'," he said, "but in every rescue the outcome is to some extent at the mercy of Lady Luck. If she's not on your side, preparation and readiness can take you only so far. You might have all the men and machines you think you'll need, but you can never plan for every hitch, glitch, and screw-up."

The first unanticipated problem had occurred when Kenneth Matz discovered that the couplings of Coast Guard fire hoses that he took aboard the *Prinsendam* didn't match the ship's Siamese connections. After working around this complication, he encountered a water-pressure problem that required shifting his portable pump to a float, only to see it swept away by a wave and sink. Soon after this disaster, the plan to use the remaining motor launch to shuttle people from the lifeboats to the *Williamsburgh* had to be abandoned because the forty-foot climb up the Jacob's ladder was deemed by Petty Officer Oliverson to be too risky for the elderly and too time-consuming to meet the deadline of rescuing everyone before nightfall.

This decision required a change in tactics in which the helicopters formed a daisy-chain airlift shuttle to the supertanker that could not have been anticipated in the original rescue plan. The expectation was that all the rescued would be taken by helicopter to the reception facility that was hastily organized at Yakutat. By airlifting them to the supertanker, arrangements had to be made to receive them at Valdez, where there were no arrangements for handling an influx of hundreds of people needing medical attention, food, and clothing.

As a result of this plan alteration, the Coast Guard choppers would have to make periodic diversions from the scene in order to refuel at Yakutat, unload the people they'd picked up, and return to resume hoisting. This put an additional strain on crews and helicopters that had been mobilized in the middle of the night to fly more than a hundred miles and spend several hours at the scene in unfavorable weather that was deteriorating. The prolonged process of hoisting and multiple flights also affected the C-130 on-scene commander and the air force Hercules that refueled the USAF chopper of Captain John Walters. Changed circumstances had required him to not only make his first landing on a ship at sea to place Dr. Hudson, blankets, and other supplies on the *Williamsburgh*, but to drop two of his parajumpers, Sergeants John Cassidy and José Rios, into the water to aid lifeboat number six people into the hoisting basket. Several hours later, with all but eighteen of sixty of the lifeboat's occupants airlifted, Walters received an order to suspend hoisting from number six to stand by at the *Prinsendam* for the expected imminent arrival of the cutter *Boutwell,* and possibly help evacuate the *Prinsendam's* officers and volunteer crewmen who'd remained on the ship to continue the fire-fighting operation.

At about the same time, the pilot of the air force Hercules, Captain Dave Briski, was directed to leave his refueling location and head east and south to assist a Canadian Air Force Labrador helicopter that had lost electrical instrumentation and was having difficulty navigating in worsening weather. Using directional-finding and search radar, Briski located the Canadian in an area of low visibility and had to escort it to Yakutat. The second 442 Squadron copter, piloted by Captain Gary Flath and designated Rescue 303, lifted sixteen passengers to the *Williamsburgh*. Low on fuel after three trips, it went to Yakutat, arrived with its fuel gauge on empty and landed barely a minute before the engines shut down. The rescue unit's action that day would earn it the Canadian government's Chief of Defence Staff Unit Commendation for outstanding devotion to duty.

When Captain Walters' helicopter returned to number six to resume hoisting, a twenty-foot swell caught the basket and swept it under the rear of the lifeboat. This resulted in the hoisting cable becoming tangled with the boat's rudder and breaking. Rendered unable to hoist, the helicopter was running low on fuel. Without access to Captain Briski's midair gas station, and the landing pads of the *Williamsburgh* occupied in handling choppers carrying people from lifeboats, Walters had no recourse but to set down on the helicopter pad of the more distant SOHIO *Intrepid*.

For the *Williamsburgh*'s skipper, Captain Arthur Fertig, October 4, 1980, had become a day in which his emotions shifted with each change in the situation. As a mariner learning that a ship was in distress, he'd felt a surge of sympathy for what its captain faced, not only in having to send out a call for help and the possibility of losing his ship, but the ordeal that would surely ensue. During an inevitable investigation, there would be a need, if not a demand, to assign the responsibility, if not blame. When Fertig was informed that a cruise ship had an engine room fire, the plight of his fellow sea captain and the fate of his ship became secondary to evaluating practicalities of how the *Williamsburgh* could assist in the event it was summoned to join in the saving of lives. Factors to be weighed were the relative locations of the supertanker and cruise ship and how much time would be needed to change course and reach the *Prinsendam*, considering weather and conditions upon arrival. Would he find a slowly sinking ship?

One that was going down rapidly? Might she have already gone down? Would the *Williamsburgh* find people in lifeboats? In the sea? Bodies? Would there be hazardous debris in the water? Upon arriving a few miles from the crippled cruise ship, the plan called for a Coast Guard helicopter to set down on one of the helipads and pick up firefighting equipment. This was aborted when Captain Wabeke ordered abandonment of his ship. After the Coast Guard plan for lifeboats to be towed to the *Williamsburgh*, with survivors boarding by ladder, proved unfeasible, the plan was changed again. Designating the supertanker primary receiver of hundreds of airlifted people, the Coast Guard thrust Fertig and his thirty-one crewmen center-stage in a high-seas rescue drama unequaled in maritime history.

Beneficiaries of the *Williamsburgh*'s conversion from supertanker to a combination of heliport, medical emergency room, and a hostel handling an influx of unexpected guests voiced only praise for the manner in which they were received. "They did everything in their power to make us comfortable," wrote Betsy Price. "The officers and crew gave up their cabins and day-rooms, their blankets and clothes. Sandwiches were brought to us. The cold cuts on plain white bread tasted like the best gourmet food ever!" Another passenger said, "The crew acted as if getting hundreds of unexpected guests was commonplace. The tanker's crew, assisted by some of the *Prinsendam* personnel, met every helicopter with cups of coffee and tea."

Concerned about dehydration, Dr. Hudson, Isabella Brex, and other medical personnel kept the hot liquids flowing. Hudson found people "as cold as marble and totally unresponsive." A few staggered into walls. One man was so disoriented that he said to Hudson, "I think I'll have the caviar, then a prime rib of beef, medium rare." A woman in pajamas was "deeply depressed because she'd left behind a large diamond ring that represented most of her life's savings." Feeling better a few hours later, she said to Hudson, "What's a diamond ring matter? I'm alive. I can start over."

By late afternoon, Hudson had dispensed nearly one hundred nitroglycerine tablets to people with heart conditions and scores of seasickness pills, but fewer than a dozen tranquilizers. "We were lucky," he said. "If some of them had been out in the boats for several more hours, I'm sure they would have succumbed."

The *Williamsburgh* crew handed out clothing from the ship's supply and from their own lockers. Giving size-8 women men's size-38 jeans, extra-large T-shirts and men's size-10 shoes, one of the crewmen joked, "One size fits all!"

Recalling having dieted so she could outfit herself for the trip with the very-latest-style clothing, Jeannie Gilmore said, "After I had a shower, I put on a pair of sailors' jeans and was thrilled that they were too big for me! In those baggy pants and a too-large Coast Guard shirt, I felt like Mary Martin in *South Pacific.*"

By late afternoon, with virtually all of the *Prinsendam*'s passengers and many of its crew and some officers taken aboard, Captain Fertig announced that the *Williamsburgh* was cleared by the Coast Guard to leave the scene. The supertanker would make way for Juan de Luca Strait, the entrance to Puget Sound, a voyage of about forty-eight hours, and then make port at Seattle. But two hours later, he advised that the plan had been changed. The tanker would be heading to Valdez, a trip of only twenty-four hours.

"With this news," said Betsy Price, "we settled down for the night." Although the crew gave up their sleeping quarters, there were not enough beds to accommodate nearly four hundred people, so Betsy rolled up her sweater for a pillow, her raincoat for a blanket and went to sleep with the steel deck for her bed.

Octogenarian Elsa Hutson, who had given a childhood blessing to Richard Steele, went looking for a place to sleep and found a bed occupied by a young, crying woman. Recognizing her as one of the singers, Elsa tried to comfort her.

"You're very kind," said the young woman.

"No more tears now," said Elsa. "Promise?"

The young woman smiled. "You remind me of my grandma, and I love her very much."

"Well, would you mind moving over to make room so Grandma can crawl in with you?"

CHAPTER 30

This Is What We Do

Almost exactly at the estimated time of arrival that Captain Leroy Krumm had calculated, the *Boutwell* came into sight of the burning *Prinsendam* at one forty-five p.m. The cutter had covered three hundred miles of the Gulf of Alaska on a rescue mission that all hands on board sensed would be not only memorable personally, but probably historic. Crew members whose duties permitted were on deck, gazing in wonderment and sadness. Much of the starboard side of the sharply listing white cruise ship was scorched. Flashes of fire were visible through black clouds of smoke that billowed from its shattered portholes and drifted aft. A motor launch dangled precariously at a steep angle, its bow pointing up.

On deck when the *Boutwell* arrived, Seaman Apprentice Dave Hughes peered through the rain. Remembering feeling both amazed and excited, he said, "It was a big air rescue."

Twenty-four years after the most dramatic experience during his Coast Guard service, he recalled, "I saw a huge oil tanker and several helicopters in the air. The *Prinsendam* was listing. Lifeboats were bobbing all over the place. We immediately put our motor surfboat in the water with a couple of boatswain mates and deck hands in them to tow lifeboats and take people out of them onto our cutter. When that got to be too dangerous, we pulled alongside a boat and lowered a Jacob's ladder with a couple of guys to help people onto it. We would try to catch the waves, the swells, to where we could pluck these folks out of the boat."

Among the rescue personnel was Chief Warrant Officer William Ham. "He was an Old Salt, about five feet eight with a sharp, trimmed salt-and-pepper beard and a very thin face with a piercing look that reminded me of Captain Ahab in *Moby Dick*," recalled Hughes. "He was out there in control and barking out commands. At one point, we couldn't grab hold of the lifeboat because the sea was too rough for our guys to be in the water. He waited for a swell, and when it was just right, he jumped from our ship into that lifeboat. I was a young kid and all I could think of was, 'Wow!' That was one of the most heroic things I've ever seen."

To retrieve people from lifeboats, the *Boutwell* launched its motor surf boats. Because of the rolling waves, this was not easy. Pete Marcucci recalled, "You have to time lowering them with the movement of the rollers, while making sure that the surf boat is kept level while it's going down. If it's released forward but not aft, or vice-versa, the men in it are dumped into the water. We dropped the boats and they brought people from the lifeboats back, but the *Boutwell* was listing so much from side to side, and pounding up and down, because the waves were so enormous, that we couldn't manage to do it. This meant that we had to use life slings. Most of us in the deck department were on the small side, so we got beefcake guys like the front line of a football team from the engineering department. They just laid on the deck and pulled people up in the horse collar sling."

When this system proved too dangerous because of the rough sea, the *Boutwell*'s surf boats went out to the lifeboats to tow them to the cutter. "We'd tie the lifeboats alongside hard," Marcucci explained, "and lift the people out one at a time."

This plan went amiss because of the behavior of some Indonesian crewmen from the *Prinsendam*. Marcucci recalled, "They were so scared, so afraid to die, that they would leap from the surf boat onto the ship. We had to snatch a bunch of them from the side of the ship. Finally, we told the boatswain in each surf boat to keep everyone seated."

Recounting unloading the first of the lifeboats full of elderly people the *Boutwell* aided, Hughes was still angry as he depicted Indonesian crewmen "shoving elderly people aside to get onto the cutter."

Except for the behavior of a few *Prinsendam* crewmen, Pete Marcucci's most memorable moment during the lifting of people from the surf boats was a woman in only a bathrobe. "She appeared to be in her forties," he recalled. "She's in a life sling. She swings away from the ship and as she swings back in, the robe goes flying off and there she is in all her naked glory. When she got to the deck, she grabbed hold of my pal Tim Stanton and hugged him like a death grip. She was completely naked and totally happy."

Taking over as on-scene commander, the *Boutwell* responded to a message from Kenneth Matz in the wheelhouse of the *Prinsendam* that efforts to put out the fire had failed. He asked assistance in removing himself, Captain Wabeke, and fifty officers and crew from the ship. This would involve helicopters, including Walters' air force chopper, taking them to the *Boutwell*'s helicopter pad. With three choppers alternating lifts of twelve men each, the hoisting of fifty weary, grimy individuals from the bridge took more than two hours. The last to leave the wheelhouse, Wabeke was assisted into the lift basket and hoisted slowly into Walters' helicopter. When it settled onto the cutter, he remained seated for a moment with a dazed expression and slowly shook his head. With a sigh, he rose, shook hands with Walters and copilot Gillam, thanked them, and stepped onto the deck of the *Boutwell.* Looking skyward, he gave a salute, presumably to God, and then clasped his hands high above his head as if he were a victorious boxer after a lengthy bout.

With confirmation by Kenneth Matz that everyone was off the ship, Walters headed back to lifeboat number six, only to lose the forest penetrator, run out of fuel, and have to set down on the *Intrepid.* Guided by the *Boutwell* in half-mile visibility and forty-five-knot crosswinds, he landed and shut down the engines at 4:57 p.m.

An hour and a half later, the *Boutwell* informed the RCC in Juneau that the last of the lifeboats and rafts had been located, emptied, and marked with a painted X to indicate it had been checked. The cutter had 84 survivors on board. The *Williamsburgh* reported having taken on 380. In the first stage of the operation, 62 had been airlifted to Yakutat. The *Mellon* and the *Woodrush* had arrived and were standing by. As the on-scene commander, Captain Krumm was told to make an account of the resources that had been used throughout the mission (a task that was put into the hands of Chris Macneith and his staff) and to compile a list of the names of survivors on board the *Boutwell.*

Working from the *Boutwell*'s report, the *Prinsendam* manifest and Holland America and Customs records, the RCC reported at eight p.m. that everyone from the *Prinsendam* had been rescued. The *Williamsburgh, Intrepid, Portland,* and *Greenland* were released. Helicopters and C-130s were cleared to return to their bases. The *Boutwell* was relieved of on-scene duty to take its survivors to Sitka.

"Everybody has come out of this mess okay," said Commander Schoel as he gazed at the map on the wall of his headquarters. "Nobody's dead. Nobody's seriously injured."

An observer noted that "quiet jubilation" rippled through the RCC.

It didn't last.

At 9:16 p.m., a cable landed on Schoel's desk. From Lieutenant Colonel Bill Langley, commander of the 71st ARCC at Elmendorf Air Force Base, it asked, "Where are my PJs?"

The men in question, Schoel was informed, were Sergeants Cassidy and Rios. They had been dropped into the sea in the early afternoon from Captain Walters' air force helicopter to aid the hoisting from lifeboat number six. Langley reported the copter had then gone to the *Prinsendam* to assist in the evacuation of the wheelhouse. Because the refueling plane had been sent to the aid of the disabled and lost Canadian helicopter to guide it to Yakutat, when Walters' chopper ran low on fuel, it had been forced to land on the SOHIO *Intrepid*. The response from Walters to an inquiry from RCC Juneau reported, "Pararescuers were left in lifeboat approximately two miles W. of Tanker Williamsburgh at approximately 142250Z [2:22:50 p.m. Z stands for "Zulu," the international code for Greenwich Mean Time]. These men left with twenty survivors from the *Prinsendam*. Also, these two men were equipped with a PRC 90 radio and Mark 13 flares. This is all the information we have."

Shocked and alarmed that a lifeboat with twenty persons and two air force parajumpers was missing, Schoel immediately ordered the *Boutwell* to break off its course to Sitka and launch a search. A C-130 Hercules from Kodiak was also ordered back to assist.

Meanwhile, the storm associated with the predicted cold front was closing in with a vengeance, bringing forty-knot winds that kicked up giant swells and waves, rain, temperatures below freezing, banks of fog, a low ceiling, and severely limited visibility.

As the cutter reversed course shortly after nine thirty p.m., the passengers in lifeboat number six had been adrift for about sixteen hours. Cassidy and Rios had joined them in the early afternoon to assist them into the lift. Shaped like an artillery projectile, it was opened into a seat into which the passenger had to be securely buckled. To assure this, Rios had climbed into the boat. To keep the device from hitting the lifeboat, Cassidy had stayed in the water.

Witnesses of Cassidy's heroism told *Reader's Digest* writer Joseph Blank that after he'd pulled the penetrator to the boat more than twenty times, he was "utterly spent," sick from having swallowed sea water and being slammed repeatedly against the side of the boat.

Contending with the effects of not having had insulin injections, Irving Brex watched in awe as Cassidy was helped aboard. "He was deathly sick," Brex noted. "He'd go to the side of the boat to throw up, then turn around to comfort us." With Cassidy out of the water, the hoist man in Captain Walters' helicopter had to maneuver the penetrator to where Cassidy and Rios could haul it aboard. After the helicopter departed to aid in evacuating the *Prinsendam*'s bridge, rain began to mix with sleet, and mounting seas interfered with the precision of the lift.

As Rios was buckling the fiftieth passenger into the lift basket, a wave had lifted the boat high and swung its bow. The cable snagged between the rudder and stern, and as the boat slid down into a wave trough the cable snapped as if it were a thread.

It was at this point that Walters' helicopter was low on fuel and was forced to land on the *Intrepid*. When the chopper didn't return, Cassidy tried in vain to use a radio he'd brought with him to make contact with any helicopter. When he heard an aircraft droning toward the boat in thickening fog, he knew from experience that it was pointless to fire a flare. "Some of the people kept telling us to use them," Rios reported, "but we didn't want to until we actually had a ship or aircraft in sight."

Cassidy activated an electronic beacon, but the signal did not last long enough for the aircraft to locate it. As the sound of the aircraft faded into the distance, one of the passengers said, "They've forgotten us. They're going to leave us to die."

Cassidy replied, "Oh, no. Our air force people know we're out here. Rescue is just a matter of time."

Fighting a powerful, churning, and frigid ocean, with bone-chilling strong headwinds that drove stinging sleet, the *Boutwell* had been at sea for more than seventeen hours. Some officers and crew who had spent the previous night partying in Juneau had been awake for more than a day and a half. Hard going since leaving Juneau and the excitement of being abruptly sent to sea to rescue a cruise ship had made resting virtually impossible. After assisting in evacuating the last of the people from the *Prinsendam*, they'd thought the worst of the mission was over. Now they were ordered back to sea to search for a missing lifeboat.

With few people left in number six after the loss of the lifting capability by Captain Walters' helicopter, Cassidy and Rios had gathered them in the front and pulled a tarpaulin over them to ward off rain and spray. Cassidy explained, "Your body heat will build up under here." Ship photographer Terry Allen would say, "They literally saved lives."

With the huddled passengers covered, Cassidy and Rios remained in the open stern to be battered by 35-knot blasts of wind and pelting rain and sleet on swells that rose to thirty feet. After seven hours of hopefully scanning the black sea and sky, Cassidy spotted a distant rotating white light. Rios fired a flare. Cassidy yanked a mirror from his survival kit to reflect the beam of what could only be the searchlight of a Coast Guard cutter.

As the *Boutwell* came in view, the C-130 switched on its Aldis lamp, turning sky and sea as bright as high noon. The *Boutwell*'s log noted that lifeboat number six, with two parajumpers and twenty passengers safe, was found at 57-47 degrees North and 141-18 degrees West on Sunday, 05 October 1980 at 0115 hours.

Eighteen-year-old Seaman Apprentice Tom Ice of Akron, Ohio, had been in the Coast Guard eight months. As the *Boutwell* looked for lifeboat number six, he was standing "flying bridge watch" and one of a team that alternated manning the cutter's powerful searchlight. "The night was pitch black," he recalled, "but now and then the light found a bank of gray fog that seemed to be as solid as a concrete wall. We knew we were in the area where the lifeboat was last reported, but the sea was rough."

There was no telling how far the lifeboat might have drifted. With such huge swells, it was possible that when the light swept an area, the boat could be in a deep trough.

"We had to hope that the light caught the boat on a rise," said Ice. "We were prowling like a one-eyed tiger in the dark on a hunt for an elusive prey, but we were looking for a tiny boat in the Gulf of Alaska in brutal wintry weather."

The searchlight's beam had pierced the darkness and swept turgid water like a long, thin finger and poked into drifting swirls of fog for nearly seven hours. Swinging in the direction of the flare fired by José Rios, the light that caught the lifeboat on the crest of a high wave instantly switched the *Boutwell*'s mission from search to rescue.

"Try to imagine it," said Ice. "The lifeboat and our ship are riding the swells. One second you can almost reach out and touch the lifeboat, and suddenly it's thirty to fifty feet below you. Your timing has to be pretty good or people can get seriously hurt."

Pulling within reach of the lifeboat, the *Boutwell* crew deployed the Jacob's ladder and put the cutter's motor surf boat into the water. With it secured to the lifeboat with a rope, Chief Warrant Officer Bill Ham jumped into number six.

Sergeant Cassidy pointed to Irving Brex and said, "This man's in really bad shape. He's in diabetic shock. He goes first."

Brex shook his head and said, "I can't stand up."

After Cassidy, Ham, and Rios lifted him into the surf boat, six *Boutwell* crew, including Dave Hughes, waited for a swell to lift the surf boat to near-deck level. Grabbing Brex by the arms, they dragged him aboard. "My first impression," said Hughes, "was that he was dead."

Rushed to the cutter's sick bay and placed on an examination table, Brex was stripped, given intravenous fluid and insulin, bathed, wrapped in blankets and carried to a bunk. He would later exclaim, "I never felt so mothered in my entire life."

Describing assisting people from lifeboats, Yeoman Chris Macneith said, "It was really, really cold. In some cases we had to use a device like a horse collar to pull them into our boat. As they came out, I'd assist them on and down to the mess deck. It was almost like a bucket brigade. People would be waiting inside the hatch to be helped below deck. This went on for several hours."

The last man out of lifeboat number six, Cassidy climbed onto the *Boutwell*'s deck at two thirty a.m. With the surf boat retrieved, number six was left to drift. The *Boutwell* had rescued a pair of pararescuers and more than eighty passengers, crew, and officers of the *Prinsendam*, including Captain Wabeke. "We wrapped them in blankets and brought them into the mess deck cafeteria and gave them warm drinks," Hughes noted, "then we sat with them and tried to make them feel comfortable. We gave up our bunks and blankets. My pal Bill Thibodeaux let a young Indonesian crewman have his bottom bunk, but the kid got sick and threw up all over it."

Because several women had been rescued, Monyee Wright found herself called from her duty in the engine room to help care for them. She recalled, "Some were dressed in nightgowns and coats. They were shaking from cold and shock. They were sick and very dirty. I tried to calm them and helped them shower. I gave them some of my clothes and let them use the two beds in the stateroom I shared with Lieutenant Burgess, who'd been left in Juneau. I slept on a grate in the floor directly over the engine room. The floor was warm, so I didn't need a blanket. I could feel the vibrations from the engine room."

"After a while it seemed like a big family reunion," said Chris Macneith. "Some of the survivors asked to buy anything that had the name *Boutwell* on it, or just the letters USCG. They wanted cigarette lighters, baseball caps, pens, writing paper, bumper stickers—you name it. I think they really wanted to party and celebrate not being on a burning and sinking cruise ship."

Looking back after a quarter of a century to all that had transpired following the order to return to his ship to rescue the *Prinsendam*, Dave Hughes mused, "When you're doing these things, you really don't think about it, because in the Coast Guard, this is what we do."

CHAPTER 31

The Boat People

With survivors' names recorded and everyone settled down, the *Boutwell* again headed for Sitka. At a distance of 170 nautical miles from the burning *Prinsendam*, the town boasted that it was the oldest and most culturally significant community in Alaska. Its claim that visitors had been enjoying its "ancient art of hospitality for almost 8,000 years" was about to be put to an extreme test. In addition to the more than eighty men and women aboard the *Boutwell*, the town was braced to receive eighty-seven survivors who had been picked up at the outset of the rescue operation and airlifted to Yakutat.

After the ninety-minute flight of 138 air miles, the Coast Guard helicopter that had carried Muriel Marvinney, Agnes Lilard, and twelve others in the first of several airlifts to Yakutat set down at a few minutes past five p.m. on Saturday, October 4. "Our ordeal in the lifeboat had lasted ten hours," Muriel recalled. "All around us after we'd landed were strong, gentle hands. The wonderful Coast Guard men somehow weren't strangers. They were like fathers, brothers, sons! They wrapped us in blankets and gave us hot coffee. I was vaguely aware of someone snapping pictures. After I had warmed up a bit, I looked in a mirror. My hair was a mass of corkscrews. I didn't know whether to cry or laugh. I phoned my children to tell them I was all right."

For the people of the fishing village, rallying to provide assistance to survivors of a sea disaster was a first. Awakened when state trooper Warren Grant rang the town's fire bell, nearly half the five hundred residents who gathered at the small airport were following a disaster plan that had been in existence but unused in the ten years since the village became incorporated. "What Yakutat did," noted a newspaper account, "was make tuna fish, ham, and peanut butter sandwiches and took shifts serving them and hot coffee to groups of cold, wet, and weary passengers. Others, like Alice Bethel, cooked up a giant order of vegetable soup and took it to the airport."

Mallotts General Store and Ryman's Department Store gave away jeans and socks. The Lakeside Chapel, St. Ann's Catholic Church, and Yakutat Presbyterian Church donated clothes. An early morning Alaska Airlines flight provided blankets. Lani Mapes, wife of a commercial fisherman, said there was initially "a state of controlled chaos." Although she noted "everyone knew what had to be done but nobody knew what anybody was doing," Fire Chief Jerry Pond said, "Things went as smoothly as could be expected, and then some."

After being examined by medical personnel and fed, the Yakutat survivors were flown to Sitka and taken by bus to a hotel. Following "a long hot bath," Muriel Marvinney and Agnes Lilard "went to a lovely little store across the street and purchased outfits," courtesy of Holland America Lines. "After dinner at our hotel, we retired. That first night we slept like logs. The bad nights wouldn't start until Sunday when, the minute we'd turn the lights out, it would all come rushing back. Then we'd have to turn the lights on and talk. We needed to feel the warmth of human contact, to know that we were safe and warm and would be returning to our loved ones in a day or so."

When she and Agnes went down for breakfast on Sunday morning, they were told that a lifeboat was missing and the twenty people on board were presumed dead. "Suddenly the cheerful dining room seemed like a tomb," Muriel recalled. "Those of us who had survived needed one another, but we needed those others too." Learning in the afternoon that the lifeboat had been found and all its occupants were on a Coast Guard cutter heading to Sitka, she "rejoiced" that all the other passengers were on board the supertanker bound for Valdez.

In an account of the 24-hour journey to Valdez aboard the *Williamsburgh* provided to the magazine *Steamboat Bill,* Betsy Price wrote that the survivors had gotten little rest and by four thirty a.m. Sunday, October 5, "we were all wide awake, and soon the sandwiches came around again. Cheese!" Shortly thereafter, an announcement was made that the last people had been picked up and "everyone–passengers and crew–were accounted for and safe."

After she and the others had a breakfast of scrambled eggs and "a tasty lunch and dinner" served by Indonesian crewmen who had "taken over the kitchen and were cooking, making dinner, and serving food," the *Williamsburgh* sailed up the Valdez narrows, escorted by tugboats, a few pleasure craft and airplanes. Following docking, they were helped across the oil- and rain-slicked decks by crewmen to waiting buses.

"We were all tagged and numbered before disembarkation," Betsy wrote, "the first of many identification and manifest checks."

Although fully awake after being rendered unconscious when struck on the head by the hoist basket, Marjorie Czeikowitz was rushed to the hospital, examined, and found not to have been seriously injured. Given a wheelchair to replace the one that had been thrown overboard, she asked, "How do I go about returning it?" A hospital staffer replied, "Don't worry. We'll pick it up at the airport after you leave."

Subscribers to the Worcester, Massachusetts, *Sunday Telegram* would read an account of the *Williamsburgh*'s arrival in Valdez by Richard Steele. He recalled, "The Holland America agents who meet us in Valdez are doing everything possible to make us comfortable and secure. Nerves are on edge, but the agents are superb in their patience, courtesy, and understanding. Some people never stop complaining–most never start. When one is handed back one's life, the loss of worldly goods is unimportant."

This was not true for all the survivors. Steele observed, "We are invited to visit a general store to select any necessities we desire. Most people are modest about their needs. Some take enough to start a new store. The greeting we receive in Valdez is totally unexpected. It's Sunday. At church, the religious leaders organize the collection of clothing and food for the *Prinsendam* refugees. Homes and hearts are opened. As we emerge from our bus at the Sheffield House hotel, scores of people applaud."

Betsy Price wrote, "The townspeople stood in pouring rain to welcome us with cheers and kisses. We were assigned four to a room. We put our belongings inside (the emergency kit given us by Alaskan Airlines contained a toothbrush, toothpaste, comb, etc.) and we went immediately to the bar and dining room. Everything was on the house and the drinks and salmon dinner with wine were gorgeous! The local merchants opened their shops so passengers could be outfitted in clothing; many still had the nightclothes and blankets with which they left the ship."

Awaiting the influx of *Prinsendam* survivors by sea and air in Valdez and Sitka were not only Holland America officials, but a horde of reporters, photographers, and TV news crews. Among the Valdez crowd was Ellis E. Conklin of the *Anchorage Times*. His story for the next day's edition (October 6) caught the mood of both groups exactly. "Hundreds of disheveled, sea-weary warriors trudged slowly into Valdez hotel rooms, filling them beyond capacity. They were exhausted but glad to be alive. For the 383 passengers and crewmen who had just experienced one of the greatest sea rescues in modern times, a long, old nightmare had come to an end. As they peeled off buses and walked a short distance through steady rain into the glare of television lights and a battalion of anxious reporters who had huddled in hotel entrance ways few realized the headlines they had been making."

Since the first bulletin that a cruise ship was on fire in the Gulf of Alaska, the plight of the *Prinsendam* and questions about the fate of her passengers had dominated the news on radio and television and taken precedence over all other events on the front pages of newspapers from coast to coast. In San Francisco, Richard and Louise Steele's daughter Ginny learned of the fire in a phone call from Richard's secretary in Worcester. Unsatisfied with "scanty reports" on the radio, she got the phone number for the Coast Guard in Juneau and soon found herself talking to Ray Massey. "I called every hour," Ginny noted in an interview for this book, "He was just great. He told me exactly what was going on. Then I'd turn on the news on the radio and TV and they were getting it all wrong, so I'd call the stations and correct their information." Lois Berk wrote to the Coast Guard Commandant that her daughter phoned the Juneau RCC "every two hours for about twenty-six hours" and found the Coast Guardsman who answered the phone "constantly courteous, well informed, and generous with his information." Carole Gilmore also worked the telephone, alternating calls to the Coast Guard in Alaska and local radio and TV newsrooms until she was told that Jeannie had been picked up and was safe on the *Williamsburgh*.

Reporting the arrival of the survivors, Ellis Conklin wrote, "Like conquering heroes, the passengers–many in their seventies and eighties–were patted on the back by smiling city officials while curious on-lookers shook their hands and held them tightly. Some of them shouted, 'Welcome to Valdez.'"

The final head count of the rescued noted by the Coast Guard accounted for all of the passengers and ship's officers and crewmen, thirteen cruise staff and two pararescuers. A *Boutwell* Coastie said, "This was a miracle."

The sentiment would be repeated many times by many people.

Noted one veteran reporter as he gazed at the raw emotion of the survivors arriving in the Sheffield House lobby, "It's like they just walked on the moon for the first time. Many of the passengers were eager to tell of their unforgettable odyssey. Others headed straight for the bar."

Waving aside a reporter, Rosemary Riggs said, "Oh, do I need a drink!"

A photographer recalled the Coast Guard's rescue at sea of refugee "boat people" from Cuba earlier in 1980 and assigned the same term to those from the *Prinsendam*. Most accepted the designation with good humor and pride. Notebooks, radio tape machines, and television news cameras were soon recording tales of what more than one reporter and headline writer who had a familiarity with Walter Lord's book and subsequent movie about the sinking of *Titanic* called another "night to remember."

Writers Don Hunter and Bob Shallit of the *Anchorage Daily News* reported from Valdez, "The end of the ordeal for 359 passengers and crewmen from the *Prinsendam* came at the terminus of the trans-Alaska pipeline on a dreary, rainy Sunday evening. Having left behind possessions ranging from shoes and money, to teeth and eyeglasses, the bedraggled refugees straggled into rooms at four Valdez hotels about eight p.m., some three hours after the supertanker *Williamsburgh* pulled into port at the Alyeska Pipeline Service Company terminal. At the Sheffield House, they walked almost one-by-one through a cordon of news reporters and photographers, in hallways brightly-lit for television crews." Louise Peyrot of Lake West, Florida, was "in fairly good spirits" as she told them, "At first we didn't take it seriously. We thought we'd be rescued in about an hour. I got scared toward the end."

Would she take more cruises?

"Sure. This can't happen every day."

Edna Marcus of Cleveland told a reporter of "gagging and coughing" because of thick smoke on the Promenade Deck, then chuckled as she described seeing a "petite woman in her seventies who calmly sat on the deck and took swigs from a bottle of liquor she'd had in her purse." Earl Andrews said, "I went through World War II and it wasn't as bad as this."

Like war correspondents eager for stories from battlefield survivors, reporters waited to interview boat people together or singly in the lobby and bar of the Sheffield House, or anyone else anywhere who might provide a different colorful angle. Dave Carpenter of the *Anchorage Times* noted "bustling" tour representatives "handed out toothpaste, shaving cream, razors, cigarettes, and hair brushes to the weary guests as well as plastic garbage bags as makeshift suitcases." Sitka tour guide John Linton said, "I think people are thankful that everybody's safe."

Reporters and photographers stationed themselves outside smaller hostelries, rooming houses, and private homes that accommodated the overflow. An Alaskan reporter covering the story for the *New York Times* spoke with "several passengers, some still wearing their pajamas and many without shoes" who were "shopping for clothes in two stores that were opened for them." Thomas Tussimardi of Silver Spring, Maryland, was "neatly dressed in a suit and beige cap." But "not so lucky" was seventy-seven-year-old Stanislas Czetwertynski of North Carolina, "wearing a sweater and a blanket as he tried on hats in the store." Tussimardi said that his lifeboat was "so full there were people under my feet" as he sat next to an eighty-five-year-old woman. "We were packed so tight," he said, "she couldn't move and I couldn't either." Czetwertynski said his lifeboat was "completely crowded" and that he had prayed, "Dear God, this is a silly way to die."

Comedian Roger Ray said, "In the end we were all praying because we didn't think we would be picked up that night. If we hadn't been, I don't think we would have lasted."

"We were so cold," said forty-eight-year-old Sonna Criss of Toronto, who'd been taken from lifeboat number six, "I don't believe we could have survived the night. It was a nightmare."

Of eleven passengers who reported injuries or distress and were taken to Sitka Community Hospital to be examined, one was admitted for treatment for exposure. The other was James Flynn, the mortician who was reluctant to tell Jeannie Gilmore his profession. Without naming him, Dr. Paul White informed reporters. "The worst case was a man complaining of back and abdominal pains from being knocked about pretty badly in a lifeboat."

Flynn would later tell the newsmen that he'd gotten hurt when "a hefty woman" fell on him when the lifeboat was hit by a twenty-five-foot wave. "I'm just thankful we got out alive," he said. "We can be very thankful it happened when we were one hundred miles off shore. If it happened one thousand miles out we would have been gone."

Dr. White phoned Flynn's son Colin to inform him that Flynn had no broken bones, but would be kept in the hospital for observation for a few days, and that Kitty Flynn was fine and had been one of the first to be rescued and flown to Yakutat.

Dave Carpenter of the *Anchorage Times* wrote, "Most were elderly. Their widely varied attire reflected the suddenness of the early morning warning from the ship's captain that 'We have a small fire on board.'" He found John Gyorokos "dressed in a black velvet, three-piece tuxedo suit and shiny black shoes." A red bathrobe "protruded beneath one man's overcoat." Several women "wore only bedroom slippers on their feet."

In the hotel dining room, Mrs. Henry Fields of Dorset, Vermont, sat facing away from a picture window overlooking the ocean. "I've seen enough water," she said, "and I've got my fill of fresh air for a year." Accompanied by a new shipboard friend, Teddie Freidlinger of Detroit, she said that in getting into lifeboats there was "no panic" and no "disagreeableness," although she said that she'd heard from other passengers that "a handful of crew members jumped in front of passengers and there had been an occasional scramble for a blanket in a lifeboat."

Reporters who picked up other references to misbehavior by some of the *Prinsendam* crew sensed a good story and went looking for confirmation. They got it from Jack Barclay. "It just made me sick to see that," said the oil company executive from

Calgary, Canada. "They were pushing elderly women out of the way in order to get into the lifeboats and then to get into the helicopters."

Unexpected verification came from two *Prinsendam* officers. "I saw it, and I know who they were," said Third Officer Paul Welling. Second Officer Matthew Oosterwijk exclaimed, "They were just cowards. I think they were so scared that they jumped into the boats. We kicked a few out. We had always told crew members that passengers go first."

Jeannie Gilmore was forgiving of the Indonesians, calling them "boys" who were "just as scared as everyone else." Betsy Price was also understanding. "They were so young," she said, "and so frightened by their ordeal–not having been trained as seamen, but so well trained as stewards, cooks, and waiters. You couldn't help but feel sorry for them."

Freshly clothed, fed, rested, and re-counted again, the group that now called themselves "the Sitka boat people" were taken by airplane to Anchorage to board another plane that would convey them to Seattle connections to hometowns or anywhere else anyone wished to go.

CHAPTER 32

Burial at Sea

Accompanying a photograph in the *Anchorage Daily News* taken in Sitka on October 6 as a forlorn-looking Captain Cornelius Wabeke came down the gangplank of the *Boutwell* was a story headlined, "True to tradition the captain was last to leave the ship." Reporters Bob Shallit and Don Hunter wrote, "True to nautical form, the captain of the pleasure cruiser *Prinsendam* was the last man to leave the ill-fated vessel Saturday, hoisted through billowing smoke to an Air Force rescue helicopter." The chopper's copilot, Bill Gillam, told the *Daily News* reporters, "It was nothing glorious or grand."

In the same edition of the newspaper, reporter John Greely noted that the U.S. Coast Guard had begun "gearing down" after "the biggest peacetime sea rescue in modern history, an operation that caught the attention of most of the world." Greely's story continued, "Meanwhile, a salvage tug was reported to be en route to the flaming *Prinsendam*, still floating 'high in the water' and under observation by two Coast Guard cutters. Prospects for salvaging the seven-year-old ship may hinge on whether the fire spread to its fuel tanks."

"If the fire gets there," said Coast Guard spokesman Petty Officer First Class Phillip Franklin, "the ball game might be over for the ship."

With the *Boutwell* making its way to Sitka with its load of survivors, and cutters *Mellon* and *Woodrush* assigned to stay with the abandoned burning ship, Holland America was taking steps to determine if she could be saved. Officials of the firm first contacted the Seattle salvage company Foss Launch and Tug. Told that it did not have a suitable vessel available, Holland America turned to Riv Tow Straits Ltd. of Vancouver. It sent the ocean tug *Commodore Strait* from Prince Rupert, British Columbia. The company's costal coordinator, George DeVore, said that the tug's commander, Captain Ted Sheppard, had instructions to tow the *Prinsendam* to Vancouver, a trip that in good weather would take about eight days. When the tug arrived at the scene early Sunday night, the *Prinsendam* was drifting northwesterly at about two knots and still burning. The Coast Guard said the ship could not be moved until the fire was out.

With sea conditions worsening, the *Mellon* stood a mile-and-a-half away. Aboard were Captain Wabeke, Chief Engineer Albertus Boot, Holland America Vice President Arie Van Voort (a former first-mate and skipper of the *Prinsendam*), the fire chief of Kodiak, and Coast Guard firefighters that had been brought in from Sitka. An attempt to put them on the *Prinsendam* had been called off because of "intense heat in the vessel" and concerns that thick columns of black smoke indicated that the fire might have reached her fuel tanks. Captain Wabeke also suspected that the fire had reached fifteen rolls of carpeting that had been stored on the top two decks.

On Monday, October 7, with only a wisp of white smoke visible on the Main Deck and with the sea calmed to four-foot swells and winds moderated, it was decided that the ship was safe to board. At eleven fifteen a.m., a helicopter placed four Coast

Guard firefighters, Wabeke, Boot, the Kodiak fire chief, the *Mellon*'s damage control officer, and Van Voort onto the stern. The ship was stable with ten-second rolls. They made their way forward and used torches to cut the ship's anchor chains. After rigging a towing bridle so the ship could be connected by a tow line to the *Commodore Strait*, they set out to assess the extent of the damage.

On the starboard side, they found smoke, but no heat, from a fan-room vent under the bridge; smoke coming from the main stairway; and upper decks buckled as much as nine inches. The Promenade Deck was hot and smoking at lifeboat stations two, four, and six with a possible fire below. The Bridge Deck had one cracked window and an inside temperature of three hundred degrees Fahrenheit. The four-hundred-gallon emergency generator was intact, but the wiring was damaged. The front of the funnel was warm.

Because the engine room had been sealed and flooded with CO_2, the team assumed that the fire there had been extinguished, but not before it spread upward to the dining room and then throughout the ship. Captain Wabeke expressed surprise that the blaze caused so much damage in such a short time. The survey resulted in a list of alternatives for fighting the fire that included towing the ship to a port and putting a large team of professional civilian firefighters on board or trying to put it out at sea. The team recommended the latter.

By the time the survey was completed, adverse wind conditions ruled out taking the men off the ship by helicopter until daylight. For shelter, they inflated a raft with a canopy and set it up next to the empty swimming pool on the Lido Terrace. This plan had to be abandoned at five fifteen a.m. when two portholes at midship on the port side of B Deck were blown out with a tremendous burst of fire and smoke. This forced the boarding team to call for evacuation, but five minutes after the helicopter that was called from Yakutat took off at six thirty, its cockpit filled with smoke, forcing the chopper to land. With the problem fixed, it resumed the flight and was over the *Prinsendam* at seven thirty. By eight sixteen, everyone was off a ship that was now listing severely.

The plan now changed from trying to fight the fire at sea to requesting permission from the State of Alaska to tow the burning ship to Sitka, a distance of 225 miles. This proposal was rejected by Holland America. The company wanted the *Prinsendam* taken to Portland in the hope that it could be repaired, refitted, and returned to service. Under this plan, the government of Alaska demanded that the ship be kept at least fifty miles from the coast. To assist in the lengthy tow, a second ship, *Salvage Chief,* was to be dispatched from Astoria, Oregon, with its earliest arrival estimated at October 10.

Within twenty-four hours of the evacuation of the survey team, the *Prinsendam*'s list had grown to thirty degrees. The ship was slowly rolling, submerging the starboard side and allowing water to pour through open portholes. When it tipped to port, clouds of steam rose as the cold sea sloshed against hot metal. Unable to do anything but watch, her stunned and grieving officers gazed in dismay at her scorched paint and burned-out wheelhouse, bridge, and Promenade and Main decks. Recalling the ship's maiden voyage when he'd been chief mate and later her skipper, Van Voort said, "She was like a child to me."

On October 9, the rolls were thirty degrees to starboard, and water flooded through broken portholes from bow to stern. Southeast winds were measured at twenty-five knots, whipping up swells of ten feet with low overcast and frequent rain. The next day, the ship was down at the bow with a thirty-degree starboard list. On October 11, a week after greaser Ali reported "plenty fire" in the engine room, the list was forty degrees, raising the portside stabilizer out of the water. The *Mellon* reported, "She's taking on some water, the deck fires are extinguished but there is evidence of interior fire deep within her."

Because listing and flooding caused the *Prinsendam* to lose stability, she could no longer be towed straight ahead, placing extreme strain on the tow lines. With all hope of saving her gone, they were severed at eight thirty a.m., October 11, 1980. Three minutes later, Captain Wabeke watched from the *Commodore Strait* as his ship capsized to starboard in heavy seas. She sank quickly seventy-nine miles west of Sitka in 1,473 fathoms of water. The *Mellon* put the location at 55-52.8 degrees North, 136-26.6 West. When she was gone, the only visible remnants of her existence were a lifeboat and bits of debris. Fears that her fuel tanks would rupture under pressure and leak two hundred thousand gallons of oil into the Gulf of Alaska proved unfounded.

As the *Prinsendam* settled to the bottom and became one more unmarked grave in the watery cemetery that had claimed so many previous venturers and reaped hundreds of lives, she did so without taking human beings with her. That everyone had been rescued in the race to save the *Prinsendam* would be described in countless accounts by passengers, officers, and crew in stories in newspapers and magazines and on radio and television as a miracle. The explanation was understandable. But it was a miracle in which the instruments of salvation were human beings in helicopters and C-130s, lift operators, a pair of pararescuers, medical personnel, the crews of oil tankers, the cutter *Boutwell,* and the hundreds of Coasties in work uniforms and wearing Bender Blues.

CHAPTER 33

Inquest

As the *Prinsendam* burned, lifeboats drifted, and the Coast Guard and U.S. and Canadian Air Forces mounted an unprecedented, massive air-sea rescue on the night of October 5, 1980, the vice president for reservations and tours of Holland America Cruises held a news conference at the company's New York City offices. Jan Boeren cited a series of failures that contributed to the worst disaster in the firm's 107-year history. He revealed the ship did not have a sprinkler system, that fire doors had not held back the flames, flooding the engine room with CO_2 had not worked, nor had the use of foam, and that water could not be supplied because the blaze had crippled the electrical system that ran the pumps. He also noted that there had been a demonstration of lowering lifeboats, but no fire drill involving passengers, and that the ship's smoke alarms, emergency-alert public address system, and fire-signal bells had worked effectively.

Regarding a formal investigation into the cause of the fire and subsequent actions by the officers and crew of a ship in international waters, Boeren informed the reporters that the inquest would be conducted by the Netherlands government. This was confirmed by Commander Larry Balok of the Coast Guard's Casualty Investigation Division in Washington, D.C. He said the Coast Guard would be a "very interested observer." He added that if there were "immediately recognizable deficiencies," the Coast Guard "may, from an international standpoint, push toward having these corrected on other similar vessels immediately," instead of waiting for a change in the International Convention for the Safety of Life at Sea.

While the *Prinsendam* was being towed on October 10, the Netherlands government opened the investigation at the Howard Johnson motel, Saddle Brook, New Jersey, amid what *New York Times* reporter Robert Hanley called "strict security enforced by a bevy" of guards. Patrolling the top three floors of the motel, they "evicted any outsiders who emerged from elevators" while three "shipping inspectors of the Netherlands Ministry of Transport began questioning crew members about the causes of the fire."

Hanley reported that Robert Natt, executive assistant to the president of Holland America Cruises, said the Dutch inspectors had "specifically asked to interview twenty persons from the *Prinsendam*'s engine room and deck staff. He noted that most of the crew, the captain, and top officers remained in Alaska while the crippled ship was being towed by a tugboat to a yet-to-be-determined dry dock.

Although the investigators had invited the senior officer of the Coast Guard's Marine Inspection Office, Commander Joseph J. Smith, to observe the proceedings, the chief of the Marine Safety Division in New York, Captain David J. Linde, said that the investigations of maritime accidents in American waters "are customarily open to the public. The way they're doing it gives us very little chance to get much knowledge. We're just trying to get a flavor to understand some of the things that occurred."

The Netherlands' New York consulate's press attaché, T. H. Van den Muysenberg, said that Dutch shipping law did not require a "preliminary inquiry" to be open to the public, and that the matter would be referred for further investigation to the Netherlands Shipping Court in The Hague if the investigators "found ground for reprimand of the crew."

Because the *Prinsendam* sank the next day, preventing an inspection to determine the cause of the fire, how it spread throughout the ship, and contributing elements and conditions, the investigation would have to rely on the testimony of the officers and crew and records of the ship's history, from its planning and design to its construction and seven years of service. Two days after Captain Wabeke watched his ship go to the bottom of the Gulf of Alaska, Robert Natt announced that the skipper would provide testimony to the investigators at Saddle Brook.

While Natt and other Holland America officials in New York were contending with the initial probe into the loss of the *Prinsendam*, the line's executives in the Netherlands had to face the expected negative impact of losing the ship at the start of the lucrative winter Indonesian cruise program. They hoped to locate a replacement for the *Prinsendam*, but were unable to do so. This meant the cancellation of the cruise schedule through April 13, 1981. Customers who had been booked for the *Prinsendam* were offered credit plans as incentives to transfer to cruises on other Holland America ships. As a result, the company announced "only" fifteen cancellations and that bookings for the line were up over the preceding year.

On October 22, 1980 (eleven days after the *Prinsendam* sank), the company announced that it had ordered construction of a $135 million cruise liner from Chantiers de l'Atlantique, with delivery of the unnamed ship by March 31, 1983. It was to be of medium size (thirty-two thousand tons, 689 feet long, and 89 feet wide) with top speed of twenty-one knots, a crew of 536, and a passenger capacity of 1,200. Like the *Prinsendam*, it would be registered in the Netherlands Antilles.

The same day, Jeannie Gilmore was notified (in response to her inquiry into the status of the investigation) that the secretary of the "Raad voor de Scheepvaart" (the Maritime Board of Inquiry) would commence "the public inquiry in the disaster" of the *Prinsendam* on November 16 at ten-thirty local time in "the southerly room of the 'Koopmansbeurs' at Amsterdam." In a letter dated the day before the start of the investigation, she was asked "to give us some information about your experiences." The letter from A. P. Vasser, Head of the Casualty Investigation Department, enclosed "a number of questions" to be answered. A response was desired by December 15.

In the words of a cover note of "Findings of the Netherlands Court of Inquiry," collection of answers to such queries "took quite a lot of time" because passengers and the Indonesian crew "had meanwhile dispersed all over the world." When the "preliminary investigation" was completed in June 1981, all documents were sent to the Committee of Inquiry in the Netherlands Antilles. If it concluded that "one or more officers of the ship" were to blame for the "casualty," the final determination had to be made by the Court of Inquiry in the Netherlands. Charges were brought against Captain Wabeke, Chief Engineer Boot, Chief Officer Valk, Second Engineer Officer Repko, Third Engineer Officer Van Hardeveld, and Assistant Engineer Officer Kalf.

Accordingly, the "Raad" held a five-day hearing on November 15, 17, 18, 19, and 20, 1981. In the vast amount of data collected were the *Prinsendam*'s history; transcripts of the testimony in previous hearings; drawings; diagrams; reports containing statements by Captain Wabeke, top officers of all departments of the ship, members of the crew, and passengers; newspaper clippings; and log books that were saved by the ship's officers. Experts provided reports on the construction of the ship, the fire protection and fire-fighting systems, engines and fuel supply, water pumps, and the electrical system. The chemical advisor for the shipping inspection department submitted an analysis of the combustible components of liquors, furnishings, and other materials throughout the ship, as well as heat radiation from the funnel shaft.

Also entered into the record was a detailed chronology of events and actions taken from the outbreak of the fire to the sinking. The Raad found error and fault in almost every phase. It cited numerous instances of ineptitude, laziness, unpreparedness, lack of training, acceptance of "normal" anomalies in engine-room operations, and poor or mistaken judgments in dealing with the fire and steps taken to control and fight it.

The board said of the required fire drills, "It is disappointing that the fire drills aboard the *Prinsendam* did not fulfill the demands which should be made with respect to them. Certainly in a passenger ship with five hundred people on board good drills are a must for the safety of the ship and those sailing in her. . . . The deficient leadership of the chief engineer officer is to blame for the said lack of proper drills."

Concerning the use of carbon dioxide to flood the engine room: The captain should have "expedited" the application of CO_2. "A delay of at least twenty minutes was unnecessary and not justified."

Regarding opening doors to the dining room: In doing so "the transverse fire protection of the ship was frustrated," resulting in fire breaking out.

On Wabeke's overall performance, the Court found that he acted "hesitantly or even wrongly" on "a number of points," and was therefore "partly" to blame for the casualty.

Contrary to accounts of passengers regarding getting people into lifeboats, the Court saw the abandonment of the ship, "in spite of several imperfections," to have been "successful."

As to Kenneth Matz's Coast Guard pump: It had a "proper capacity and probably could have led to the effective fighting of the fire." Therefore, it was to be "regretted" that it had to be "slung so low a level above the sea" that it could not be kept from getting wet and sinking.

The *Prinsendam*'s owners were chided for being aware of a history of "frequent high-pressure fuel leakages" and not giving "sufficient guidance and advice" to the chief engineer "as regards the general safety in the engine room."

Among recommendations were putting numbers on lifeboats that would be visible from the air (a step that Holland America had since taken), requiring refresher courses for officers and crew in conducting fire drills and in firefighting, "special attention" to construction of fuel lines and gas ducts, installation of a diesel engine–driven fire pump independent of other systems as far away from the engine room as possible, and installation of emergency equipment "as simple and easy to understand in their operation as possible."

Finally, the Court stated, "It is of importance that officers are able to act quickly and efficiently." In weighing the actions of the men charged with culpability in the losing of the *Prinsendam*, it decided Captain Wabeke was poorly served by his officers. The Court exonerated him of blame, but suspended his captain's license for three weeks.

Assistant Chief Engineer Officer Robert Kalf's qualification to sail in that capacity was also suspended for three weeks.

Second Engineer John Frederick Repko received the very same discipline.

Chief Officer Hendrik Egbert Valk was banned for one month.

Chief Engineer Albertus Marianus Boot received a two-month suspension.

Before delineating these judgments in its published findings, the Court expressed its "gratitude, and admiration for, all those who—sometimes risking their own lives—have given everything in a capable way to save those aboard the *Prinsendam*, to attend to them, to clothe them and, where necessary, to provide them with medicine. Due to this, the deplorable casualty of the *Prinsendam* led to a unique lifesaving operation, having had the fortunate result that nobody of the over five hundred persons on board lost his life or was even seriously injured."

CHAPTER 34

A Morning to Remember

"**A** note of humor is struck when we approach Anchorage," noted Richard Steele about the flight of survivors from Sitka. "The captain announces that an immigration official will pass through the cabin to examine our papers. The laughter that follows testifies that 'our papers' are long gone in the Gulf of Alaska. Another chuckle occurs as we take off from Anchorage. We are told, 'Some of this flight will be over water, so we ask you to study the lifeboat instructions.' Someone joked, 'If you don't mind, I'd rather go overland.'"

Instead of going to Anchorage and onward to Seattle with Richard, Louise Steele had found herself on a Lear Jet hired by NBC Television News to fly her and Bill Powell directly from Yakutat to Seattle to be interviewed live at the NBC-affiliated station by correspondent Bill Sternoff for the *Today Show*. In a studio in New York's Rockefeller Center with a TV monitor showing aerial shots of the burning cruise ship taken from a plane hired by NBC, Tom Brokaw reported, "There is good news this morning. More than five hundred people, many of them elderly, are now back on land after abandoning the burning cruise ship *Prinsendam* off Alaska." Following a report from David Burrington on passengers having arrived in Valdez, he introduced Louise and Powell, shown seated at a desk in the Seattle studio. Sternoff began by telling Louise that NBC had confirmed that Richard had arrived in Valdez. She explained that they had been separated because the Coast Guard helicopter that rescued her was running out of fuel and had to head back to its station.

Unable to watch Louise on *Today* because he was on a plane from Valdez to Sitka at the time of the broadcast, Richard was reunited with her in San Francisco the next day. While he traveled home to Worcester, Massachusetts, to eventually write the biggest news story of his life for his paper, she was determined to continue her Asian odyssey and meet her daughter Barbara in Hong Kong. Accompanied by daughter Ginny, she acquired a new passport and other personal documentation, then shopped for a new travel wardrobe in San Francisco's finest stores.

That Louise would be determined to complete the Asian odyssey did not surprise her daughters. "She always had a lot of spunk," Ginny remembered in an interview for this book, "and she loved designer clothes. She spent three days filling up suitcases." Barbara remembered her mother's "desperate need to do something as planned."

While Louise was accumulating the new wardrobe, Barbara and her husband were settled into a hotel room in Hong Kong. A planned reunion with her parents when the *Prinsendam* got to Singapore was to have been the culmination of an around-the-world trip that included a visit to Katmandu. While her husband trekked for a few days in the mountains, Barbara had gone on to Hong Kong. Learning of the fire in the newspapers, she contacted the Associated Press bureau chief in Hong Kong. She recalled, "Dad had given me his name, so he and I became allies in trying to get information. Once the outcome was known, I had to get word to my husband. This meant sending a general Telex message to Katmandu and hoping that he would get it when he came out of the mountains. I told him to meet me at Singapore. Informed that Mom intended to continue the trip, I arranged to meet her in Hong Kong. When her plane arrived at midnight, her baggage did not. All the bags were lost. Never to be seen again."

In Richard's only television interview, he talked in his office with reporter Mike Taibi of Boston station WNAC-TV and displayed the only thing he was able to save from the ship. It was the key to his stateroom. Grandson Jake Elwell, to whom Louise wrote "I hope it doesn't sink" on a *Prinsendam* postcard, noted that over the years she often spoke about the ordeal, but that after a period of talking about it, Richard abruptly refused to do so. Jake speculated that Richard may have suffered from post-traumatic stress disorder. He also noted that a few weeks after returning to Worcester, Dick and Lou, as the family called them, were shocked to learn they were featured in the supermarket tabloid magazine *The Globe* with the headline:

HOW WE SURVIVED LOVE BOAT INFERNO
HUSBANDS THOUGHT THEY'D NEVER SEE THEIR WIVES AGAIN

"They were so embarrassed," Jake recalled, "they said they wanted to hide in the attic."

John Courtney had the distinction of being the only passenger quoted in a *Time* magazine article on the loss of the *Prinsendam* titled "A Morning to Remember" and sub-headed "The *Prinsendam* fire kindles concern about safety at sea." It cited "experienced seamen" regarding what had "gone wrong" who asked, "If a fire can rage out of control on a ship supposedly as safe as the *Prinsendam,* is any cruise ship safe?" Reunited at Seattle,

Courtney and Edwin Ziegfeld were back in Claremont, California, exactly a week after they'd left for their Oriental odyssey. Their neighbors in the Mount San Antonio Gardens apartments organized a welcome-home reception. A story about their adventure in the Claremont *Courier* began, "It's a helluva way to finally get quoted in *Time* magazine."

When Jack and Beatrice Malon returned to their apartment in Queens, New York, they found it ransacked, belongings scattered all over and jewelry missing. The police surmised the burglary was done by someone who'd read about the couple being on the *Prinsendam*. Malon said, "I feel much more affected by this than seven hours in a lifeboat. Cold. Wet. Sick. With every wave a lifetime. When they pulled me into the helicopter, I escaped a disaster, but found one waiting for me at home."

In nearly as many places as the *Prinsendam* had passengers, what had been national news throughout the weekend became a story of hometown folks. Typical of the local slant was the October 7 headline in the Las Vegas, Nevada, *Review-Journal*: "Vegans will never forget Alaska sea ordeal." The story by Diane Russell stated, "Three Las Vegans who were among passengers forced to abandon a cruise ship and spend about eleven hours in lifeboats in the Gulf of Alaska during the weekend described their ordeal as a frightening event they will never forget." Wayne Parkinson, his wife, June, and comedian Roger Ray were interviewed by phone in Sitka. Ray said, "I'll never forget that sight, looking back at the burning ship as we drifted away. Have you ever seen the movie *Lifeboat*? I kept thinking about the *Titanic* and *Lusitania*."

Betsy Price looked back in an article in *Steamboat Bill*, a periodical devoted to subjects of ships and maritime history. "I left as a passenger and returned as a survivor," she wrote. "It was a day (or days) that I will never forget, and it was truly a modern day miracle."

When Muriel Marvinney and Agnes Lilard arrived at Newark International Airport on Tuesday, October 9, to "a tearful, joyous scene" a friend presented them with blue T-shirts with I SURVIVED THE PRINSENDAM screened in white. In an article for *Guideposts,* with a photo showing them displaying the shirts, Muriel wrote, "We did more than survive, you know. Agnes and I both grew from our harrowing experience on the sea." It had to do, she thought, with the bond they felt with everyone in those lifeboats. She learned "that we are all part of one another. When the crunch comes, it doesn't matter whether you're single, married or widowed, or parent of one child or two. We're all part of the human family and we are deeply responsible for one another. And so we are never alone. And it had to with the courage of the Coast Guard and the U.S. Air Force—all those brave, wonderful men who played a part in our rescue."

After the debarking of survivors at Sitka, Captain Leroy Krumm set the *Boutwell*'s course for its home port of Seattle. Having become the most famous cutter in the world because of the news coverage of the *Prinsendam* rescue, she was saluted all along the way by flyovers of planes of the Canadian and U.S. Air Forces. When she entered Seattle's harbor, everyone on deck was in Bender Blues. Fire boats spouted streams of water in tribute as she pulled up to her home pier, number thirty-six. With a navy band playing and cannons firing salutes, the dock was crowded with hundreds of cheering and waving civilians and Coasties, including the commandant and Seattle's mayor. "That's when the magnitude of what we in the Coast Guard had done hit us," said Dave Hughes. "Before that our attitude was 'it's our job.'"

In a letter to a Seattle newspaper, citizen William S. Benedict took note of the news coverage of the "miracle at sea" and how "the Coastguardsmen gave their own clothes, worked day and night to ensure the safety, comfort and well-being of the survivors." Pointing out that the average salary of a Coast Guardsman was $7,500 a year, he wrote, "Stack that up against the people who were paying not less than five thousand dollars a person for the thirty-day cruise." Proposing that Seattleites write to their congressmen and demand better pay for members of the Coast Guard, he said, "You can also thank God that there are people in this country who work for less than most, are willing at two o'clock in the morning to answer a general Quarters alarm, work around the clock, give up their personal possessions, to help save another human life, and suffer through the separation from loved ones and family while on a thirty-plus-day Alaskan patrol."

In authorizing the "Coast Guard Unit Commendation Ribbon" to "all personnel attached to and serving with the USCG *Boutwell* for at least 50 percent of the cited period," Vice Admiral J. S. Gracey, Commander, Pacific Area, signed a citation for each Coastie that noted "exceptionally meritorious service while engaging in its search and rescue operations in the support of the M/V PRINSENDAM fire and subsequent abandoning ship by all personnel." Calling the situation the "perfect setting for a major maritime disaster," the commendation noted that officers and crew of the *Boutwell* exhibited "valiant persistence, professional skill and untiring efforts" and "devotion to duty and excellent performance" in keeping with "the highest traditions of the United States Coast Guard."

On January 5, 1981, California Congressman Glenn M. Anderson introduced House Concurrent Resolution 2 "to express the thanks of the Congress of the United States to those persons who, during the period of October 4 through 6, 1980, directly participated in the rescuing of five hundred and ten people aboard the burning passenger vessel *Prinsendam* off the coast Alaska." The measure was referred to the House Subcommittee on Coast Guard and Navigation. When it became Public Law 97-136 on December 29, 1981, everyone who had taken part in the rescue received from the Clerk of the House a "Certificate of Recognition" that expressed "the Thanks of the Congress of the United States."

After the *Boutwell*'s sister cutter *Mellon* moved to a new home port in Seattle in 1981, she participated in the rescue of four survivors in a crash of a C-130 on Attu Island. Reconfigured along with the other cutters of its type in a Fleet Rehabilitation and Modernization program to prolong their useful life, she was given the latest command-and-control technologies. In 1990, she was given the Coast Guard Unit Commendation Medal for successful execution of military readiness missions, including a successful test firing of a Harpoon anti-ship missile. In 1991, on a visit to Vladivostok, Russia, she joined in the celebration of Russia's Maritime Border Guard's seventy-third anniversary. In 1992, *Mellon* represented the Coast Guard at the launching of the city of Portland, Oregon's, "Just Say No to Drugs" campaign and received the Coast Guard Foundation Admiral John B. Hayes award, presented to a Pacific Area unit demonstrating commitments to "excellence and professionalism embodied in the traditions and lore of the Coast Guard." In the international arena, *Mellon* conducted professional exchanges with the navies of Costa Rica and Panama in 1993 involving training in international law, defensive tactics, countering narcotics trafficking, boarding procedures, and medical training. In the spring of 1994, she engaged in two hot-pursuit chases of Russian fishing boats suspected of fishing in the U.S. Exclusive Economic Zone. In October 1999, achievements in gunnery operations earned the unit the Commandant's Gunnery Award. Since then, *Mellon* divided her patrol time between the Bering Sea and the Pacific Ocean adjacent to Mexico and Guatemala. In the Bering Sea, this typically involved enforcement of laws and regulations related to the preservation of U.S. fisheries stocks. From time to time, she patrolled the Maritime Boundary Line between the United States and Russia. The ship was often called upon to assist a disabled vessel or transport an injured crew member ashore by helicopter and played a key part in a national strategy known as "Steel Web" to interdict maritime narcotics smugglers.

After ninety-seven years of service, and more than twenty years' duty in Alaskan waters, the *Woodrush* was decommissioned in March 2001. Noting in a proclamation of "Woodrush Day" that she was the last of the Coast Guard's 180-foot oceangoing buoy tender fleet, Governor Tony Knowles cited the cutter's "proud history" and "impressive record" in "plying the often-unforgiving waters" of Alaska's panhandle on search-and rescue missions.

The *Boutwell's* next spectacular rescue occurred two months after the *Prinsendam,* but two thousand miles at sea. It involved the oil rig "Dan Prince." While being towed to the South Pacific it had been caught in a storm and began sinking. With the crewmen taken off, it went down at a point equally distant from Alaska, Hawaii, and the West Coast of the United States. Following the extensive cutter renovation and modernization project in 1990, *Boutwell* was assigned a new homeport in Alameda, California.

Throughout the 1990s, as part of the "Strategic Goals of Safety, Protection of Natural Resources, Mobility, Maritime Security, and National Defense," she had missions ranging over a wide area of the Pacific. From the Bering Sea to Central and South America, she made numerous seizures of illegal drugs in Alaskan and Central American waters. In 1998, she was deployed for 201 days and forcibly seized a Chinese fishing vessel in the North Pacific for using illegal indiscriminate nets, termed high-seas drift nets. From 2001 to 2002 she seized more than $100 million in cocaine using a new "Hitron" helicopter. In 2003, she participated in the Iraq conflict by defending oil terminals off the coast of Iraq and Iran.

The first Coast Guardsman to board the *Prinsendam*, Kenneth Matz, died on August 12, 2003, at the age of sixty-two of a heart attack The first survivor to die, Paul Noyes, passed away in a Seattle hospital a week after the rescue of complications related to the head injury he suffered prior to the trip. Captain Wabeke died in September 2003 at the age of ninety. Two decades after Pararescuer José Rios was lauded for his heroism in lifeboat six, he was killed in an automobile accident. Year after year, newspapers across the United States and those in towns and cities in other countries noted deaths of local residents who were deemed deserving of more than a routine obituary because they had once been newsworthy as part of a spectacular and historic rescue at sea.

Typical of the coverage at the time was an article in the October 9, 1980, edition of the Santa Cruz, California, *Sentinel*. Titled "Chat with a Prinsendam Survivor" and based on an interview with Jeannie Gilmore after her return to Burlingame, it observed, "This is a scary tale, one filled with human valor, trust, and blaring mismanagement," tempered with the fact that everyone of the *Prinsendam* was saved. Jeannie was also interviewed by George Golding of the San Mateo, California, *Times*. Her husband Bill noted for another paper that he'd learned Jeannie's ship was on fire while he was listening to the news on his car radio on his way to work.

"Having attended several 'emergency at sea' situations during World War II," he wrote, "I was concerned as to the exact situation aboard the *Prinsendam*. They referred to the Coast Guard being in attendance and this was comforting to say the least."

When Jeannie Gilmore and her mother arrived at San Francisco International Airport, they were greeted not only by Bill, daughter Carole, other family members and friends, but by a crowd of reporters, photographers, and TV camera crews. They found her outgoing and appealing manner and appearance ideal for their purposes. Over the next week, television and newspaper reporters went to her home seeking interviews and pictures, including a shot of her wearing the bunny hat and too-large work jeans and shirt she'd been given on the *Williamsburgh*.

In a letter to friends, she referred to her and her mother as "temporary media celebrities," and said that "some of the most gratifying requests for interviews" were from former students, each of which "seemed to have a favorite part of our rather soggy experience." Because she and fifteen other survivors lived in San Mateo County, she noted, *Reader's Digest* roving editor Joseph Blank "descended" on the area to tape-record interviews for an article. (Published two years later as a "Feature Condensation" titled "Last Cruise of the *Prinsendam*," it was one of only two lengthy accounts to appear in national magazines. The other, "The *Prinsendam* Fire: History's Greatest Sea Rescue," by Joseph Eppinger, was published in *Popular Mechanics* in April 1981 and subsequently reprinted in the June 1981 regional magazine *Pacific Northwest*.)

One of Jeannie's most prized accounts of her experience was written in 2004 by a young neighbor, eight-year-old Sean Thomas. For a school assignment he was required to write a short essay on the subject of a hometown hero. He wrote, "Jeannie was on a cruise to Alaska when the ship caught fire. She had to abandon ship and get off into a crowded lifeboat. The typhoon made the waves huge and the people got seasick. After fourteen hours in the lifeboat a helicopter rescued her. It was a miracle no one died. Jeannie kept the people in her lifeboat from being scared to death. She wasn't afraid. She knew she was going to survive."

On August 17, 2003, Jeannie told her story at the Burlingame Historical Society in a program titled "Abandon Ship! The True Tales of Burlingame Resident Jeannie Gilmore And Her Rescue At Sea."

Twenty-two years after Commander Richard Schoel ordered the cutter *Boutwell* and all other available assets to sea and into the air to save a cruise ship in distress, a new *Prinsendam* began sailing the seas. Built in 1988 for the Royal Viking Line and eventually taken over by the Seabourn Line and named *Seabourn Sun,* Holland America acquired the thirty-eight-thousand-ton, 669-foot ship. Refurbished and renamed for European, Pacific, and American cruises, and reconfigured to carry 793 passengers and a crew of 443 at twenty-two knots, she had amenities that were not available in her ill-fated predecessor in the pre–personal computer era. Offering an Internet café with e-mail service, she was extolled in Holland America Line advertising as an "elegant explorer" and a "very special experience to those who voyage with her."

In 2006, the fourth year of the new *Prinsendam*'s life, hardly any of the men and women who had sailed in her namesake on the last day of September 1980 for the trip of a lifetime were still around to talk about how everyone on her predecessor had been saved because the Coast Guard mobilized people, ships, and aircraft of two countries to execute the largest ocean rescue since the first human dared to make a boat and set out to conquer the seas.

Names of People
Rescued by the *Boutwell*

Henry Aeberli	Johnny Dawin
Mohamad Ali	Bonaficio Dela Cruz
Mr. Audi	Achmme Dgwbaidi
Ann Benton	Moh Farchani
A. E. Bestic	Richard Farnsworth
L. Blackman	Hanri Field
Albertus Boot	Fred Foxbenton
W. R. Boyce	Lester Frieginger
Irving Brex	Colin Gildarthrop
Francis Burrowski	Nancy Gilderthrop
Lynn Bush	John Graham
F. R. Carris	Mr. and Mrs. Grayland
Sergeant John Cassidy	Randall Green
Douglass Centers	Ed Harrison
E. S. Chapman	Ralph Herrington
Robert Colderis	Peter Kapetan
John Courtney	Max Kleeman
Michael Crespan	Abothim Kohimichlil
J. W. Dansberg	Barry Koran
Suprijade Daris	Richard Krumb
Mohs Darta	Mr. Kunsi

John Leppait

Shezo Mauuoka

Grace Miller

Paul Miller

Joseph Mishell

Lawrence Nowak

Mary O'Hagen

Robert A. Pangrey

C. W. Parker

Margaret Peladen

G. Pendell

H. Pendel

W. M. Pendell

William Powell

Sergeant José Rios

Walter Sanborn

Laurence Saville

Mavis Saville

Mr. Sirjono

Rich Spivie

Alfred Standfast

R. Stickney

Toto Subrantoko

Mas Suemirat

Etna Sueur

Kusni Sufir

Mr. Suhartoyo

Roger Allen Ternce

Peter Thomson

Ernesto Traulsen

I. Trausek

F. Vanbreterf

Hendrik Vanvuuien

Captain Cornelius Wabeke

Abdul Wahab

Freddie Walsieger

Charles Weil

Kevin Wilson

Ray Wolf

Richard Yanni

Names of People Airlifted to Sitka

Antonius Ambergen
Jack Barclay
Mrs. Arthur J. Baum
Mrs. Vicky Bennett
Mrs. W. Briggs
Richard F. Carr
Mr. J. R. Carris
Barbara Clark
Mrs. D. Connell Brownhill
Ann F. Corey
Stanislas Czetwertynski
Joan E. Davison
Howard N. Dietrich
Alfred Ellingham
Runfo Enoch
Mrs. S. Farnsworth
Mrs. R. Field
James L. Flynn
Mrs. Teddie Freidinger
Donald Goodwill
Eugene Gyorokos

John Gyorokos
Sandy Gyorokos
Virginia Gyorokos
Soeripto Hadiprayitno
Edward Halliday
Malotu Hesran
Royce E. House
John D. Huxtable Jr.
Klara H. Kaelin
Robert Kalf
William Kriss
Mrs. Kriss
Agnes Lilard
Robert Martinez
Muriel Marvinney
Herman Marx
Rully Masrui
Claude Massoulier
Jeanne Massoulier
Margaret Ann Meyers
Soebyantoro Mochamad

Mr. Msalee

Matthieu J. Oosterwijk

June Parkinson

Wayne Parkinson

Leo Pijnenburg

Lawrence A. Razete

Ronny Rosepandi

Mr. Sarkcsih

Paul W. Schol

V. D. Sluis

Mrs. Herman Solomon

Louise Steele

Mr. Sukanda

Thomas Tuccinardi

Mrs. Tuccinardi

Gerrit Ren Voorde

William B. Warner

Mrs. Elfriede Weil

Paul Welling

Timeline

1972

- Holland America Line orders two identical motor-vessel cruise ships, but cancels second
- Shipbuilding company De Merwedem Hardinxveld begins construction of hull number 606, to be named *Prinsendam*

1973

- Launching and outfitting
- Fire in a trash bin causes extensive smoke damage, delaying delivery
- November: First voyage, from the Netherlands to Singapore

1974–1980

- Cruise service in western Pacific and Alaska
- November 30, 1980: Departs Vancouver, Canada, for Alaska and Orient
- October 1, 1980: En route to Ketchikan, Alaska
- October 3, 1980:   Port call in Ketchikan; passengers go ashore
  - Cruise of Glacier Bay
  - Enters open water of Gulf of Alaska
  - Rough sea causes rampant sickness among passengers

- October 4, 12:40 a.m.
  - Oil leak in engine room causes fire; attempts to extinguish it fail
  - 1:15–2:00: Captain Cornelius Wabeke informs passengers that "small fire" in engine room is under control and orders them to go to the Promenade Deck; watertight doors between compartments closed
  - U.S. Coast Guard Coordination Center in Juneau, Alaska, organizes rescue operation
  - Crew of USCG cutter *Boutwell* rounded up from 24-hour shore leave; gets underway with partial crew
  - Supertanker *Williamsburgh* changes course to assist, along with tanker SOHIO *Intrepid*
  - U.S. and Canadian Air Force units respond
  - Emergency distress message XXX transmitted
  - Power loss hampers firefighting
  - Main lounge and Lido Restaurant opened for passenger comfort
  - 2:00–6:00 Aircraft from Kodiak and Sitka locate the *Prinsendam*
  - Fire breaks out in dining room, directly below Main Lounge
  - Passengers moved outside
  - SOS signal is sent
  - Order to abandon ship
  - First passengers board *Williamsburgh*
  - Hoisting from lifeboats
  - Coast Guard fire specialist Kenneth Matz boards the *Prinsendam*

- Some passengers taken to Yakutat
- 11:00 Winds pick up to twenty-five knots, with waves of fifteen feet
- 1:00–4:00 p.m. Parajumpers Cassidy and Rios go into water to aid lifeboat number six
- Airlifts continue
- Matz and ship's officers and crew taken off the *Prinsendam* by helicopter
- *Boutwell* is on scene
- 5:30 USCG cutters *Woodrush* and *Mellon* are on scene
- 9:00 Coast Guard reports all passengers removed from lifeboats
- Lifeboat number six is unaccounted for, search begins

- October 5
  - 2:30 a.m. Missing lifeboat located and occupants removed to *Boutwell*
  - 4:00 a.m. *Williamsburgh* leaves for Valdez, Alaska
  - *Boutwell* heads to Sitka

- October 6–7
  - Salvage tugboat *Commodore Straits* arrives
  - Damage survey team boards the *Prinsendam*
  - Towing operation fails
  - Boarding team evacuated

- October 8–10
  - The *Prinsendam* continues to burn under tow
  - Preliminary investigation begins in Saddle Brook, New Jersey

- October 11
  - 8:30 a.m. The *Prinsendam* sinks

1981

- June
  - Preliminary investigation concludes

- November
  - Hearings by Dutch Court of Inquiry at The Hague, Netherlands

- December 7
  - Court finds Captain Wabeke partly to blame for loss of ship, Suspensions of officers Kalf and Repko for three weeks, Valk for one month and Boot for two months

2002

- Holland acquires *Seabourn Sun,* refurbishes and renames her
- The new *Prinsendam* goes into service

INDEX

MBI Publishing Company   We'd Like Your Input!

Thank you for buying this book! In an effort to continue providing you with quality books, we want to learn more about you, your interests, and your thoughts about this book. Please take a few moments to answer the questions below.

Your name: _____

Your address: _____

Your E-mail address: _____

Type of car and/or motorcycle you own: _____

☐ Please keep me informed of new books and calendars

1. Book title: _____

2. Purchased from: _____

3. What comments do you have about this book?
   (likes, suggested improvements, etc.) _____

4. What other books would you like to see us publish? _____
   _____

5. Would you consider yourself . . . ?

   ☐ Enthusiast *(I spend most of my free time with my . . .)*
   ☐ Occasional hobbyist *(I enjoy it when it's convenient)*
   ☐ Distant admirer *(I'm not really into this but I know people who are)*

6. Which magazines do you read? _____

7. Which enthusiast shows do you like to attend? _____

8. Which enthusiast clubs do you belong to? _____

For 40 years, MBI Publishing Company has proudly produced books that quickly become the authoritative texts in their respective fields.

If you would like more information, go to www.mbipublishing.com, www.motorbooks.com or call 1-800-826-6600.